Betty Crocker's

ANNUAL RECIPES

2·0·0·4

Bac-Os, BETTY CROCKER, Betty Crocker Dessert Decorations, Betty Crocker Original Supreme, Betty Crocker Rich & Creamy, Betty Crocker Snackin' Cake, Betty Crocker Suddenly Salad, Betty Crocker SuperMoist, Betty Crocker Supreme, Bisquick, Gold Medal, Green Giant, Honey Nut Cheerios, Lloyd's, Old El Paso, Progresso and Yoplait are registered trademarks of General Mills, Inc.

This edition published by arrangement with Wiley, Inc.

General Mills, Inc.

Betty Crocker Kitchens

Manager, Books: Lois Tlusty

Recipe Development: Betty Crocker Kitchens Home Economists

Food Stylists: Betty Crocker Kitchens Food Stylists

Photography: Photographic Services Department

Editor: Shea Zukowski

Book Designer: Tracey J. Hambleton

For consistent baking results, the Betty Crocker Kitchens recommend Gold Medal Flour.

ISBN 1-57954-757-5

Printed in the United States of America

10 9 8 7 6 5 4 3 2   hardcover

Cover: Grilled Steak with Feta (page 208)

For more great ideas, visit www.bettycrocker.com.

C O N T E N T S

Fiesta Taco Casserole (page 219)

Introduction

You asked for more recipes and ideas for pleasing your family and friends, and here they are! In this, the third edition of *Betty Crocker's Annual Recipes*, we've once again assembled over 240 of your favorites from the past year of *Betty Crocker* magazine into one convenient collection of simple, satisfying dishes for all occasions. We've packed it full of new information, such as all the latest on heirloom tomatoes and varietal potatoes, as well as innovative hints for making your meals extra special. And with a beautiful color photograph for every recipe, you'll know in an instant that these are foods to be savored and enjoyed.

Even if you're short on time, we show you how to prepare dozens of dishes that minimize the fuss but never the flavor. Whip up a special breakfast with Praline Peach Pancakes or plan ahead the night before with Overnight French Toast or Do-Ahead Breakfast Bake. Come home to dinner with easy slow cooker favorites like Turkey Breast with Wild Rice Stuffing or Black-Eyed Pea and Sausage Soup.

And speaking of convenience, you'll find a variety of delicious recipes for quick and easy grilling—including great foil-packet dishes that let you expand the sort of foods you grill. Try the Mediterranean Chicken Packets or the Caribbean Salmon Packets. You'll be amazed how simple they are to prepare—and after dinner, cleanup is a breeze!

You'll also find a number of recipes that let you cook ahead and extend part of one meal into a completely new dish later in the week. Make the Kid-Pleasin' Chili meal one night, and you're already halfway done preparing the Fiesta Taco Casserole for the next. To find more recipes that work together like this, look for the "Meal 1" and "Meal 2" labels on recipes that are right next to one another.

As with past editions, you'll also find a "Quick" label on all the recipes that can be ready in under 30 minutes. If you are looking for meals with less fat, main dishes with the "Low Fat" label have 6 grams of fat or less per serving; side dishes and desserts have 3 grams or less. And to help you sort through this year's collection of recipes, we've again included a list of recipes arranged by season, as well as a list of inspiring menu suggestions for easy entertaining.

We hope you enjoy this edition of *Betty Crocker's Annual Recipes*. Here's to good cooking!

Inspired Entertaining

INNOVATIVE MENUS FOR EVERY OCCASION

Gatherings with family and friends are all the more memorable when you can share delicious food you've prepared yourself. Use these creative menu ideas to lend your own signature style to your special occasions. Whether you're planning to throw the next big Super Bowl party or a summer barbecue—or perhaps a romantic dinner for two— you'll find lots of great ways to combine the recipes in this book and create meals everyone is sure to remember.

On a Snowy Evening

Cajun Beef Stew (page 112)

Betty's Classic Cheddar Cheese Biscuits (page 261)

Dutch Apple Wedges (page 274)

Hot Chocolate, Coffee or Hot Tea

Game Day!

Chicken Wings with Dipping Sauces (page 44)

Barbecue Beef Sandwiches (page 86)

Chocolate Chip Cookie Dough Brownies (page 247)

Beer and Assorted Sodas

Breakfast in Bed

Jeweled Fruit Salad (page 5)

Overnight French Toast (page 7)

Honey-Mustard Ham (page 14)

Orange Juice and Coffee or Tea

Get Well Soon

Orange Frost (page 3)

After-Work Chicken Noodle Soup (page 102)

Easy Puff Twists (page 261)

Hot Tea, Ginger Ale or Orange Juice

Girls' Night In

Shrimp Quesadillas (page 35)

Garden-Fresh Linguine and Vegetables (page 138)

Chocolate Pecan Pie (page 276)

White Sangria (page 22)

Spring Fever Supper

Extra-Special Caesar Salad (page 55)

Lemony Fish over Vegetables and Rice (page 129)

Light 'n' Creamy Tropical Dessert (page 284)

White Wine

Lunch with Friends

Grilled Chicken Salad with Raspberries (page 64)

French Onion Soup (page 100)

Double-Chocolate Cake with Broiled Topping (page 267)

Iced Tea

Just the Two of You

Easy Toasted Coconut Shrimp (page 37)

Asian Grilled Tuna with Wasabi Aioli (page 118)

Green Beans with Shiitake Mushrooms (page 231)

Mini Almond Cheesecakes (page 269)

Wine, Cocktails or Champagne

Seasonal Selections

Looking for the perfect salad to take advantage of your seasonal vegetables? Perhaps you need an irresistible dessert to take to a potluck or picnic. Use this helpful list of recipes, grouped by season, to select just the right dish—any time of year.

Spring

Summer

Fall

Winter

Anytime

Good Mornings

Sunny Breakfast Ideas

Mixed-Berry Smoothie (page 2)

Do-Ahead Breakfast Bake (page 16)

Mixed-Berry Smoothie

Prep: 10 min
Photo on page 1

1 cup strawberry or raspberry low-fat yogurt
1 cup fat-free (skim) milk
1 tablespoon powdered sugar
1 bag (14 to 16 ounces) frozen mixed berries (strawberries, blackberries, blueberries and raspberries), slightly thawed

1. Place yogurt, milk and powdered sugar in blender or food processor. Cover and blend on high speed about 30 seconds or until smooth.

2. Add half of the berries. Cover and blend on high speed 1 minute. Add remaining berries. Cover and blend on high speed about 1 minute, adding a small amount of additional milk if necessary, until smooth. Serve immediately.

3 servings.

1 Serving: Calories 175 (Calories from Fat 20); Fat 2g (Saturated 1g); Cholesterol 5mg; Sodium 90mg; Carbohydrate 38g (Dietary Fiber 6g); Protein 7g
% Daily Value: Vitamin A 6%; Vitamin C 74%; Calcium 24%; Iron 2%
Exchanges: 1 Starch, 1 Fruit, ½ Skim Milk

BETTY'S TIPS

◎ **Substitution**
If you can't find frozen mixed berries at your supermarket, substitute 1½ cups each of frozen unsweetened strawberries and unsweetened red raspberries.

◎ **Special Touch**
Pour smoothie into insulated mugs or other covered drink carriers and add drinking straws so the kids can enjoy these on the way to soccer practice!

Merry Mimosas

Prep: 5 min
Photo on page iii

3 tablespoons sugar
2 cups fresh orange juice, chilled
1 cup cranberry juice
2 bottles (750 milliliters each) champagne or Catawba grape juice, chilled
8 orange slices

1. Place sugar and orange juice in blender. Cover and blend on medium speed about 15 seconds or until foamy.

2. Place 2 tablespoons cranberry juice in each of 8 tall glasses. Pour ¼ cup orange juice into each glass; add about 1 cup champagne to each glass. Garnish with orange slice.

8 servings.

1 Serving: Calories 180 (Calories from Fat 0); Fat 0g (Saturated 0g); Cholesterol 0mg; Sodium 10mg; Carbohydrate 45g (Dietary Fiber 0g); Protein 1g
% Daily Value: Vitamin A 2%; Vitamin C 48%; Calcium 2%; Iron 4%
Exchanges: 3 Fruit

BETTY'S TIPS

◎ **Success Hint**
You'll want to whip up these cocktails just before serving, so guests can enjoy the airy lightness of the orange juice foam.

◎ **Serve-With**
Serve champagne and juices separately at the table to accommodate guests who might prefer one or the other. Serve juice from a glass pitcher with slices of lime and orange.

◎ **Special Touch**
For a pretty garnish, use a citrus zester to make strips around an orange; then, cut into slices.

Orange Frost

Prep: 10 min

¾ cup milk
¾ cup water
1 can (6 ounces) frozen orange juice concentrate
8 ice cubes
¼ cup sugar
1 teaspoon vanilla

1. Place all ingredients in order listed in blender.

2. Cover and blend on high speed about 30 seconds or until mixture is smooth and foamy. Serve immediately.

3 servings.

1 Serving: Calories 210 (Calories from Fat 10); Fat 1g (Saturated 1g); Cholesterol 5mg; Sodium 35mg; Carbohydrate 47g (Dietary Fiber 1g); Protein 4g
% Daily Value: Vitamin A 6%; Vitamin C 100%; Calcium 10%; Iron 2%
Exchanges: 2½ Fruit, ½ Skim Milk

BETTY'S TIPS

✿ Health Twist
This recipe is a terrific example of a guilt-free indulgence. The shake is virtually fat free and is an excellent source of vitamin C. Bottoms up!

✿ Variation
A wide variety of frozen juice concentrates could be used for this recipe. Look for a new family favorite! Try a tropical blend such as pineapple-orange-banana or orange-peach-mango.

Orange Frost

Baked Apple Oatmeal

Jeweled Fruit Salad

Jeweled Fruit Salad

Prep: 15 min

    1   cup vanilla yogurt
    1   tablespoon mayonnaise or salad dressing
  ¼   teaspoon grated orange peel
    2   tablespoons orange juice
    1   pint (2 cups) strawberries, sliced
    1   medium kiwifruit, peeled and chopped
1½   cups seedless green grapes, cut in half
    1   can (11 ounces) mandarin orange segments, drained
    3   tablespoons dried cranberries

1. Mix yogurt, mayonnaise, orange peel and orange juice; set aside.

2. Mix remaining ingredients. Serve with yogurt mixture.

8 servings.

1 Serving: Calories 90 (Calories from Fat 20); Fat 2g (Saturated 0g); Cholesterol 0mg; Sodium 30mg; Carbohydrate 19g (Dietary Fiber 2g); Protein 2g
% Daily Value: Vitamin A 4%; Vitamin C 74%; Calcium 6%; Iron 2%
Exchanges: 1 Fruit, ½ Fat

Baked Apple Oatmeal

Prep: 15 min Bake: 45 min

2⅔   cups old-fashioned oats
  ½   cup raisins
    4   cups milk
  ⅓   cup packed brown sugar
    2   tablespoons butter or margarine, melted
    1   teaspoon ground cinnamon
  ¼   teaspoon salt
    2   medium apples, chopped (2 cups)
  ½   cup chopped walnuts, if desired
        Additional milk, if desired

1. Heat oven to 350°. Mix oats, raisins, 4 cups milk, the brown sugar, butter, cinnamon, salt and apples in 2-quart casserole.

2. Bake uncovered 40 to 45 minutes or until most liquid is absorbed. Top with walnuts. Serve with additional milk.

8 servings.

1 Serving: Calories 260 (Calories from Fat 65); Fat 7g (Saturated 4g); Cholesterol 15mg; Sodium 140mg; Carbohydrate 44g (Dietary Fiber 4g); Protein 9g
% Daily Value: Vitamin A 6%; Vitamin C 2%; Calcium 18%; Iron 8%
Exchanges: 1 Starch, 1 Fruit, 1 Skim Milk, 1 Fat

BETTY'S TIPS

✪ **Variation**
The yogurt mixture also makes a wonderful party dip to serve with fruit. Try it with strawberries, grapes and chunks of melon.

✪ **Do-Ahead**
Prepare the yogurt mixture a day ahead and refrigerate in a covered container. Cut up fruit in advance.

BETTY'S TIPS

✪ **Substitution**
For variety, substitute chopped pear for the apple.

✪ **Serve-With**
Serve this hot oatmeal with bowls of toppers such as walnuts, chopped dried apricots, banana slices, chocolate chips, brown sugar, yogurt and cream.

Strawberry-Banana Crepes

Prep: 15 min Cook: 9 min

Crepes (right)
1½ cups whipping (heavy) cream
¼ cup sugar
2 to 3 bananas, sliced
1 pint (2 cups) fresh strawberries, sliced, or 1 package (10 ounces) frozen strawberries, partially thawed
¼ cup chopped walnuts

1. Make Crepes.

2. Beat whipping cream and sugar in chilled medium bowl with electric mixer until stiff. Spoon about 3 tablespoons whipped cream down center of each crepe; top with 4 or 5 banana slices. Roll up; top each crepe with whipped cream, strawberries and walnuts.

About 12 crepes.

Crepes
1 cup Original Bisquick® mix
¾ cup milk
2 eggs

Stir all ingredients until blended. Grease 6- or 7-inch skillet with shortening (or spray with cooking spray before heating); heat over medium-high heat. For each crepe, pour 2 tablespoons batter into skillet; rotate skillet until batter covers bottom. Cook until golden brown. Gently loosen edge with metal spatula; turn and cook other side until golden brown. Stack crepes as you remove them from skillet, placing waxed paper over each. Keep crepes covered to prevent them from drying out.

1 Crepe: Calories 220 (Calories from Fat 125); Fat 14g (Saturated 7g); Cholesterol 70mg; Sodium 170mg; Carbohydrate 20g (Dietary Fiber 1g); Protein 4g
% Daily Value: Vitamin A 8%; Vitamin C 12%; Calcium 6%; Iron 4%
Exchanges: 1 Starch, ½ Fruit, 2½ Fat

BETTY'S TIPS

❂ **Substitution**
Use whatever berries you have on hand—raspberries, blueberries, blackberries or a combination. All will be delicious in these sweet crepes.

❂ **Do-Ahead**
Crepes can be frozen up to 3 months. Stack cool unfilled crepes with waxed paper between. Wrap in aluminum foil or place in an airtight plastic freezer bag; label and freeze. Thaw at room temperature about 1 hour or in refrigerator 6 to 8 hours.

Strawberry-Banana Crepes

Overnight French Toast

Prep: 35 min Chill: 8 hr Cook: 10 min per batch

4   eggs
½   cup half-and-half or milk
⅓   cup orange juice
3   tablespoons orange-flavored liqueur or orange juice
2   tablespoons sugar
¼   teaspoon vanilla
¼   teaspoon salt
16   slices French bread, each ¾ inch thick
      Glorious Orange Sauce (below)

1. Beat eggs, half-and-half, orange juice, liqueur, sugar, vanilla and salt in small bowl with fork. Dip bread into egg mixture, soaking thoroughly; place in un-greased rectangular pan, 15 × 10 × 1 inches. Pour any remaining egg mixture over bread. Cover loosely and refrigerate at least 8 hours but no longer than 24 hours.

2. Make Glorious Orange Sauce; keep warm.

3. Heat griddle to 375° or heat skillet over medium heat; grease with butter (or spray with cooking spray be-fore heating). Cook bread 4 to 5 minutes on each side or until golden brown. Serve with sauce.

8 servings (2 slices each).

Glorious Orange Sauce
   ½   cup butter or margarine
   ⅓   cup sugar
   ⅓   cup frozen (thawed) orange juice concentrate
   ¼   cup pomegranate seeds, if desired

Melt butter in 1-quart saucepan over medium heat. Add sugar and orange juice concentrate, stirring until sugar is dissolved. Remove from heat; cool slightly. Beat with wire whisk until thick and shiny. Stir in pomegranate seeds.

2 Slices: Calories 370 (Calories from Fat 160); Fat 18g (Saturated 10g); Cholesterol 140mg; Sodium 480mg; Carbohydrate 45g (Dietary Fiber 1g); Protein 8g
% Daily Value: Vitamin A 14%; Vitamin C 18%; Calcium 8%; Iron 10%
Exchanges: 3 Starch, 3 Fat

BETTY'S TIPS

☻ **Success Hint**
Pomegranates are known as nature's most labor-intensive fruit. Inside are hundreds of seeds packed in compartments separated by bitter, cream-colored membranes. To use, cut the pomegranate in half and pry out the pulp-encased seeds, removing any of the light-colored membrane that adheres.

☻ **Special Touch**
Instead of passing the sauce separately, you may want to spoon it over the French toast slices and top with additional pomegranate seeds.

Overnight French Toast

Praline Peach Pancakes

Prep: 10 min Cook: 15 min

Praline Peach Syrup (right)
2   cups Reduced Fat Bisquick® mix
1   cup fat-free (skim) milk
2   tablespoons pecan pieces
1   tablespoon packed brown sugar
1   egg
1   container (6 ounces)Yoplait® Original peach yogurt (⅔ cup)

1. Make Praline Peach Syrup; keep warm. Heat griddle to 375° or heat skillet over medium heat; grease with shortening if necessary (or spray with cooking spray before heating).

2. Stir remaining ingredients until blended. Pour batter by slightly less than ¼ cupfuls onto hot griddle.

3. Cook until edges are dry. Turn; cook other sides until golden brown. Serve with syrup.

About 12 pancakes.

Praline Peach Syrup
½   cup maple-flavored syrup
¼   cup pecan pieces
1   medium peach, peeled and chopped (¾ cup)

Heat all ingredients in 1-quart saucepan over low heat, stirring occasionally, until hot.

1 Pancake: Calories 175 (Calories from Fat 45); Fat 5g (Saturated 1g); Cholesterol 20mg; Sodium 240mg; Carbohydrate 28g (Dietary Fiber 1g); Protein 4g
% Daily Value: Vitamin A 2%; Vitamin C 0%; Calcium 8%; Iron 6%
Exchanges: 1 Starch, 1 Fruit, 1 Fat

BETTY'S TIPS

❂ **Substitution**
You can also use nectarines if you prefer them. An added bonus: no need to peel them!

❂ **Do-Ahead**
Looking for a hot weekday breakfast? You can make these pancakes, stack them between sheets of waxed paper and then freeze in a plastic bag or container. Pop them into your toaster or toaster oven, like commercially frozen pancakes or waffles, for piping-hot pancakes in minutes. Make the syrup as the pancakes reheat.

Praline Peach Pancakes

Granola Whole Wheat Waffles with Double-Berry Sauce

Granola Whole Wheat Waffles with Double-Berry Sauce

Prep: 10 min Cook: 12 min

Double-Berry Sauce (below)
1½ cups Original Bisquick mix
½ cup granola cereal
½ cup Gold Medal® whole wheat flour
1½ cups milk
3 tablespoons vegetable oil
2 eggs
1 container (6 ounces) Yoplait Original strawberry yogurt (⅔ cup)

1. Make Double-Berry Sauce; keep warm. Heat waffle iron; grease with shortening if necessary (or spray with cooking spray before heating).

2. Stir remaining ingredients until blended. Pour batter by ⅔ cupfuls onto center of hot waffle iron; close lid.

3. Bake 2 to 3 minutes or until steaming stops and waffle is golden brown. Carefully remove waffle. Serve with sauce.

Twenty-four 4-inch waffles.

Double-Berry Sauce

⅔ cup maple-flavored syrup
⅔ cup raspberry jam or preserves
1 cup strawberries, cut into fourths

Heat syrup and jam to boiling in 1½-quart saucepan, stirring occasionally. Stir in strawberries; remove from heat.

1 Waffle: Calories 135 (Calories from Fat 35); Fat 4g (Saturated 1g); Cholesterol 20mg; Sodium 135mg; Carbohydrate 23g (Dietary Fiber 1g); Protein 2g
% Daily Value: Vitamin A 0%; Vitamin C 4%; Calcium 4%; Iron 2%
Exchanges: 1 Starch, ½ Fruit, ½ Fat

BETTY'S TIPS

⊙ **Substitution**
You can use almost any flavor of yogurt in these waffles. We suggest raspberry, vanilla or strawberry-banana as great alternatives.

⊙ **Success Hint**
Waffle irons come in a variety of shapes and sizes. Each waffle iron uses a different amount of batter, so you may end up with a few less or a few more waffles.

⊙ **Time-Saver**
If you prefer, skip making the Double-Berry Sauce and top these waffles with a dollop of yogurt and a sprinkle of additional granola.

Peanut Butter Waffle Toast

Prep: 5 min   Cook: 15 min

1¼ cups milk

1 cup Original Bisquick mix

½ cup peanut butter

2 tablespoons granulated sugar

1 teaspoon vanilla

1 egg

6 to 8 slices bread

6 to 8 tablespoons miniature semisweet chocolate chips

Powdered sugar, if desired

1. Heat waffle iron; grease with shortening if necessary (or spray with cooking spray before heating).

2. Stir milk, Bisquick mix, peanut butter, granulated sugar, vanilla and egg until well blended. Carefully dip bread into batter on both sides. Place in waffle iron; close lid.

3. Cook about 2 minutes or until steaming stops and "toast" is golden. Carefully remove waffle toast. Sprinkle each waffle with 1 tablespoon chocolate chips and powdered sugar.

6 to 8 servings.

1 Serving: Calories 395 (Calories from Fat 180); Fat 20g (Saturated 6g); Cholesterol 40mg; Sodium 560mg; Carbohydrate 42g (Dietary Fiber 3g); Protein 12g
% Daily Value: Vitamin A 2%; Vitamin C 0%; Calcium 14%; Iron 12%
Exchanges: 3 Starch, ½ High-Fat Meat, 2½ Fat

BETTY'S TIPS

☺ Success Hint

The peanutty batter covering the bread is thick so it clings to the bread. If it seems a little too thick, add a small amount of milk. When you coat the bread, use your fingers to turn the slices (messy) or try using a spatula (less messy). Either way, the toast turns out delicious!

How many slices of waffle toast you'll actually make will depend on the type of bread you use.

☺ Did You Know?

This waffle toast is a cross between French toast and a waffle. The bread is dipped in a peanut butter batter and then cooked in a waffle iron.

Peanut Butter Waffle Toast

Banana Split Pancakes

Prep: 10 min Cook: 15 min

2 cups Original Bisquick mix

1¼ cups milk

¼ cup chocolate-flavor syrup

1 egg

2 medium bananas, sliced

2 cups sliced strawberries

Whipped topping, if desired

Chopped peanuts, if desired

Additional chocolate-flavor syrup, if desired

Maraschino cherries, if desired

1. Heat griddle to 375° or heat skillet over medium heat; grease with shortening if necessary (or spray with cooking spray before heating). Stir Bisquick mix, milk, ¼ cup chocolate syrup and the egg in medium bowl until blended (batter may be thin).

2. Pour batter by slightly less than ¼ cupfuls onto hot griddle.

3. Cook until edges are dry. Turn; cook other sides until golden brown. Serve with bananas, strawberries, whipped topping, peanuts, chocolate syrup and maraschino cherries.

About 16 pancakes.

1 Pancake: Calories 105 (Calories from Fat 25); Fat 3g (Saturated 1g); Cholesterol 15mg; Sodium 230mg; Carbohydrate 18g (Dietary Fiber 1g); Protein 2g
% Daily Value: Vitamin A 0%; Vitamin C 10%; Calcium 6%; Iron 4%
Exchanges: 1 Starch, ½ Fat

BETTY'S TIPS

⊛ **Success Hint**
Don't flip 'em more than once! Repeated cooking on both sides toughens rather than browns the pancakes.

⊛ **Special Touch**
Serve with luscious Caramel-Banana Topping. To make, heat 1 cup caramel topping until warm. Gently stir in 2 medium bananas, sliced.

Banana Split Pancakes

Quick

Honey-Mustard Ham

Prep: 10 min Cook: 16 min

2 fully cooked ham slices, about 1 inch thick (2 pounds)
½ cup water
⅓ cup honey mustard
1 cup sour cream
4 medium green onions, sliced (¼ cup)

1. Cut each ham slice into 4 serving pieces. Mix water and honey mustard in 12-inch skillet. Add ham.

2. Cover and heat to boiling; reduce heat. Simmer about 15 minutes, turning ham once, until ham is hot. Remove ham from skillet; keep warm.

3. Stir sour cream into mixture in skillet; heat 1 minute. Pour over ham. Sprinkle with onions.

8 servings.

1 Serving: Calories 295 (Calories from Fat 145); Fat 16g (Saturated 7g); Cholesterol 85mg; Sodium 1750mg; Carbohydrate 11g (Dietary Fiber 0g); Protein 27g
% Daily Value: Vitamin A 4%; Vitamin C 0%; Calcium 4%; Iron 10%
Exchanges: 1 Starch, 3 Medium-Fat Meat

BETTY'S TIPS

⊕ **Substitution**
Can't find honey mustard at your local market? Just stir 2 tablespoons honey into ¼ cup Dijon mustard and you're set!

⊕ **Health Twist**
Use reduced-fat or fat-free sour cream for a slightly lighter honey-mustard sauce.

Crab Strata

Prep: 25 min Chill: 2 hr Bake: 45 min Stand: 10 min

4 cups cubed firm bread (6 slices)
2 cans (6 ounces each) crabmeat, drained, cartilage removed and flaked
1 cup shredded Swiss cheese (4 ounces)
1 cup shredded Cheddar cheese (4 ounces)
¼ cup capers, drained, if desired
3 medium green onions, chopped (3 tablespoons)
6 eggs, slightly beaten
1⅓ cups milk
¼ cup dry sherry or apple juice
1 tablespoon Dijon mustard
½ teaspoon Worcestershire sauce
  Additional chopped green onions, if desired
  Chopped red bell pepper, if desired

1. Grease 2-quart casserole with shortening. Mix bread cubes, crabmeat, cheeses, capers and onions in casserole. Mix remaining ingredients except additional onions and bell pepper; pour over bread mixture. Cover tightly and refrigerate at least 2 hours but no longer than 24 hours.

2. Heat oven to 350°. Bake uncovered about 45 minutes or until knife inserted in center comes out clean. Let stand 10 minutes before serving. Sprinkle with additional onions and bell pepper.

12 servings.

1 Serving: Calories 195 (Calories from Fat 90); Fat 10g (Saturated 5g); Cholesterol 150mg; Sodium 400mg; Carbohydrate 9g (Dietary Fiber 0g); Protein 17g
% Daily Value: Vitamin A 8%; Vitamin C 0%; Calcium 22%; Iron 6%
Exchanges: ½ Starch, 2 Medium-Fat Meat

BETTY'S TIPS

⊕ **Substitution**
Twelve ounces of frozen cooked crabmeat (thawed) can be used in place of the canned crabmeat.

⊕ **Special Touch**
For an elegant presentation, sprinkle a couple tablespoons of red caviar over the strata.

Crab Strata

Honey-Mustard Ham

Do-Ahead Breakfast Bake

Prep: 12 min Chill: 4 hr Bake: 35 min Stand: 10 min

1   cup diced fully cooked ham

2   packages Betty Crocker® hash brown potatoes

1   medium green bell pepper, chopped (1 cup)

1   tablespoon instant chopped onion

2   cups shredded Cheddar cheese (8 ounces)

3   cups milk

1   cup Original or Reduced Fat Bisquick mix

½   teaspoon salt

4   eggs

1. Spray rectangular baking dish, 13 × 9 × 2 inches, with cooking spray. Mix ham, potatoes, bell pepper, onion and 1 cup of the cheese. Spread in baking dish.

2. Stir milk, Bisquick mix, salt and eggs until blended. Pour over potato mixture. Sprinkle with remaining 1 cup cheese. Cover and refrigerate at least 4 hours but no longer than 24 hours.

3. Heat oven to 375°. Uncover and bake 30 to 35 minutes or until light golden brown around edges and cheese is melted. Let stand 10 minutes before cutting.

12 servings.

1 Serving: Calories 350 (Calories from Fat 110); Fat 12g (Saturated 6g); Cholesterol 100mg; Sodium 610mg; Carbohydrate 45g (Dietary Fiber 3g); Protein 15g
% Daily Value: Vitamin A 8%; Vitamin C 8%; Calcium 20%; Iron 6%
Exchanges: 3 Starch, 1 Medium-Fat Meat, 2 Fat

BETTY'S TIPS

⚙ **Time-Saver**
You can save a few minutes of prep time by looking for packaged cubed fully cooked ham at the grocery store.

⚙ **Serve-With**
This is a perfect make-ahead dish for a crowd. Serve with Cinnamon Bubble Loaf (page 259) or Blueberry-Banana Oat Bread (page 258) and a platter of fresh fruit.

⚙ **Variation**
Stir in sliced fresh mushrooms or jarred Green Giant® sliced mushrooms with the potatoes, or sprinkle on ¼ to ½ cup Bac-Os® bacon flavor bits or chips with the remaining cheese.

Do-Ahead Breakfast Bake

Turkey Sausage Quiche

Prep: 20 min Bake: 35 min Stand: 10 min

1¼ cups Original Bisquick mix

¼ cup butter or margarine, softened

2 tablespoons boiling water

1 cup shredded Italian-style cheese blend (4 ounces)

1 cup cooked turkey sausage

4 medium green onions, sliced (¼ cup)

1½ cups half-and-half

3 eggs

1 teaspoon chopped fresh basil leaves

¼ teaspoon ground red pepper (cayenne)

1. Heat oven to 400°. Spray pie plate, 9 × 1¼ inches, with cooking spray. Stir Bisquick mix and butter until blended. Add boiling water; stir vigorously until soft dough forms. Press dough on bottom and up side of pie plate, forming edge on rim of pie plate.

2. Sprinkle cheese, sausage and onions over crust. Beat half-and-half and eggs; stir in basil and red pepper. Pour into crust.

3. Bake uncovered 30 to 35 minutes or until knife inserted in center comes out clean. Let stand 10 minutes before cutting.

6 servings.

1 Serving: Calories 305 (Calories from Fat 215); Fat 24g (Saturated 13g); Cholesterol 175mg; Sodium 440mg; Carbohydrate 8g (Dietary Fiber 0g); Protein 14g
% Daily Value: Vitamin A 18%; Vitamin C 2%; Calcium 22%; Iron 4%
Exchanges: ½ Starch, 2 High-Fat Meat, 1 Fat

BETTY'S TIPS

✲ **Substitution**
Cooked Italian sausage can be substituted for the turkey sausage.

✲ **Variation**
For **Ham and Cheese Quiche**, use 1 cup chopped Canadian-style bacon and 1 cup shredded Swiss cheese in place of the turkey sausage and Italian-style cheese blend. Omit the basil, too.

Turkey Sausage Quiche

Holiday Hash Browns

Prep: 15 min Bake: 45 min

1 bag (1 pound 4 ounces) refrigerated Southwest- or home-style shredded hash brown potatoes

1 medium bell pepper, finely chopped (1 cup)

1 medium onion, finely chopped (½ cup)

2 tablespoons grated Parmesan cheese

½ teaspoon salt

¼ teaspoon pepper

1 tablespoon butter or margarine, melted

1 tablespoon vegetable oil

Additional grated Parmesan cheese, if desired

6 servings.

1 Serving: Calories 190 (Calories from Fat 45); Fat 5g (Saturated 2g); Cholesterol 5mg; Sodium 260mg; Carbohydrate 36g (Dietary Fiber 4g); Protein 4g
% Daily Value: Vitamin A 4%; Vitamin C 26%; Calcium 4%; Iron 4%
Exchanges: 2 Starch, 1 Vegetable

BETTY'S TIPS

❂ **Do-Ahead**
This recipe is a true sanity saver. Just mix it, spread it, cover it and refrigerate it for up to 24 hours before baking.

❂ **Special Touch**
Bake in a round casserole dish and garnish with a wreath made from fresh rosemary sprigs and a bow made from roasted red bell pepper strips.

1. Heat oven to 350°. Toss together potatoes, bell pepper, onion, cheese, salt and pepper. Pour butter and oil into 1½-quart casserole or rectangular pan, 13 × 9 × 2 inches; tilt casserole to cover bottom. Spread potato mixture in casserole.

2. Bake uncovered about 45 minutes, stirring once, until golden brown. Sprinkle with additional cheese before serving.

Holiday Hash Browns

Wonderful
Warm-Ups

Beverages and Appetizers

Roasted Red Pepper and Artichoke Dip (page 26)

Peanutty Snack Mix (page 26)

"Cran-tinis"

"Cran-tinis"

Prep: 5 min

1 cup cranberry juice (8 ounces)
½ cup citrus vodka or plain vodka (4 ounces)
¼ cup orange-flavored liqueur or orange juice (2 ounces)
1 teaspoon lime juice
 Fresh cranberries, if desired
 Lime slices, if desired

1. Fill martini shaker or 3-cup covered container half full with ice. Add all ingredients except cranberries and lime slices; cover and shake.

2. Pour into martini or tall stemmed glasses, straining the ice. Garnish glasses with fresh cranberries and lime slices on picks.

4 servings.

1 Serving: Calories 140 (Calories from Fat 0); Fat 0g (Saturated 0g); Cholesterol 0mg; Sodium 0mg; Carbohydrate 14g (Dietary Fiber 0g); Protein 0g
% Daily Value: Vitamin A 0%; Vitamin C 26%; Calcium 0%; Iron 0%
Exchanges: 1 Fruit

BETTY'S TIPS

☺ **Success Hint**
Cran-tinis are sweeter than regular martinis. True martini drinkers may want to cut the cranberry juice in half.

☺ **Variation**
For a slightly less potent drink, serve Cran-tinis on the rocks and add a splash of sparkling water.

☺ **Special Touch**
Place strip of lime peel in the bottom of each glass.

Frozen Cranberry Margaritas

Prep: 10 min Freeze: 24 hr
Photo on page ix

1 can (11½ ounces) frozen cranberry juice cocktail concentrate, thawed
2 cans (12 ounces each) lemon-lime soda pop
5 cups water
1 cup tequila
¼ cup lime juice

1. Pour all ingredients into 3-quart plastic container; beat with wire whisk or spoon until well blended.

2. Cover and freeze at least 24 hours until slushy. Serve in margarita or cocktail glasses.

15 servings (⅔ cup each).

⅔ Cup: Calories 85 (Calories from Fat 0); Fat 0g (Saturated 0g); Cholesterol 0mg; Sodium 10mg; Carbohydrate 21g (Dietary Fiber 0g); Protein 0g
% Daily Value: Vitamin A 0%; Vitamin C 22%; Calcium 0%; Iron 0%
Exchanges: 1½ Fruit

BETTY'S TIPS

☺ **Keep It Casual**
Serve in colorful plastic beverage glasses. Attach large dots or stripe stickers (available at office supply stores) to the glasses and let guests write their names on the stickers to identify their glasses.

☺ **Make It Extra Special**
For fun, rub the cut side of a lime or lemon on the rims of the glasses, then dip the rims into a shallow dish of coarse red sugar. Garnish with fresh cranberries on a beverage pick. If desired, thread sew-on gems, jewels or elegant beads (available at craft stores) onto thin silver wire and wrap around the stem of the glass.

White Sangria

Prep: 10 min

½ cup sugar
1 cup orange-flavored liqueur or orange juice
1 cup vodka or lemon-lime soda pop
2 medium peaches or nectarines, thinly sliced
1 medium orange, thinly sliced
1 lemon, thinly sliced
1 lime, thinly sliced
1 bottle (750 milliliters) dry white wine, nonalcoholic white wine or white grape juice, chilled (3½ cups)
1 bottle (1 liter) club soda, chilled (4 cups)

1. Stir sugar, orange liqueur and vodka in half-gallon glass or plastic pitcher until sugar is dissolved. Pour half of vodka mixture into another half-gallon glass or plastic pitcher. Divide fruits and wine evenly between pitchers.

2. Refrigerate until serving. Just before serving, pour half of club soda into each pitcher; stir gently to mix. Serve immediately. Serve over ice if desired.

12 servings (about ¾ cup each).

¾ Cup: Calories 85 (Calories from Fat 0); Fat 0g (Saturated 0g); Cholesterol 0mg; Sodium 5mg; Carbohydrate 21g (Dietary Fiber 0g); Protein 0g
% Daily Value: Vitamin A 0%; Vitamin C 20%; Calcium 0%; Iron 2%
Exchanges: 1½ Fruit

BETTY'S TIPS

⚙ **Pack 'n Go**
If you're bringing this drink to a potluck, pour the vodka mixture into two large Thermoses. Carry the club soda separately and mix just before serving.

⚙ **Success Hint**
The nice thing about this fruity, refreshing drink is that inexpensive liqueur, vodka and wine can be used because the flavor doesn't rely solely upon alcohol. Try Triple Sec for the orange liqueur and a Chablis Blanc or Chardonnay for the dry white wine.

Watermelon Lemonade with Kiwifruit Splash

Prep: 20 min Freeze: 1 hr

4 kiwifruit, peeled and cut into fourths
1 tablespoon sugar
8 cups cubed seedless watermelon
2 cans (12 ounces each) frozen lemonade concentrate, thawed
4 cups water

1. Place kiwifruit and sugar in blender. Cover and blend on medium speed just until smooth. Freeze 1 to 2 hours or until firm.

2. Place watermelon in blender or food processor (blender will be full until blended). Cover and blend on medium speed until smooth. Place lemonade concentrate and water in large pitcher. Add watermelon mixture; mix well.

3. Pour watermelon lemonade into glasses. Spoon dollop of frozen kiwifruit on top. Serve immediately.

12 servings (1 cup each).

1 Cup: Calories 190 (Calories from Fat 10); Fat 1g (Saturated 0g); Cholesterol 0mg; Sodium 5mg; Carbohydrate 46g (Dietary Fiber 2g); Protein 1g
% Daily Value: Vitamin A 12%; Vitamin C 78%; Calcium 2%; Iron 4%
Exchanges: 3 Fruit

BETTY'S TIPS

⚙ **Pack 'n Go**
Blend the watermelon ahead of time and pour into a Thermos, then mix with the lemonade concentrate and water on site.

⚙ **Success Hint**
Don't worry if you find a few seeds in your watermelon. Seedless watermelons actually do have a few seeds; however, they are usually small and edible and will be virtually undetectable by the time you blend the mixture.

⚙ **Special Touch**
Garnish each drink with a slice of watermelon and kiwifruit. If you like, moisten rims of the glasses and dip in coarse sugar crystals, then fill with watermelon lemonade.

White Sangria

Watermelon Lemonade with Kiwifruit Splash

Betty... ON WHAT'S NEW

A Toast to Beverages

Jazz up liquid refreshments at holiday gatherings with these indispensable ideas. Whether you're serving coffee, cocktails or wine, just follow your taste buds and add a splash of creativity for outstanding holiday drinks!

HOT STUFF

Tradition, comfort. What better words to describe a cup of hot coffee or a mug of steaming cocoa? Add a contemporary twist to these favorites with these ideas:

- To coffee, stir in about 1 tablespoon chocolate syrup, crème de cacao, hazelnut liqueur or syrup, caramel topping or a small scoop of your favorite ice cream.

- Add pieces of vanilla bean, a cardamom pod and/or cinnamon stick to a pot or cups of coffee or hot chocolate for a spicy flavor and aroma.

- To hot chocolate, add about 1 tablespoon crème de menthe, orange-flavored liqueur, cherry syrup, coffee liqueur or syrup, caramel topping, toasted coconut or a small scoop of your favorite ice cream.

DRINK DAZZLERS FOR HOT BEVERAGES

- Drizzle chocolate syrup inside glass (use a small squeeze bottle or spoon).

- Use a vanilla bean pod, cinnamon stick or peppermint stick as a stirrer.

- Top with whipped cream and garnish with chocolate-covered coffee beans, shaved chocolate, chopped nuts, chocolate chips or crushed candies or cookies. Or drizzle with crème de menthe, cherry syrup or maple syrup.

- Flavor your sweetened whipped cream with 1 to 2 tablespoons cocoa, spices (ground cinnamon, nutmeg or even a pinch of ground red pepper), ground nuts, crushed peppermint or a small amount of flavored liqueur.

A TWIST ON BEER

Enjoying a cold beer while mowing the lawn or listening to the ball game is great. But when the holidays roll around, it's fun to jazz up beer.

- To a tall glass of beer, add a shot (1 to 2 ounces) of whiskey, gin or vodka.

- Spike a full glass of beer with a couple tablespoons of lemon or lime juice. Start with a small amount and add more if you like.

- Mix equal parts of chilled beer and either chilled tomato juice, ginger ale or orange juice for a colorful, flavorful beer drink.

FINE WINES

Wine is a year-round favorite. Enjoy it served straight from the bottle or embellish it for fun results.

- To enjoy "wine coolers," mix equal parts of white wine and fruit juice. You can also add a shot of fruit-flavored liqueur if you like.

- Add honey and spices such as cinnamon, cardamom and cloves to red wine, then heat slowly for a mulled wine.

SPIRITED DRINKS

- Spiked gelatin cubes, with their colorful, wiggly shapes and dazzling flavors, are the rage. Prepare any 4-serving-size package of flavored gelatin using 1 cup boiling water.

  After the gelatin is dissolved, stir in ¾ cup of your favorite spirit, perhaps rum, brandy, vodka, gin or champagne. Spray ice-cube trays with cooking spray. Pour gelatin mixture into ice-cube trays and refrigerate until set. Remove from the trays and serve the cubes in small glasses.

A CLASSIC COCKTAIL

Surrounded with nostalgia and romance, the martini holds a certain place of honor with those who enjoy cocktails. As a result, this simple, sophisticated drink is popular again.

- A traditional dry martini is 1½ to 2 ounces of gin with a splash (about 2 teaspoons) of dry vermouth. It is shaken (or stirred, if you prefer) with ice to make it refreshingly cold. The ice is strained and an olive or two added. The less vermouth a martini has, the "drier" it is. Be sure to chill the martini glasses or add ice while making the martinis (and then remove before serving).

- Those with adventurous palates have expanded on the classic and created Vodka Martinis (substitute vodka for gin), Cosmopolitans (vodka with orange-flavored liqueur, cranberry juice and lime juice), Mintinis (substitute white crème de menthe for the vermouth) and Tequinis (substitute tequila for the gin).

DRINK DAZZLERS FOR MIXED DRINKS

- Glass rims can be rubbed with the cut side of a lime or lemon and then dipped into salt or sugar. Spice the salt or sugar, or use colored sugar crystals for a fun touch.

- Make ice cubes out of juices for a colorful effect: cranberry juice for red cubes, grape juice for purple cubes and mango juice for yellow.

- Instead of the traditional olive garnish, try a fruit garnish. Use fresh berries, cherries, citrus twists, kiwifruit slices or melon wedges.

Holiday Spritzer

  2 cups chilled dry white wine, nonalcoholic wine or apple juice

  1 cup chilled cranberry-apple juice drink

  1 cup chilled **sparkling water**

1. Mix wine, juice drink and sparkling water.

2. Serve over ice. Garnish with apple slices and mint if desired.

6 servings (about ¾ cup each).

Peanutty Snack Mix

Prep: 7 min Bake: 10 min Cool: 1 hr
Photo on page 19

5	cups Honey Nut Cheerios® cereal
1	cup pretzel sticks
¼	cup creamy peanut butter
2	tablespoons butter or margarine
1	cup raisins
1	cup honey-roasted peanuts
1	cup dried banana chips
1	cup candy-coated chocolate candies

1. Heat oven to 350°. Mix cereal and pretzels in large bowl.

2. Heat peanut butter and butter to boiling in 1-quart saucepan, stirring occasionally; pour over cereal mixture. Toss until evenly coated. Spread in ungreased rectangular pan, 13 × 9 × 2 inches.

3. Bake uncovered 10 minutes, stirring occasionally. Remove from oven; stir in raisins and peanuts. Spread over waxed paper; cool completely, about 1 hour.

4. Stir in banana chips and candies. Store in airtight container.

9 cups snack.

½ Cup: Calories 240 (Calories from Fat 100); Fat 11g (Saturated 5g); Cholesterol 5mg; Sodium 300mg; Carbohydrate 33g (Dietary Fiber 3g); Protein 5g
% Daily Value: Vitamin A 4%; Vitamin C 4%; Calcium 2%; Iron 12%
Exchanges: 2 Starch, 2 Fat

BETTY'S TIPS

❂ **Substitution**
Miniature pretzel twists can be used instead of the pretzel sticks.

❂ **Success Hint**
If you buy the ingredients in the bulk-food section of the grocery store, you can purchase only the amount you need.

❂ **Special Touch**
Serve this kid-pleasin' snack mix in colorful ice-cream cones.

Quick

Roasted Red Pepper and Artichoke Dip

Prep: 10 min
Photo on page 19

1	jar (6 to 7 ounces) marinated artichoke hearts, drained
½	cup drained roasted red bell peppers (from 7-ounce jar)
1	package (3 ounces) cream cheese, softened
½	cup sour cream
¼	cup chopped fresh parsley
	Assorted crackers or vegetable chips, if desired

1. Place artichoke hearts and bell peppers in food processor. Cover and process until coarsely chopped.

2. Add cream cheese, sour cream and parsley. Cover and process just until blended. Garnish with additional chopped fresh parsley, if desired. Serve with crackers.

16 servings (2 tablespoons each).
2 Tablespoons: Calories 45 (Calories from Fat 35); Fat 4g (Saturated 2g); Cholesterol 10mg; Sodium 55mg; Carbohydrate 2g (Dietary Fiber 1g); Protein 1g
% Daily Value: Vitamin A 10%; Vitamin C 20%; Calcium 2%; Iron 2%
Exchanges: 1 Fat

BETTY'S TIPS

❂ **Success Hint**
Different brands of marinated artichoke hearts have slightly different flavors, and this will affect the flavor of the dip. Some taste more vinegary than others, so be sure to use your favorite brand.

Make sure you use marinated artichoke hearts instead of just canned artichokes. The marinated artichoke hearts add lots of flavor to this quick dip.

Greek Marinated Roasted Peppers, Olives and Feta

Prep: 55 min Stand: 20 min

5 large red bell peppers
¼ cup olive or vegetable oil
3 tablespoons lemon juice
½ cup chopped fresh parsley
¼ cup finely chopped red onion
2 tablespoons chopped fresh or 2 teaspoons
   dried oregano leaves
2 cloves garlic, finely chopped
2 cups pitted Kalamata olives
8 ounces feta cheese, cut into ½-inch cubes
   (1 cup)
   Baguette slices, if desired

1. Set oven control to broil. Place bell peppers on cookie sheet. Broil with tops about 5 inches from heat, turning occasionally, until skin is blistered and evenly browned. Place peppers in a plastic bag and close tightly. Let stand 20 minutes.

2. Meanwhile, shake oil, lemon juice, parsley, onion, oregano and garlic in tightly covered container.

3. Remove skins, stems, seeds and membranes from peppers. Cut peppers into 1-inch pieces. Place peppers, olives and cheese in glass bowl or jar. Pour marinade over pepper mixture. Serve with slotted spoon. Serve with baguette slices.

32 servings (¼ cup each).

¼ Cup: Calories 155 (Calories from Fat 110); Fat 12g (Saturated 5g); Cholesterol 20mg; Sodium 530mg; Carbohydrate 10g (Dietary Fiber 3g); Protein 5g
% Daily Value: Vitamin A 100%; Vitamin C 100%; Calcium 16%; Iron 10%
Exchanges: 2 Vegetable, 2 Fat

BETTY'S TIPS

⊕ **Success Hint**
For the very best flavor, use Kalamata or Gaeta olives, but you can also use large pitted ripe olives if you prefer.

⊕ **Do-Ahead**
Store this appetizer in a tightly covered container in the refrigerator for up to 1 week.

Greek Marinated Roasted Peppers, Olives and Feta

Bloody Mary Shrimp Cocktail

Prep: 30 min Cook: 8 min Marinate: 2 hr

1½ pounds cooked peeled deveined medium shrimp (about 60), thawed if frozen

½ cup tomato juice

¼ cup vodka, if desired

½ teaspoon red pepper sauce

½ teaspoon sugar

½ teaspoon celery salt

2 tablespoons chopped fresh parsley

1 cup cocktail sauce

¼ cup finely chopped green olives

1. Arrange shrimp in single layer in rectangular glass or plastic dish, 11 × 7 × 1½ inches.

2. Heat tomato juice, vodka and pepper sauce to boiling in 1-quart saucepan over medium-high heat. Stir in sugar; reduce heat. Simmer uncovered 5 minutes, stirring occasionally. Stir in celery salt and parsley; pour over shrimp. Cover and refrigerate 2 to 3 hours.

3. Mix cocktail sauce and olives; pour into small serving bowl. Remove shrimp from marinade with slotted spoon; arrange on serving platter. Serve shrimp with cocktail sauce and toothpicks.

About 60 appetizers.

1 Appetizer: Calories 10 (Calories from Fat 0); Fat 0g (Saturated 0g); Cholesterol 20mg; Sodium 105mg; Carbohydrate 1g (Dietary Fiber 0g); Protein 2g
% Daily Value: Vitamin A 2%; Vitamin C 0%; Calcium 0%; Iron 2%
Exchanges: 1 Serving is a Free Food

BETTY'S TIPS

❂ **Success Hint**
Don't marinate the shrimp more than 3 hours; a longer time in the tomato juice will toughen the shrimp.

❂ **Keep It Casual**
Serve shrimp in a divided glass bowl or cylinder with cocktail sauce. Serve condiments such as celery sticks, lime wedges, pickles and olives in separate low-ball glasses. Place the bowl and glasses on a large tray.

❂ **Make It Extra Special**
Place shrimp in an oversized martini glass (about 12 to 14 inches in diameter). Pour cocktail sauce mixture over shrimp and garnish like a Bloody Mary with a skewer of colossal olives, small lime wedges and a celery stick.

Bloody Mary Shrimp Cocktail

Chipotle Deviled Eggs

Prep: 20 min

8   hard-cooked eggs
¼   cup mayonnaise or salad dressing
½   teaspoon lemon juice
2   medium green onions, chopped
    (2 tablespoons)
2 to 3   teaspoons finely chopped chipotle chilies in
    adobo sauce (from 7-ounce can), drained
⅛   teaspoon salt
    Paprika

1. Peel eggs; cut lengthwise in half. Slip out yolks and mash with fork.

2. Stir mayonnaise, lemon juice, onions, chilies and salt into yolks. Fill egg whites with egg yolk mixture, heaping it lightly. Sprinkle with paprika.

16 appetizers.

1 Appetizer: Calories 60 (Calories from Fat 45); Fat 5g (Saturated 1g); Cholesterol 110mg; Sodium 75mg; Carbohydrate 1g (Dietary Fiber 0g); Protein 3g
% Daily Value: Vitamin A 2%; Vitamin C 0%; Calcium 0%; Iron 2%
Exchanges: ½ High-Fat Meat

BETTY'S TIPS

⊙ **Special Touch**
To easily pipe the yolk mixture into the egg whites, spoon yolk mixture into a resealable plastic food-storage bag, seal the bag and cut off a corner.

Place small flags in the eggs with pictures of chilies or words to indicate "hot" to your guests.

Chipotle Deviled Eggs

Double-Cheese Fondue

Prep: 15 min Cook: 15 min

1½ cups shredded Havarti cheese (6 ounces)

 1 cup shredded sharp Cheddar cheese
    (4 ounces)

 2 tablespoons Gold Medal all-purpose flour

 ⅓ cup chicken broth

 ⅓ cup milk

 ½ cup sliced drained sun-dried tomatoes in oil

 4 medium green onions, sliced (¼ cup)
    Crisp breadsticks, if desired
    Cut-up fresh vegetables, if desired

1. Place cheeses and flour in resealable plastic food-storage bag. Shake until cheese is coated with flour. Heat broth and milk in fondue pot just to a simmer over warm/simmer setting.

2. Add cheese mixture, about 1 cup at a time, stirring with wire whisk until melted. Cook over warm/simmer setting, stirring constantly, until slightly thickened. Stir in tomatoes and onions.

3. Keep warm over warm/simmer setting. Serve with breadsticks and vegetables.

20 servings (2 tablespoons each).

2 Tablespoons: Calories 65 (Calories from Fat 45); Fat 5g (Saturated 3g); Cholesterol 15mg; Sodium 125mg; Carbohydrate 1g (Dietary Fiber 0g); Protein 4g
% Daily Value: Vitamin A 4%; Vitamin C 2%; Calcium 8%; Iron 0%
Exchanges: ½ High-Fat Meat

BETTY'S TIPS

⚙ **Success Hint**
Transport this dip to a party in a resealable container. Once you arrive, pour into the fondue pot and turn the heat to warm/simmer setting.

⚙ **Serve-With**
Breadsticks and a variety of veggies, such as cauliflower, baby broccoli and bell pepper, are perfect accompaniments to this bubbly hot appetizer.

Double-Cheese Fondue

Festive Cheese Trio

Prep: 45 min Chill: 24 hr

1 package (8 ounces) cream cheese, softened
1 package (3 ounces) cream cheese, softened
1 package (6 ounces) chèvre (goat) cheese
1½ tablespoons chopped fresh chives
2 tablespoons finely chopped yellow bell pepper
2 tablespoons finely chopped walnuts, toasted
2 tablespoons chopped pitted Kalamata or Spanish olives
2 tablespoons grated Parmesan cheese
1 jar (2 ounces) diced pimientos, drained
  Crackers or cocktail breads, if desired

1. Line three 6-ounce custard cups or molds with plastic wrap. Beat cream cheese and chèvre cheese with electric mixer on medium speed until smooth. Divide mixture into three equal portions (about ⅔ cup each).

2. Stir chives into one portion of cheese mixture. Spoon half of mixture evenly into a lined cup. Sprinkle with bell pepper. Top with remaining chives mixture. Cover and refrigerate at least 24 hours but no longer than 3 days.

3. Stir walnuts into another portion of cheese mixture. Spoon half of mixture evenly into a lined cup. Top with olives. Top with remaining walnut mixture. Cover and refrigerate at least 24 hours but no longer than 3 days.

4. Stir Parmesan cheese into remaining portion of cheese mixture. Spoon half of mixture evenly into remaining lined cup. Top with pimientos. Top with remaining Parmesan mixture. Cover and refrigerate at least 24 hours but no longer than 3 days.

5. Turn cups upside down onto serving plate; carefully remove cups and plastic wrap from cheese mixtures. Serve with crackers.

16 servings (2 tablespoons each).

2 Tablespoons: Calories 110 (Calories from Fat 90); Fat 10g (Saturated 6g); Cholesterol 30mg; Sodium 200mg; Carbohydrate 1g (Dietary Fiber 0g); Protein 4g
% Daily Value: Vitamin A 8%; Vitamin C 8%; Calcium 8%; Iron 2%
Exchanges: 1 Medium-Fat Meat, 1 Fat

BETTY'S TIPS

✿ **Success Hint**
To toast walnuts, bake uncovered in an ungreased shallow pan in 350° oven about 10 minutes, stirring occasionally, until golden brown.

✿ **Special Touch**
Make little flags to insert into the tops of the unmolded spreads that identify the flavors of each cheese. Place cheese spreads in a row on long narrow platter (about 12 × 5 inches). Garnish with edible white flowers.

Festive Cheese Trio

Dilled Scallops with Orange-Chive Mayonnaise

Prep: 20 min Grill: 10 min

Orange-Chive Mayonnaise (below)
½ cup butter or margarine, melted
¼ cup chopped fresh or 1 tablespoon dried dill weed
2 tablespoons orange-flavored liqueur or orange juice
½ teaspoon salt
2 pounds sea scallops

1. Heat coals or gas grill for direct heat. Spray hinged wire grill basket with cooking spray or brush with vegetable oil.

2. Make Orange-Chive Mayonnaise.

3. Mix butter, dill weed, liqueur and salt in medium bowl. Stir in scallops until well coated with butter mixture. Place scallops in basket.

4. Cover and grill scallops 4 to 6 inches from medium heat 8 to 10 minutes or until scallops are white. Serve with Orange-Chive Mayonnaise.

4 servings.

Orange-Chive Mayonnaise

1 cup mayonnaise or salad dressing
2 tablespoons chopped fresh chives or green onion tops
2 teaspoons grated orange peel

Mix all ingredients. Cover and refrigerate until serving but no longer than 24 hours.

1 Serving: Calories 370 (Calories from Fat 305); Fat 34g (Saturated 11g); Cholesterol 65mg; Sodium 530mg; Carbohydrate 3g (Dietary Fiber 0g); Protein 13g
% Daily Value: Vitamin A 12%; Vitamin C 2%; Calcium 8%; Iron 10%
Exchanges: 2 Lean Meat, 6 Fat

BETTY'S TIPS

✪ **Serve-With**
Serve these simply elegant scallops with hot cooked angel hair pasta or linguine tossed with melted butter, chopped fresh parsley and freshly ground pepper.

✪ **The Finishing Touch**
Place orange slices on large platter. Place scallops on orange slices and sprinkle with chopped fresh dill weed. Serve with Orange-Chive Mayonnaise.

Dilled Scallops with Orange-Chive Mayonnaise

Shrimp Quesadillas

Prep: 10 min Cook: 16 min

8 flour tortillas (8 to 10 inches in diameter)

2 cups shredded Monterey Jack cheese with jalapeño peppers (8 ounces)

1 large tomato, chopped (1 cup)

½ cup real bacon pieces (from 3-ounce jar)

1 package (4 ounces) frozen cooked salad shrimp, rinsed and thawed

1. Heat 10-inch nonstick skillet over medium-high heat. Place 1 tortilla in skillet. Sprinkle with ¼ cup of the cheese and one-fourth each of the tomato, bacon and shrimp. Sprinkle with additional ¼ cup of the cheese. Top with another tortilla.

2. Cook 1 to 2 minutes or until bottom is golden brown; turn. Cook 1 to 2 minutes longer or until bottom is golden brown.

3. Repeat 3 more times with remaining ingredients. Cut quesadillas into wedges.

8 servings.

1 Serving: Calories 280 (Calories from Fat 125); Fat 14g (Saturated 7g); Cholesterol 60mg; Sodium 500mg; Carbohydrate 25g (Dietary Fiber 2g); Protein 15g
% Daily Value: Vitamin A 10%; Vitamin C 4%; Calcium 26%; Iron 12%
Exchanges: 1 Starch, 1 High-Fat Meat, 2 Vegetable, 1 Fat

BETTY'S TIPS

⊙ **Substitution**
Use up your extra garden vegetables in this easy sandwich. Try red or green bell peppers instead of the tomato or add chopped zucchini or green onions.

Shrimp Quesadillas

Easy Toasted Coconut Shrimp

Tomato-Basil Crostini

— Quick & Low Fat —

Easy Toasted Coconut Shrimp

Prep: 10 min

½ cup apricot preserves or orange marmalade
¼ cup Dijon mustard
1 pound cooked peeled deveined medium shrimp (about 40), thawed if frozen
1½ cups shredded coconut, toasted*

1. Mix preserves and mustard in small serving bowl. Cover and refrigerate until serving time.

2. Arrange shrimp on serving platter.

3. Dip shrimp first into preserves mixture and place on individual serving plate; sprinkle or spoon coconut onto shrimp.

About 40 shrimp.

*To toast coconut, bake uncovered in ungreased shallow pan in 350° oven 5 to 7 minutes, stirring occasionally, until golden brown. Or cook in ungreased heavy skillet over medium-low heat 6 to 14 minutes, stirring frequently until browning begins, then stirring constantly until golden brown.

1 Shrimp: Calories 15 (Calories from Fat 10); Fat 1g (Saturated 0g); Cholesterol 5mg; Sodium 5mg; Carbohydrate 1g (Dietary Fiber 0g); Protein 1g
% Daily Value: Vitamin A 0%; Vitamin C 2%; Calcium 0%; Iron 0%
Exchanges: 1 Serving is a Free Food

BETTY'S TIPS

✪ **Substitution**
Coarse-grained, country-style or spicy brown mustard can be used in place of the Dijon mustard.

✪ **The Finishing Touch**
Split fresh coconuts in half with a hammer and screwdriver. Drain the liquid and fill halves with the preserves and coconut for dipping.

— Quick —

Tomato-Basil Crostini

Prep: 20 min Bake: 5 min

32 slices French bread, ¼ inch thick
¼ cup olive or vegetable oil
3 roma (plum) tomatoes, diced (2 cups)
3 cloves garlic, finely chopped
½ cup shredded Parmesan cheese
2 tablespoons chopped fresh basil leaves
½ teaspoon salt

1. Heat oven to 425°. Place bread on ungreased cookie sheet. Brush 2 tablespoons of the oil on bread. Bake 4 to 5 minutes or until light golden brown.

2. Mix tomatoes, remaining 2 tablespoons oil, the garlic, cheese, basil and salt. Place about 1 tablespoon tomato mixture on each warm bread slice.

32 appetizers.

1 Appetizer: Calories 75 (Calories from Fat 35); Fat 4g (Saturated 1g); Cholesterol 0mg; Sodium 190mg; Carbohydrate 9g (Dietary Fiber 1g); Protein 2g
% Daily Value: Vitamin A 2%; Vitamin C 2%; Calcium 4%; Iron 2%
Exchanges: ½ Starch, 1 Fat

BETTY'S TIPS

✪ **Keep It Casual**
Omit 2 tablespoons of the oil and don't toast the bread. Serve tomato mixture in a small glass bowl and let guests help themselves.

✪ **Make It Extra Special**
Substitute sourdough cocktail bread for the French bread. Serve on elegant white marble tiles.

Easy Brie Smoked Lox Torte

Prep: 5 min

1 round (8 ounces) Brie cheese
6 slices salmon lox
1 teaspoon capers
1 teaspoon chopped fresh dill weed
   Fresh dill weed sprigs, if desired
   Assorted crackers, if desired

1. Cut cheese horizontally in half. Place 5 slices of the lox on bottom half of cheese. Sprinkle with capers and chopped dill weed.

2. Top with other cheese half. Roll remaining lox slice to form a rose shape. Garnish cheese with lox rose and dill weed sprig. Serve with crackers.

8 servings.

1 Serving: Calories 85 (Calories from Fat 65); Fat 7g (Saturated 4g); Cholesterol 20mg; Sodium 260mg; Carbohydrate 0g (Dietary Fiber 0g); Protein 6g
% Daily Value: Vitamin A 4%; Vitamin C 0%; Calcium 10%; Iron 0%
Exchanges: 1 Medium-Fat Meat

BETTY'S TIPS

✿ **Success Hint**
When slicing the Brie in half, use toothpicks to mark the middle and dental floss to cut the cheese round.

✿ **Variation**
The Brie also can be served warm. Heat oven to 350°. Lightly brush cookie sheet with vegetable oil. Place filled cheese (do not add capers) on cookie sheet and bake uncovered 5 to 7 minutes or until cheese is soft and partially melted. Sprinkle with capers. Garnish as directed.

✿ **Do-Ahead**
Assemble the Brie up to 24 hours ahead; cover and refrigerate. Garnish just before serving.

Easy Brie Smoked Lox Torte

Baked Spinach, Crab and Artichoke Dip

Prep: 10 min Bake: 20 min

1   cup mayonnaise or salad dressing

1   cup grated Parmesan cheese

1   can (14 ounces) artichoke hearts, drained and coarsely chopped

1   package (9 ounces) frozen chopped spinach, thawed and squeezed to drain

1   package (8 ounces) refrigerated imitation crabmeat chunks

1   cup shredded Monterey Jack or Cheddar cheese (4 ounces)

Toasted baguette slices or assorted crackers, if desired

1. Heat oven to 350°. Mix mayonnaise and Parmesan cheese in medium bowl. Stir in artichoke hearts, spinach and crabmeat.

2. Spoon mixture into 1-quart casserole. Sprinkle with Monterey Jack cheese.

3. Cover and bake 15 to 20 minutes or until cheese is melted. Serve warm with baguette slices.

24 servings (2 tablespoons each).

2 Tablespoons: Calories 120 (Calories from Fat 90); Fat 10g (Saturated 3g); Cholesterol 15mg; Sodium 300mg; Carbohydrate 3g (Dietary Fiber 1g); Protein 5g
% Daily Value: Vitamin A 16%; Vitamin C 2%; Calcium 10%; Iron 2%
Exchanges: ½ Lean Meat, 2 Fat

BETTY'S TIPS

☺ Substitution
One cup of loosely packed, coarsely chopped fresh spinach leaves can be substituted for the frozen spinach.

☺ Do-Ahead
This sensational, simple-to-prepare dip can be made and refrigerated before baking up to 24 hours ahead. Bake as directed.

Baked Spinach, Crab and Artichoke Dip

Ham and Gouda Pastry Puffs

Prep: 30 min   Bake: 22 min

1¼ cups finely diced fully cooked ham
½ cup shredded Gouda cheese (2 ounces)
¼ cup sun-dried tomatoes in oil, drained and chopped
2 tablespoons sour cream
4 medium green onions, chopped (¼ cup)
2 packages (17.3 ounces each) frozen puff pastry, thawed

1. Heat oven to 400°. Mix all ingredients except pastry.

2. Cut pastry into circles with 2½- to 3-inch round cookie cutter or pastry wheel. Spoon about 1 rounded teaspoon ham mixture on center of each circle; brush edges with water. Fold each circle over filling, pressing edges to seal.

3. Place in ungreased rectangular pan, 15 × 10 × 1 inch. Bake 18 to 22 minutes or until golden brown. Serve warm.

About 36 appetizers.

1 Appetizer: Calories 107 (Calories from Fat 110); Fat 12g (Saturated 4g); Cholesterol 35mg; Sodium 160mg; Carbohydrate 13g (Dietary Fiber 0g); Protein 4g
% Daily Value: Vitamin A 0%; Vitamin C 0%; Calcium 2%; Iron 8%
Exchanges: 1 Starch, 2 Fat

BETTY'S TIPS

✿ **Do-Ahead**

Prepare and bake puffs up to a day ahead of time. Cool completely, then cover and refrigerate no longer than 24 hours. Reheat in 400° oven 6 to 8 minutes or until heated through.

You can also freeze unbaked puffs. Place waxed paper or cooking parchment paper between layers of puffs. Cover tightly and freeze up to 1 week. Bake as directed.

Ham and Gouda Pastry Puffs

Creamy Chicken and Peppers Enchilada Dip

Caribbean Chicken Wings

Low Fat

Caribbean Chicken Wings

Prep: 10 min Bake: 1 hr

½ cup pineapple juice
½ cup ketchup
¼ cup packed brown sugar
¼ cup teriyaki marinade and sauce
¼ cup honey
2 cloves garlic, finely chopped
2 pounds chicken drummettes (about 24)

1. Heat oven to 350°. Line rectangular pan, 13 × 9 × 2 inches, with aluminum foil.

2. Heat all ingredients except chicken to boiling in 1-quart saucepan, stirring occasionally. Place chicken in pan; pour sauce over chicken.

3. Bake uncovered about 1 hour, turning chicken 2 to 3 times, until juice of chicken is no longer pink when centers of thickest pieces are cut.

4. Spray inside of 3½-inch slow cooker with cooking spray. Place chicken in slow cooker. Cover and keep warm on low heat setting.

24 appetizers.

1 Appetizer: Calories 60 (Calories from Fat 25); Fat 3g (Saturated 1g); Cholesterol 10mg; Sodium 115mg; Carbohydrate 4g (Dietary Fiber 0g); Protein 4g
% Daily Value: Vitamin A 0%; Vitamin C 0%; Calcium 0%; Iron 0%
Exchanges: ½ High-Fat Meat

Creamy Chicken and Peppers Enchilada Dip

Prep: 15 min Cook: 10 hr + 30 min

2 pounds boneless, skinless chicken thighs
1 can (10 ounces) enchilada sauce
1 can (4 ounces) chopped green chilies, undrained
1 medium red bell pepper, chopped (1 cup)
1 medium green bell pepper, chopped (1 cup)
2 packages (8 ounces each) cream cheese, cut into cubes and softened
4 cups shredded Cheddar cheese (16 ounces)
  Large tortilla chips, if desired

1. Place chicken, enchilada sauce and chilies in 3½- to 4-quart slow cooker.

2. Cover and cook on low heat setting 8 to 10 hours or until juice of chicken is no longer pink when centers of thickest pieces are cut.

3. Stir in bell peppers, cream cheese and Cheddar cheese. Cover and cook on low heat setting about 30 minutes, stirring once or twice, until cheese is melted. Serve with tortilla chips.

32 servings (¼ cup each).

¼ Cup: Calories 250 (Calories from Fat 170); Fat 19g (Saturated 11g); Cholesterol 80mg; Sodium 310mg; Carbohydrate 3g (Dietary Fiber 1g); Protein 18g
% Daily Value: Vitamin A 24%; Vitamin C 20%; Calcium 12%; Iron 10%
Exchanges: 3 Medium-Fat Meat

BETTY'S TIPS

⊕ **Do-Ahead**
You can prepare and bake these yummy drummettes up to 24 hours ahead. Cover with foil and refrigerate. Reheat them in the slow cooker.

⊕ **Keep It Casual**
Serve the chicken wings in the slow cooker with plenty of paper napkins and plates.

⊕ **Make It Extra Special**
For a real Caribbean feel, add 1 cup chopped fresh pineapple and ¼ cup chopped green or red bell pepper to the chicken and serve in a silver chafing dish.

BETTY'S TIPS

⊕ **Substitution**
No red bell peppers? Use 2 green bell peppers.

⊕ **Success Hint**
For an extra burst of flavor and heat, add 2 finely chopped chipotle chilies in adobo sauce or 2 seeded and finely chopped jalapeño chilies.

Chicken Wings with Dipping Sauces

Prep: 10 min Bake: time will vary

Zesty Italian Dip (below)
Maple-Dijon Sauce (right)
2 pounds purchased ready-to-eat or frozen seasoned chicken wings

1. Make Zesty Italian Dip and Maple-Dijon Sauce; cover and refrigerate until serving.

2. Reheat ready-to-eat wings if necessary; if using frozen wings, bake as directed on package. Serve with Zesty Italian Dip and Maple-Dijon Sauce.

8 servings.

Zesty Italian Dip

1 cup sour cream
¼ cup finely chopped cucumber
4 medium green onions, thinly sliced (¼ cup)
2 tablespoons milk
1 teaspoon Italian seasoning
⅛ teaspoon salt
⅛ teaspoon ground red pepper (cayenne)
1 clove garlic, finely chopped

Mix all ingredients.

Maple-Dijon Sauce

⅓ cup olive or vegetable oil
⅓ cup real maple syrup
⅓ cup Dijon mustard

Beat all ingredients with wire whisk.

1 Serving: Calories 495 (Calories from Fat 335); Fat 37g (Saturated 12g); Cholesterol 80mg; Sodium 1120mg; Carbohydrate 21g (Dietary Fiber 1g); Protein 21g
% Daily Value: Vitamin A 10%; Vitamin C 4%; Calcium 4%; Iron 12%
Exchanges: 1 Starch, 3 High-Fat Meat, ½ Fruit, 2 Fat

BETTY'S TIPS

❂ **Substitution**
Maple-flavored syrup can be used in place of real maple syrup.

❂ **Success Hint**
Pick up hot, ready-to-eat wings at your favorite fast-food restaurant or grocery store deli. Using frozen seasoned wings is another option; they're convenient and handy—just heat, eat and enjoy!

Chicken Wings with Dipping Sauces

Cheesy Herb and Beef Bites

Prep: 15 min

10   thin slices roast beef, about 4 inches in diameter (from 6-ounce package)

¼   cup herb-and-garlic spreadable cheese

¼   cup finely chopped red bell pepper

40   bite-size garlic-flavor or regular bagel chips or round buttery crackers

Chopped fresh parsley or chives, if desired

1. Unfold each beef slice so that it is flat. Spread each slice with 1 teaspoon cheese and 1 teaspoon red bell pepper. Carefully roll up. Cut each roll into 4 pieces.

2. Place each beef roll on bagel chip. Garnish with parsley. Serve immediately.

40 appetizers.

1 Appetizer: Calories 35 (Calories from Fat 10); Fat 1g (Saturated 1g); Cholesterol 20mg; Sodium 75mg; Carbohydrate 4g (Dietary Fiber 0g); Protein 3g
% Daily Value: Vitamin A 0%; Vitamin C 0%; Calcium 0%; Iron 2%
Exchanges: ½ Medium-Fat Meat

BETTY'S TIPS

⊙ **Substitution**
Turkey, ham or pastrami slices can be substituted for the roast beef.

⊙ **Do-Ahead**
To jump-start preparation of these bite-size snacks, follow step 1 to the point of carefully rolling up each beef slice, but do not cut. Cover and refrigerate rolls up to 8 hours. Cut into 4 pieces and continue as directed.

Cheesy Herb and Beef Bites

Betty...
ON BASICS

Hummus

Prep: 5 min

1   can (15 to 16 ounces) garbanzo beans, drained and
    ⅓ cup liquid reserved
3   tablespoons lemon juice
½   cup sesame seed
1   clove garlic, crushed
1   teaspoon salt
    Chopped fresh parsley
    Raw vegetables or crackers, if desired

1. Place beans, reserved bean liquid, lemon juice, sesame seed, garlic and salt in blender or food processor. Cover and blend on high speed, stopping blender occasionally to scrape sides if necessary, until uniform consistency.

2. Spoon dip into serving dish. Sprinkle with parsley. Serve with vegetables.

16 servings (2 tablespoons each).

2 Tablespoons: Calories 65 (Calories from Fat 25); Fat 3g (Saturated 0g); Cholesterol 0mg; Sodium 190mg; Carbohydrate 8g (Dietary Fiber 3g); Protein 4g
% Daily Value: Vitamin A 0%; Vitamin C 2%; Calcium 2%; Iron 6%
Exchanges: ½ Starch, ½ Fat

Cover and blend until mixture is uniform consistency.

Hummus-Olive Spread

~ Quick & Low Fat ~

Hummus-Olive Spread

Prep: 10 min

Hummus (opposite) or 2 containers (7 ounces each) plain hummus

¾ cup pitted Kalamata and/or Spanish olives, chopped

2 tablespoons Greek vinaigrette

Pita bread wedges or baby carrots, if desired

1. Spread hummus on 8- to 10-inch serving plate.

2. Mix olives and vinaigrette. Spoon over hummus. Serve with pita bread wedges.

22 servings (2 tablespoons each).

2 Tablespoons: Calories 65 (Calories from Fat 25); Fat 3g (Saturated 0g); Cholesterol 0mg; Sodium 190mg; Carbohydrate 7g (Dietary Fiber 2g); Protein 3g
% Daily Value: Vitamin A 0%; Vitamin C 0%; Calcium 2%; Iron 6%
Exchanges: ½ Starch, ½ Fat

BETTY'S TIPS

✿ **Substitution**

A 4¼-ounce can of chopped ripe olives, drained, can be substituted for the Kalamata olives.

Zesty Italian dressing can be substituted for the Greek vinaigrette.

Roast Beef Bruschetta

Prep: 20 min Bake: 5 min Cool: 5 min

1 loaf (8 ounces) French bread, cut into thirty ¼- to ½-inch slices

2 tablespoons olive or vegetable oil

½ cup soft cream cheese with chives and onions

8 ounces thinly sliced cooked deli roast beef

¼ teaspoon coarsely ground pepper

4 roma (plum) tomatoes, thinly sliced

8 medium green onions, sliced (½ cup)

1. Heat oven to 375°. Brush both sides of bread slices with oil. Place on ungreased cookie sheet. Bake about 5 minutes or until crisp. Cool 5 minutes.

2. Spread cream cheese over each slice. Top with beef; sprinkle with pepper. Top with tomato slice and green onions.

30 appetizers.

1 Appetizer: Calories 60 (Calories from Fat 25); Fat 3g (Saturated 1g); Cholesterol 10mg; Sodium 60mg; Carbohydrate 5g (Dietary Fiber 0g); Protein 3g
% Daily Value: Vitamin A 2%; Vitamin C 2%; Calcium 0%; Iron 2%
Exchanges: ½ Starch, ½ Fat

BETTY'S TIPS

☺ Pack 'n Go
You can make these appetizers ahead, but add the tomato slices and green onions just before serving.

To transport, arrange bruschetta on a large serving platter and cover tightly with plastic wrap.

☺ Do-Ahead
You can toast the bread up to a day ahead of time. Store loosely covered at room temperature.

Roast Beef Bruschetta

Straight from the Garden

A Refreshing Medley of Salads

Thai Chicken Peanut Salad (page 62)

Pesto Potato Salad (page 50)

Pesto Potato Salad

Prep: 10 min
Photo on page 49

1 quart deli potato salad (4 cups)
½ cup basil pesto
½ cup chopped red bell pepper
2 tablespoons pine nuts, toasted (page 57)

1. Mix potato salad, pesto and bell pepper in large bowl.

2. Just before serving, sprinkle with pine nuts.

9 servings (½ cup each).

½ Cup: Calories 240 (Calories from Fat 170); Fat 19g (Saturated 3g); Cholesterol 10mg; Sodium 400mg; Carbohydrate 16g (Dietary Fiber 2g); Protein 3g
% Daily Value: Vitamin A 12%; Vitamin C 34%; Calcium 6%; Iron 4%
Exchanges: 1 Starch, 3½ Fat

BETTY'S TIPS

❂ **Serve-With**
This basil-accented potato salad would taste great with grilled steak, pork chops or chicken breasts.

❂ **The Finishing Touch**
Make this salad extra special by placing individual servings in colorful red radicchio leaves.

Betty's Classic Potluck Potato Salad

Betty's Classic Potluck Potato Salad

Prep: 15 min Cook: 40 min Chill: 4 hr

6 medium round red or white potatoes (2 pounds), peeled
1½ cups mayonnaise or salad dressing
1 tablespoon white or cider vinegar
1 tablespoon yellow mustard
1 teaspoon salt
¼ teaspoon pepper
2 medium stalks celery, chopped (1 cup)
1 medium onion, chopped (½ cup)
4 hard-cooked eggs, chopped

1. Place potatoes in 3-quart saucepan; add enough water just to cover potatoes. Cover and heat to boiling; reduce heat to low. Cook covered 30 to 35 minutes or until potatoes are tender; drain. Let stand until cool enough to handle. Cut potatoes into cubes.

2. Mix mayonnaise, vinegar, mustard, salt and pepper in large glass or plastic bowl. Add potatoes, celery and onion; toss. Stir in eggs. Cover and refrigerate at least 4 hours to blend flavors and chill.

10 servings.

1 Serving: Calories 340 (Calories from Fat 250); Fat 28g (Saturated 5g); Cholesterol 105mg; Sodium 480mg; Carbohydrate 19g (Dietary Fiber 2g); Protein 5g
% Daily Value: Vitamin A 4%; Vitamin C 12%; Calcium 2%; Iron 4%
Exchanges: 1 Starch, 1 Vegetable, 5 Fat

BETTY'S TIPS

❂ **Success Hint**
For foolproof hard-cooked eggs, place eggs in medium saucepan and cover with cold water (at least 1 inch above eggs). Heat water to boiling; remove from heat. Cover and let stand 18 minutes. Immediately cool in cold water.

❂ **Variation**
For **Dilled Potato Salad**, omit mayonnaise mixture. Mix ¾ cup Italian dressing, 1 tablespoon chopped fresh or 1 teaspoon dried dill weed, ½ teaspoon salt and ¼ cup chopped green onions. Toss with potatoes, celery and onion. Stir in eggs. Cover and refrigerate at least 2 hours to blend flavors.

Betty's Classic Creamy Coleslaw

Prep: 15 min Chill: 1 hr

½ cup sour cream

¼ cup mayonnaise or salad dressing

1 tablespoon sugar

2 teaspoons lemon juice

2 teaspoons Dijon mustard

½ teaspoon celery seed

¼ teaspoon pepper

½ medium head cabbage, finely shredded or chopped (4 cups)

1 small carrot, shredded (½ cup)

1 small onion, chopped (¼ cup)

1. Mix all ingredients except cabbage, carrot and onion in large glass or plastic bowl. Add remaining ingredients; toss until evenly coated.

2. Cover and refrigerate at least 1 hour to blend flavors.

8 servings.

1 Serving: Calories 100 (Calories from Fat 70); Fat 8g (Saturated 3g); Cholesterol 15mg; Sodium 90mg; Carbohydrate 7g (Dietary Fiber 2g); Protein 2g
% Daily Value: Vitamin A 26%; Vitamin C 32%; Calcium 4%; Iron 2%
Exchanges: 1 Vegetable, 1½ Fat

BETTY'S TIPS

✿ **Pack 'n Go**
Clean, plastic takeout containers are a great way to transport salads such as this creamy coleslaw. Look for the containers at a paper or party supply store.

✿ **Time-Save**
Forget about shredding the cabbage and carrot. Instead pick up a package of coleslaw mix in the produce department of the grocery store.

✿ **Special Touch**
Toss in red grapes, crumbled blue cheese and toasted walnuts for extra-special flavor and crunch.

Betty's Classic Creamy Coleslaw

Greek Salad

Prep: 10 min

1 small head Bibb lettuce, torn into bite-size pieces

8 to 10 ounces fresh baby spinach, torn into bite-size pieces

1 small red onion, thinly sliced

1 can (15 to 16 ounces) garbanzo beans, rinsed and drained

1 can (5¾ ounces) pitted ripe olives, drained

¼ cup Greek vinaigrette

1 jar (6 to 7 ounces) marinated artichoke hearts, undrained

1 cup crumbled feta cheese (4 ounces)

1. Toss lettuce, spinach, onion, beans and olives in large bowl.

2. Toss with vinaigrette and artichoke hearts. Sprinkle with cheese.

6 servings.

1 Serving: Calories 265 (Calories from Fat 135); Fat 15g (Saturated 5g); Cholesterol 25mg; Sodium 830mg; Carbohydrate 30g (Dietary Fiber 10g); Protein 13g
% Daily Value: Vitamin A 80%; Vitamin C 30%; Calcium 26%; Iron 26%
Exchanges: 1 Starch, 1 Medium-Fat Meat, 3 Vegetable, 1 Fat

BETTY'S TIPS

⊘ **Substitution**
Bags of salad greens are convenient to use, but they do cost a bit more money. If you prefer, use a 16-ounce bag of ready-to-eat lettuce and an 8- to 10-ounce bag of ready-to-eat spinach.

One-fourth cup of Italian dressing can be substituted for the Greek vinaigrette.

⊘ **Success Hint**
Cut the artichoke hearts in half if desired.

Greek Salad

Club Pasta Salad

Prep: 10 min Cook: 15 min

1 package Betty Crocker Suddenly Salad® ranch & bacon pasta salad mix

½ cup mayonnaise or salad dressing

1½ cups cut-up cooked chicken or turkey

4 cups bite-size pieces lettuce

½ cup cherry tomatoes, cut into fourths

1. Empty pasta mix into 3-quart (or larger) saucepan ⅔ full of boiling water. Gently boil uncovered 15 minutes, stirring occasionally. Drain; rinse well with cold water. Shake to drain well.

2. Stir Seasoning mix and mayonnaise in large bowl. Stir in pasta and chicken. Arrange lettuce on 4 salad plates. Top with pasta mixture and tomatoes.

4 servings.

1 Serving: Calories 470 (Calories from Fat 250); Fat 28g (Saturated 4g); Cholesterol 60mg; Sodium 560mg; Carbohydrate 34g (Dietary Fiber 2g); Protein 23g
% Daily Value: Vitamin A 22%; Vitamin C 10%; Calcium 4%; Iron 14%
Exchanges: 2 Starch, 2 Medium-Fat Meat, 1 Vegetable, 3 Fat

BETTY'S TIPS

❂ **Success Hint**
Rinsing the pasta under cold running water removes the excess starch and keeps the pasta from sticking together.

Be sure to thoroughly drain the cooked pasta. Excess cooking water clinging to the pasta will dilute the dressing.

❂ **Special Touch**
Top with ½ cup of thin strips of Cheddar cheese.

Club Pasta Salad

Extra Special Caesar Salad

Extra-Special Caesar Salad

Prep: 20 min

2 cloves garlic, cut in half

1 can (2 ounces) anchovy fillets, cut up

⅔ cup olive or vegetable oil

6 tablespoons lemon juice

2 teaspoons Worcestershire sauce

½ teaspoon salt

½ teaspoon ground mustard

 Freshly ground pepper

2 large bunches romaine, torn into bite-size pieces (20 cups)

2 cups garlic-flavored croutons

⅔ cup grated Parmesan cheese

Serve with One or More of These Toppings:

8 grilled or broiled boneless, skinless chicken breast halves, sliced diagonally (serve warm or chilled)

2 pounds grilled or broiled peeled deveined large shrimp or sea scallops (serve warm or chilled)

1. Rub large wooden salad bowl with cut cloves of garlic. Allow a few small pieces of garlic to remain in bowl if desired.

2. Mix anchovies, oil, lemon juice, Worcestershire sauce, salt, mustard and pepper in salad bowl. Add romaine; toss until coated. Sprinkle with croutons and cheese; toss. Serve with desired Toppings.

8 servings.

1 Serving: Calories 275 (Calories from Fat 205); Fat 23g (Saturated 5g); Cholesterol 15mg; Sodium 750mg; Carbohydrate 11g (Dietary Fiber 3g); Protein 9g
% Daily Value: Vitamin A 60%; Vitamin C 60%; Calcium 20%; Iron 14%
Exchanges: 2 Vegetable, 5 Fat

BETTY'S TIPS

☺ **Substitution**
Two teaspoons of anchovy paste can be substituted for the anchovy fillets.

☺ **The Finishing Touch**
Here's an easy way to add bread to this meal. Serve prepared salad and topping on individual ready-to-serve pizza crusts. The pizza crust "salad holders" make dinner portable for your guests.

TIMETABLE FOR GRILLING TOPPINGS

Topping	Grilling Time	Doneness
Chicken Breast Halves	Heat coals or gas grill for direct heat. Brush chicken with olive or vegetable oil; season if desired. Cover and grill 4 to 6 inches from medium heat 15 to 20 minutes, turning once.	Cook chicken until juice is no longer pink when centers of thickest pieces are cut.
Shrimp and Scallops	Heat coals or gas grill for direct heat. Brush shrimp and/or scallops with olive or vegetable oil; season if desired. Spray hinged wire grill basket with cooking spray or brush with vegetable oil. Place shrimp and/or scallops in basket. Cover and grill 5 to 10 minutes, turning once.	Cook shrimp until pink and firm. Cook scallops until white.

Betty...
ON BASICS

Quick

Balsamic Vinaigrette

Prep: 10 min

$\frac{1}{3}$ cup olive or vegetable oil
$\frac{1}{4}$ cup balsamic or red wine vinegar
2 tablespoons sugar
1 clove garlic, finely chopped
1 teaspoon Dijon mustard

Beat all ingredients with wire whisk until smooth.

$\frac{2}{3}$ cup vinaigrette.

1 Tablespoon: Calories 75 (Calories from Fat 65); Fat 7g
(Saturated 2g); Cholesterol 0mg; Sodium 20mg; Carbohydrate 5g
(Dietary Fiber 0g); Protein 0g
% Daily Value: Vitamin A 0%; Vitamin C 0%; Calcium 0%; Iron 0%
Exchanges: $1\frac{1}{2}$ Fat

Christmas Salad with Balsamic Vinaigrette

Prep: 20 min

Balsamic Vinaigrette (opposite)
1 bag (10 ounces) mixed baby greens or Italian-blend salad greens
1 avocado, pitted, peeled and sliced
⅓ cup pistachio nuts
¼ cup dried cranberries

1. Make Balsamic Vinaigrette.

2. Toss vinaigrette and remaining ingredients just before serving.

6 servings.

1 Serving: Calories 235 (Calories from Fat 125); Fat 20g (Saturated 3g); Cholesterol 0mg; Sodium 35mg; Carbohydrate 14g (Dietary Fiber 3g); Protein 3g
% Daily Value: Vitamin A 30%; Vitamin C 18%; Calcium 4%; Iron 6%
Exchanges: 3 Vegetable, 3½ Fat

See the chart at right for examples of delicious ingredient combinations to toss with greens and Balsamic Vinaigrette.

Variation 1
2 cups quartered strawberries
1 package (4 ounces) goat cheese crumbles
⅓ cup slivered almonds, toasted

Variation 2
1 medium green apple, chopped (1 cup)
4 ounces Gorgonzola or blue cheese, crumbled (½ cup)
⅓ cup walnuts, toasted

Variation 3
2 cups fresh mushrooms, sliced
1½ cups grape tomatoes, cut in half
⅓ cup finely sliced purple onion

BETTY'S TIPS

✿ Success Hint
To toast nuts, heat oven to 350°. Spread nuts in ungreased shallow pan. Bake about 10 minutes, stirring occasionally, until golden brown and fragrant. Watch carefully because nuts brown quickly. Or cook nuts in ungreased heavy skillet over medium-low heat 5 to 7 minutes, stirring frequently until browning begins, then stirring constantly until golden brown and fragrant.

Gazpacho Pasta Salad with Tomato-Lime Dressing

Prep: 20 min

Tomato-Lime Dressing (below)
1   package (8 ounces) farfalle (bow-tie) pasta
1   large tomato, seeded and coarsely chopped (1 cup)
1   small cucumber, coarsely chopped (¾ cup)
1   small bell pepper, coarsely chopped (½ cup)
4   medium green onions, sliced (¼ cup)
½   green Anaheim chili, seeded and chopped
1   can (2¼ ounces) sliced ripe olives, drained
¼   cup chopped fresh cilantro

1. Make Tomato-Lime Dressing. Cook and drain pasta as directed on package.

2. Mix pasta and remaining ingredients in large bowl. Pour dressing over mixture; toss. Serve immediately or cover and refrigerate until serving.

4 servings.

Tomato-Lime Dressing
¼   cup tomato juice
2   tablespoons olive or vegetable oil
2   tablespoons lime juice
¼   teaspoon salt
⅛   teaspoon pepper
1   clove garlic, finely chopped

Shake all ingredients in tightly covered container.

1 Serving: Calories 320 (Calories from Fat 90); Fat 10g (Saturated 2g); Cholesterol 0mg; Sodium 350mg; Carbohydrate 52g (Dietary Fiber 4g); Protein 9g
% Daily Value: Vitamin A 20%; Vitamin C 32%; Calcium 4%; Iron 20%
Exchanges: 3 Starch, 2 Vegetable, 1 Fat

BETTY'S TIPS

⊕ **Success Hint**
Check out *What's New* on page 61 for moreinfo on tomatoes, including how to store them and how to seed them.

⊕ **Did You Know?**
Gazpacho, a cold, nearly fat-free soup that originated in southern Spain, is usually made from a pureed mixture of fresh tomatoes, bell peppers, onions, celery, cucumber, bread crumbs, garlic, olive oil, vinegar and lemon juice. This low-cal salad borrows from traditional gazpacho to bring you a salad bursting with nutrient-rich veggies.

Gazpacho Pasta Salad with Tomato-Lime Dressing

Italian Herb Pasta Salad

Prep: 20 min Chill: 2 hr

1 package (16 ounces) rotini pasta

1 can (8 ounces) tomato sauce

1 cup Italian dressing

1 tablespoon chopped fresh or 1 teaspoon dried basil leaves

1 tablespoon chopped fresh or 1 teaspoon dried oregano leaves

1 cup sliced mushrooms (3 ounces)

1 pint (2 cups) cherry tomatoes, cut in half

1 large cucumber, coarsely chopped (1½ cups)

½ medium red onion, cut into thin wedges and separated (½ cup)

1. Cook and drain pasta as directed on package. Rinse with cold water; drain.

2. Mix tomato sauce, dressing, basil and oregano in large glass or plastic bowl. Add pasta and remaining ingredients; toss. Cover and refrigerate about 2 hours until chilled but no longer than 24 hours.

12 servings.

1 Serving: Calories 250 (Calories from Fat 80); Fat 9g (Saturated 1g); Cholesterol 5mg; Sodium 300mg; Carbohydrate 36g (Dietary Fiber 2g); Protein 6g
% Daily Value: Vitamin A 8%; Vitamin C 14%; Calcium 4%; Iron 10%
Exchanges: 2 Starch, 1 Vegetable, 1½ Fat

BETTY'S TIPS

✿ **Pack 'n Go**
For an impromptu potluck picnic, keep a basket or bag packed with basic supplies, including plates, flatware, cups, napkins, tablecloth, paper towels and trash bags.

✿ **Success Hint**
If using pasta for a salad, rinse it under cold running water to remove the excess starch and to keep the pasta from sticking together.

✿ **Variation**
For **Pizza Pasta Salad**, toss a 3¼-ounce package of sliced pepperoni, chopped, and a 2¼-ounce can of sliced ripe olives, drained, with the pasta and other ingredients.

Italian Herb Pasta Salad

Ranch Ham and Pasta Salad

Prep: 20 min Cook: 25 min Chill: 1 hr

4 unpeeled small new potatoes, cubed (2 cups)
2 cups uncooked radiatore (nugget) pasta (6 ounces)
2 cups broccoli flowerets
1 cup diced fully cooked ham
¼ cup chopped drained roasted red bell peppers (from 7-ounce jar)
2 medium green onions, chopped (2 tablespoons)
⅓ cup mayonnaise or salad dressing
⅓ cup ranch dressing
⅛ teaspoon pepper

1. Place potatoes in 4-quart Dutch oven; add enough water just to cover potatoes. Cover and heat to boiling; boil 4 minutes. Remove potatoes from water with slotted spoon.

2. Add pasta to boiling water in Dutch oven; cook and drain as directed on package, adding broccoli for last 2 minutes of cooking. Cool potatoes, pasta and broccoli slightly. Refrigerate about 1 hour or until completely chilled.

3. Mix potatoes, pasta, broccoli, ham, bell peppers and onions in large glass or plastic bowl. Mix mayonnaise, ranch dressing and pepper; gently stir into potato mixture. Serve immediately or cover and refrigerate up to 2 hours before serving.

6 servings.

1 Serving: Calories 385 (Calories from Fat 190); Fat 21g (Saturated 4g); Cholesterol 350mg; Sodium 880mg; Carbohydrate 36g (Dietary Fiber 3g); Protein 16g
% Daily Value: Vitamin A 16%; Vitamin C 38%; Calcium 4%; Iron 14%
Exchanges: 2 Starch, 1½ Medium-Fat Meat, 1 Vegetable, 2 Fat

BETTY'S TIPS

✪ Pack 'n Go
If you're heading out for a picnic, be sure to pack perishable cold foods like this pasta salad in an insulated cooler filled with ice. While traveling, it's a good idea to keep the cooler in an air-conditioned car rather than in the trunk, where the temperature is much hotter.

✪ Success Hint
To serve this salad at an outdoor gathering, place the salad bowl in a shallow bowl filled with crushed ice.

Ranch Ham and Pasta Salad

Betty... ON WHAT'S NEW

Tomato Harvest

STORAGE

Never store tomatoes in the refrigerator. Once temperatures reach below 50°F, the quality of the tomato deteriorates with the pulp becoming mushy and the tomatoes losing their flavor. Store at room temperature instead. You can quicken ripening by placing underripe tomatoes in a brown paper bag and closing.

PEELING

To peel a tomato, heat a large saucepan of water to boiling. Carefully place the tomatoes in the boiling water for 15 to 20 seconds. Transfer with a slotted spoon or tongs to cold water, then peel skins from the tomatoes.

CORING

To remove the core, cut a small circle around the stem end with a small knife and remove the core.

SEEDING

To remove seeds, cut the tomato crosswise in half and gently squeeze or spoon seeds into a bowl. Although seeding a tomato may be beneficial to a recipe, remember that the seeds are the highest concentration of vitamin C and much of the flavor.

FREEZING

To freeze fresh tomatoes, peel, seed and chop them; do not drain. Place tomatoes in plastic containers or plastic freezer bags and freeze up to three months. Use in recipes as you would canned tomatoes.

ROASTING

To roast a tomato, insert a long-handled fork into a tomato. Hold it over a gas or charcoal grill, turning the tomato until it is charred on all sides. Let the tomato become cool enough to handle, then remove the skin.

Thai Chicken Peanut Salad

Prep: 25 min Microwave: 6 min Chill: 2 hr

¾ pound green beans
    Peanut Dressing (below)
2   cups cubed cooked chicken
1   large red bell pepper, cut into 1 × ¼-inch
    strips
4   medium green onions, sliced (¼ cup)
½   cup honey-roasted peanuts

1. Place green beans and 1 cup water in 1-quart microwavable casserole. Cover and microwave on High 4 to 6 minutes or until beans are tender; drain.

2. Make Peanut Dressing. Toss beans, chicken, bell pepper and onions in large bowl. Pour dressing over mixture; toss. Cover and refrigerate 1 to 2 hours or until chilled. Sprinkle with peanuts just before serving.

4 servings.

Peanut Dressing

¼ cup crunchy peanut butter
6   tablespoons zesty Italian dressing
3   tablespoons orange juice
½   teaspoon red pepper sauce

Beat all ingredients with wire whisk until smooth.

1 Serving: Calories 470 (Calories from Fat 290); Fat 32g (Saturated 5g); Cholesterol 65mg; Sodium 490mg; Carbohydrate 20g (Dietary Fiber 6g); Protein 31g
% Daily Value: Vitamin A 60%; Vitamin C 72%; Calcium 10%; Iron 14%
Exchanges: 3 Medium-Fat Meat, 4 Vegetable, 3 Fat

BETTY'S TIPS

✿ **Success Hint**
If you want a bit more spice, increase the red pepper sauce to ¾ teaspoon.

✿ **Time-Saver**
You can use leftover cut-up cooked chicken or pick up a rotisserie chicken at the supermarket. Remove the chicken from the bones and cut into bite-size pieces.

Thai Chicken Peanut Salad

Mandarin Chicken Salad

Prep: 15 min Cook: 5 min

2 tablespoons butter or margarine

1 package (3 ounces) Oriental-flavor ramen noodle soup mix

2 tablespoons sesame seed

¼ cup sugar

¼ cup white vinegar

1 tablespoon sesame or vegetable oil

½ teaspoon pepper

2 cups cut-up cooked chicken

¼ cup dry-roasted peanuts, if desired

4 medium green onions, sliced (¼ cup)

1 bag (16 ounces) coleslaw mix

1 can (11 ounces) mandarin orange segments, drained

1. Melt butter in 10-inch skillet over medium heat. Stir in seasoning packet from soup mix. Break block of noodles into bite-size pieces over skillet; stir into butter mixture.

2. Cook noodles 2 minutes, stirring occasionally. Stir in sesame seed. Cook about 2 minutes longer, stirring occasionally, until noodles are golden brown; remove from heat.

3. Mix sugar, vinegar, oil and pepper in large bowl. Add noodle mixture and remaining ingredients; toss.

6 servings.

1 Serving: Calories 290 (Calories from Fat 125); Fat 14g (Saturated 5g); Cholesterol 50mg; Sodium 300mg; Carbohydrate 27g (Dietary Fiber 3g); Protein 17g
% Daily Value: Vitamin A 12%; Vitamin C 34%; Calcium 6%; Iron 10%
Exchanges: 1 Starch, 1½ Lean Meat, 2 Vegetable, 1 Fat

BETTY'S TIPS

❂ **Pack 'n Go**
If you're taking this salad to a potluck, toss everything except the noodle mixture and the dressing into a large portable container. Once you arrive, add noodle mixture and dressing, then cover and gently shake or spin to "toss."

❂ **Serve-With**
Enjoy this summer salad with crispy breadsticks and tall glasses of lemon-flavored iced tea.

Mandarin Chicken Salad

Betty ...
MAKES IT EASY

Grilled Chicken Salad with Raspberries

Prep: 18 min Grill: 20 min

4   boneless, skinless chicken breast halves (about 1¼ pounds)
¾   cup raspberry or regular vinaigrette dressing
6   cups bite-size pieces mixed salad greens
1   pint (2 cups) raspberries
1   mango, peeled and sliced

Use a sharp knife to cut the mango vertically, sliding the knife along the seed on one side. Repeat on the other side, which will give you 2 large pieces. If the mango is large enough, trim the sides as well.

1. Heat coals or gas grill for direct heat. Brush chicken with 2 tablespoons of the dressing. Cover and grill chicken 4 to 5 inches from medium heat 15 to 20 minutes, turning once and brushing with 2 tablespoons dressing, until juice of chicken is no longer pink when centers of thickest pieces are cut.

2. Divide greens among 4 plates. Top with raspberries and mango. Cut chicken diagonally into ½-inch slices; place on salads. Drizzle with remaining dressing.

4 servings.

1 Serving: Calories 235 (Calories from Fat 45); Fat 5g (Saturated 1g); Cholesterol 75mg; Sodium 560mg; Carbohydrate 24g (Dietary Fiber 7g); Protein 29g
% Daily Value: Vitamin A 58%; Vitamin C 70%; Calcium 6%; Iron 14%
Exchanges: 3½ Very Lean Meat, 2 Vegetable, 1 Fruit

Cut away the remaining fruit and remove the peel from the pieces. Cut into slices.

Grilled Chicken Salad with Raspberries

— Low-Fat —

Chicken-Parmesan Couscous Salad

Prep: 35 min Cook: 6 min

1 package (5.9 ounces) Parmesan couscous mix
1 can (10 ounces) chunk chicken breast, drained
1 jar (7 ounces) roasted red bell peppers, drained and cut into strips
1 jar (6 to 7 ounces) marinated artichoke hearts, undrained
¼ cup chopped fresh parsley

1. Make couscous as directed on package. Transfer couscous to large bowl; let stand 20 minutes to cool slightly.

2. Add remaining ingredients to couscous; gently stir to mix. Serve slightly warm or at room temperature.

4 servings.

1 Serving: Calories 330 (Calories from Fat 25); Fat 3g (Saturated 1g); Cholesterol 30mg; Sodium 390mg; Carbohydrate 61g (Dietary Fiber 7g); Protein 22g
% Daily Value: Vitamin A 62%; Vitamin C 100%; Calcium 4%; Iron 12%
Exchanges: 4 Starch, 1 Very Lean Meat

BETTY'S TIPS

✿ **Substitution**
If flavored couscous is not available, cook regular couscous as directed on the package, using chicken broth and stirring in ¼ cup grated Parmesan cheese at the end.
Substitute 1½ cups cut-up cooked chicken for the canned chicken.

✿ **Time-Saver**
Keep a jar of roasted red bell peppers in the refrigerator. They add lots of great sweet-smoky flavor to salads and sandwiches.

Curried Chicken and Rice Salad

Prep: 15 min Chill: 2 hr

½ cup mayonnaise or salad dressing
½ cup plain yogurt
2 teaspoons curry powder
½ teaspoon salt
3 cups cold cooked rice
2 cups cut-up cooked chicken
2 medium mangoes, cut lengthwise in half, pitted and diced (2 cups)
2 medium stalks celery, sliced (1 cup)
1 small bell pepper, chopped (½ cup)

1. Mix mayonnaise, yogurt, curry powder and salt in large bowl. Stir in remaining ingredients.

2. Cover and refrigerate about 2 hours or until chilled.

6 servings.

1 Serving: Calories 380 (Calories from Fat 170); Fat 19g (Saturated 3g); Cholesterol 50mg; Sodium 370mg; Carbohydrate 38g (Dietary Fiber 2g); Protein 17g
% Daily Value: Vitamin A 12%; Vitamin C 52%; Calcium 6%; Iron 10%
Exchanges: 1 Starch, 2 Lean Meat, 2 Vegetable, 1 Fruit, 2 Fat

BETTY'S TIPS

✿ **Health Twist**
For 4 grams of fat and 255 calories per serving, use fat-free mayonnaise and fat-free plain yogurt.

✿ **Special Touch**
Garnish with large pieces of shaved coconut, which are available in the baking section of most large supermarkets.

Curried Chicken and Rice Salad

Chicken-Parmesan Couscous Salad

Southwestern Chicken Taco Salad

Prep: 25 min

Southwest Dressing (below)

1 bag (10 ounces) romaine and leaf lettuce

1 cup shredded Mexican cheese blend (4 ounces)

2 packages (6 ounces each) frozen cooked Southwest-flavor chicken breast strips, thawed

1 can (2¼ ounces) sliced ripe olives, drained

4 roma (plum) tomatoes, cut into fourths

1 cup chili-flavored corn chips, slightly crushed

1. Make Southwest Dressing.

2. Mix remaining ingredients except corn chips in large bowl. Toss salad with dressing until coated. Sprinkle with corn chips.

4 servings.

Southwest Dressing

½ cup salsa

½ cup Southwest sour cream dip

Beat all ingredients with wire whisk until smooth.

1 Serving: Calories 465 (Calories from Fat 245); Fat 27g (Saturated 10g); Cholesterol 110mg; Sodium 1150mg; Carbohydrate 22g (Dietary Fiber 4g); Protein 38g
% Daily Value: Vitamin A 60%; Vitamin C 64%; Calcium 30%; Iron 20%
Exchanges: 1 Starch, 5 Lean Meat, 1 Vegetable, 2 Fat

BETTY'S TIPS

۞ Substitution

If Southwest sour cream dip is not available in your supermarket, add 2 teaspoons taco seasoning to ½ cup of sour cream.

Cheddar, Colby or Monterey Jack cheese can be used instead of Mexican cheese blend, which is a combination of Colby and Monterey Jack cheeses.

Cherry tomatoes, cut in half, can be used instead of the roma tomatoes.

Southwestern Chicken Taco Salad

Sandwiches, Burgers and Pizza

New Inspirations for Midday Meals

Rustic Vegetable Baguette with Smashed Avocado (page 82)

Ham and Provolone Pinwheels (page 71)

Asian Chicken Roll-Ups

Prep: 15 min

2 tablespoons crunchy peanut butter

2 tablespoons teriyaki baste and glaze (from 12-ounce bottle)

1 tablespoon packed brown sugar

1 tablespoon hot water

1 teaspoon sesame oil or vegetable oil

4 flour tortillas (8 to 10 inches in diameter)

8 slices cooked deli chicken breast

1½ cups shredded iceberg lettuce

1½ cups shredded carrots

½ cup chopped fresh cilantro

1. Beat peanut butter, teriyaki baste and glaze, brown sugar, water and oil with wire whisk until smooth.

2. Spread about 2 tablespoons peanut butter mixture over each tortilla. Top each with 2 slices chicken, about ⅓ cup lettuce, about ⅓ cup carrots and 2 tablespoons cilantro. Roll up.

4 roll-ups.

1 Roll-Up: Calories 280 (Calories from Fat 90); Fat 10g (Saturated 2g); Cholesterol 25mg; Sodium 630mg; Carbohydrate 35g (Dietary Fiber 4g); Protein 16g
% Daily Value: Vitamin A 100%; Vitamin C 10%; Calcium 8%; Iron 14%
Exchanges: 2 Starch, 1 Lean Meat, 1 Vegetable, 1 Fat

BETTY'S TIPS

❂ **Substitution**
Stir-fry sauce can be used instead of the teriyaki baste and glaze.

❂ **Time-Saver**
Look for bags of shredded lettuce and carrots in the produce case. You can also use 3 cups purchased broccoli slaw instead of the lettuce and carrots. The broccoli slaw will add an interesting flavor twist to this recipe.

Asian Chicken Roll-Ups

Ham and Provolone Pinwheels

Prep: 10 min
Photo on page 69

¼ cup mayonnaise or salad dressing
2 cloves garlic, finely chopped
2 flour tortillas (8 to 10 inches in diameter)
1 cup fresh spinach
¼ pound thinly sliced ham
6 slices (¾ ounce each) provolone cheese
1 medium tomato, thinly sliced

1. Mix mayonnaise and garlic; spread evenly over tortillas.

2. Top tortillas with layers of spinach, ham, cheese and tomato; roll up tightly. Cut each tortilla into thirds; secure with toothpicks. Serve immediately or refrigerate until serving.

6 servings.

1 Serving: Calories 55 (Calories from Fat 35); Fat 4g (Saturated 1g); Cholesterol 10mg; Sodium 140mg; Carbohydrate 2g (Dietary Fiber 0g); Protein 3g
% Daily Value: Vitamin A 2%; Vitamin C 4%; Calcium 2%; Iron 4%
Exchanges: 1 Fat

BETTY'S TIPS

⚙ **Substitution**
In place of the ham, try regular or Cajun- or Italian-seasoned roast beef from the deli. Or use sliced cooked turkey or chicken if you prefer.

⚙ **Time-Saver**
Ready-to-use chopped garlic, available in jars in the produce section of the grocery store, is very convenient. Use 1 teaspoon of this already-chopped garlic instead of chopping the 2 cloves of garlic.

⚙ **Do-Ahead**
Wrap tortilla pinwheels individually in plastic wrap and refrigerate for up to 24 hours.

Inside-Out Beef Wraps

Prep: 10 min
Photo on page x

2 purchased regular or Italian-flavor soft breadsticks, about 7 × 1¾ inches
¼ cup soft cream cheese with onions and chives
4 slices (1 ounce each) process American cheese
4 slices deli roast beef, about 7 × 3 inches
4 large leaf lettuce leaves
8 pretzel sticks

1. Cut each breadstick crosswise in half. Cut each half lengthwise not quite through to bottom of breadstick. Spread 1 tablespoon cream cheese onto one cut side of slit.

2. Center cheese slice on beef slice. Wrap beef and cheese around breadstick, with beef on the outside. Wrap lettuce leaf around beef on breadstick. Secure with pretzel stick.

4 wraps.

1 Wrap: Calories 210 (Calories from Fat 115); Fat 13g (Saturated 7g); Cholesterol 50mg; Sodium 460mg; Carbohydrate 6g (Dietary Fiber 1g); Protein 14g
% Daily Value: Vitamin A 14%; Vitamin C 4%; Calcium 12%; Iron 8%
Exchanges: 1 Starch, 1 Medium-Fat Meat, 1 Fat

BETTY'S TIPS

⚙ **Success Hint**
Select a head of lettuce with soft, pliable, tender leaves that will roll up easily. We also recommend cutting the center rib out of each leaf, or it will crack when rolled. To cut out the rib, just slice around both sides from the leaf base to just where the tip is no longer firm; discard rib. To use for rolling, simply overlap cut sides of leaf in center.

⚙ **Special Touch**
Here's a fun and tasty idea. Check the snack section of your store for onion-flavored rings and send a few along to eat with each sandwich.

Veggie Focaccia Sandwiches

Prep: 15 min Cook: 5 min

½ medium yellow bell pepper, cut into strips
½ medium green bell pepper, cut into strips
1 small red onion, sliced
2 tablespoons balsamic vinaigrette or Italian dressing
1 round focaccia bread (8 inches in diameter)
2 tablespoons chopped fresh basil leaves
½ cup shredded mozzarella cheese (2 ounces)
2 roma (plum) tomatoes, sliced

1. Spray 8- or 10-inch skillet with cooking spray; heat over medium-high heat. Cook bell peppers, onion and vinaigrette in skillet 4 to 5 minutes, stirring occasionally, until peppers are crisp-tender; remove from heat.

2. Cut focaccia into 4 wedges; split each wedge horizontally. Spoon one-fourth of vegetable mixture onto each bottom half; sprinkle with basil and cheese. Top with tomatoes and tops of bread wedges.

4 sandwiches.

1 Sandwich: Calories 265 (Calories from Fat 100); Fat 11g (Saturated 3g); Cholesterol 10mg; Sodium 360mg; Carbohydrate 35g (Dietary Fiber 2g); Protein 9g
% Daily Value: Vitamin A 6%; Vitamin C 54%; Calcium 12%; Iron 12%
Exchanges: 2 Starch, 1 Vegetable, 2 Fat

BETTY'S TIPS

✪ Health Twist
You can use fat-free balsamic vinaigrette and reduced-fat mozzarella cheese to reduce the fat to 7 grams and the calories to 235 per serving.

✪ Variation
Heat oven to 350°. Place uncut focaccia on oven rack. Bake 5 to 7 minutes or until warm.

Veggie Focaccia Sandwiches

Salmon Sandwiches

Prep: 20 min Cook: 10 min

1 cup soft bread crumbs (about 1½ slices bread)

½ cup Original or Reduced Fat Bisquick mix

1 tablespoon Dijon mustard

¼ teaspoon pepper

8 medium green onions, finely chopped (½ cup)

2 eggs, slightly beaten

1 can (14¾ ounces) red salmon, skin and bone removed, drained and flaked

2 tablespoons butter or margarine

4 whole wheat hamburger buns, split
Lettuce leaves

4 tablespoons dill or ranch dip

1. Mix all ingredients except butter, buns, lettuce and dill dip. Shape mixture into 4 patties, using heaping ½ cupfuls for each patty.

2. Melt butter in 10-inch nonstick skillet over medium heat. Cook patties in butter over medium heat 8 to 10 minutes, turning once, until brown and cooked through.

3. Fill buns with lettuce, patties and dill dip.

4 sandwiches.

1 Sandwich: Calories 515 (Calories from Fat 190); Fat 21g (Saturated 8g); Cholesterol 180mg; Sodium 1510mg; Carbohydrate 52g (Dietary Fiber 5g); Protein 34g
% Daily Value: Vitamin A 18%; Vitamin C 6%; Calcium 40%; Iron 30%
Exchanges: 3½ Starch, 3½ Lean Meat, 1 Fat

BETTY'S TIPS

❂ **Substitution**
Do you prefer **Tuna Sandwiches**? Use two 6-ounce cans of tuna, drained, instead of the salmon.

❂ **Success Hint**
The cook time for these patties may vary slightly depending on the heat source on your range. Keep an eye on them during cooking to make sure they cook evenly on the bottom.

❂ **Do-Ahead**
Cook the salmon patties up to 24 hours before serving; cover and refrigerate. To serve, heat on a cookie sheet at 400° for 10 minutes.

Salmon Sandwiches

Betty... MAKES IT EASY

Beef, Bacon and Blues Wrap

Prep: 20 min

2   soft cracker breads, 15 inches in diameter
    (from 17-ounce package), or 3 flour tortillas
    (10 inches in diameter)
1   package (8 ounces) cream cheese, softened
1   container (4 ounces) crumbled blue cheese (1 cup)
¼   cup milk
6   slices bacon, crisply cooked and crumbled
2   tablespoons chopped fresh or 1 tablespoon freeze-
    dried chives
¼   teaspoon pepper
1   pound sliced cooked deli roast beef
2   cups lightly packed spring salad greens mix or small
    lettuce leaves
2   medium tomatoes, thinly sliced

1. Let cracker breads come to room temperature as directed on package. Meanwhile, mix cream cheese, blue cheese, milk, bacon, chives and pepper.

2. Spread half of cream cheese mixture evenly over 1 cracker bread. Layer half of roast beef, salad greens and tomatoes (in that order) on cracker bread, leaving 4 inches at one side covered only with cream cheese mixture. Beginning at side covered with fillings, roll up tightly. Repeat with remaining cracker bread, cream cheese mixture and fillings.

3. For uniform-size slices, cut ends without fillings from each roll (about 1 inch from each end). Cut remaining portion of each roll into 5 slices. Serve immediately or wrap securely with plastic wrap and refrigerate no longer than 24 hours.

10 sandwiches.

Layer roast beef, salad greens and tomatoes on cracker bread.

Roll up tightly.

1 Sandwich: Calories 280 (Calories from Fat 145); Fat 16g (Saturated 9g); Cholesterol 75mg; Sodium 460mg; Carbohydrate 13g (Dietary Fiber 1g); Protein 22g
% Daily Value: Vitamin A 20%; Vitamin C 12%; Calcium 10%; Iron 10%
Exchanges: 1 Starch, 3 Lean Meat, 1 Fat

Beef, Bacon and Blues Wrap

Southwest Chicken Sub

Prep: 15 min

1 loaf (1 pound) French bread

⅓ cup mayonnaise or salad dressing

1 tablespoon Garlic-Lime Seasoning (below) or Key West-style coarsely ground seasoning blend

6 ounces Monterey Jack cheese, sliced

1 pound sliced cooked deli chicken breast

2 cups lightly packed spring salad greens mix or small lettuce leaves

1 medium sweet onion or Bermuda onion, thinly sliced

1 medium red bell pepper, thinly sliced into rings

1. Cut bread horizontally in half. Mix mayonnaise and Garlic-Lime Seasoning; spread over cut sides of bread.

2. Layer cheese, chicken, salad greens, onion and bell pepper on bottom half of bread. Add top half of bread. Secure loaf with 6 long wooden picks or small skewers. Cut into 6 serving pieces.

6 servings.

1 Serving: Calories 520 (Calories from Fat 215); Fat 24g (Saturated 8g); Cholesterol 100mg; Sodium 1140mg; Carbohydrate 42g (Dietary Fiber 2g); Protein 37g
% Daily Value: Vitamin A 40%; Vitamin C 70%; Calcium 28%; Iron 20%
Exchanges: 2 Starch, 4 Medium-Fat Meat, 2 Vegetable, 1 Fat

Garlic-Lime Seasoning

Prep: 5 min

2 tablespoons plus ¼ teaspoon ground cumin

1 tablespoon plus 2 teaspoons grated lime peel

1¼ teaspoons garlic salt

1¼ teaspoons pepper

1. Mix all ingredients. Store covered in refrigerator up to 3 weeks.

About ¼ cup seasoning.

BETTY'S TIPS

⊘ **Pack 'n Go**
Wrap the entire loaf with waxed paper. Tie with 6 pieces of twine, spacing evenly along loaf. To serve, cut between twine into 6 serving pieces.

⊘ **Substitution**
If sweet onions are not available, slices of red onion would be equally delicious in these flavor-packed sub sandwiches.

⊘ **Success Hint**
French bread loaves vary in thickness depending on where they're purchased. If your loaf is very thick, pull out some of the soft bread in the center so the sandwich won't stack too high.

Southwest Chicken Sub

Taco Turkey Wedges

Prep: 20 min

1 round focaccia bread (about 10 inches in diameter)
½ cup chopped pitted ripe olives
2 tablespoons sour cream
2 tablespoons mayonnaise or salad dressing
1 teaspoon taco seasoning mix
1 small tomato, sliced
4 ounces thinly sliced cooked turkey
2 ounces thinly sliced Monterey Jack cheese with jalapeño peppers
2 ounces thinly sliced Cheddar cheese

1. Cut bread horizontally in half. Mix olives, sour cream, mayonnaise and taco seasoning. Spread olive mixture evenly over cut sides of bottom and top halves of bread.

2. Layer tomato, turkey and cheeses on bottom half. Top with top half. Secure loaf with toothpick or small skewer. Cut loaf into 8 wedges.

8 servings.

1 Serving: Calories 260 (Calories from Fat 125); Fat 14g (Saturated 5g); Cholesterol 25mg; Sodium 760mg; Carbohydrate 25g (Dietary Fiber 1g); Protein 10g
% Daily Value: Vitamin A 6%; Vitamin C 4%; Calcium 10%; Iron 10%
Exchanges: 1½ Starch, 1 High-Fat Meat, 1 Fat

Taco Turkey Wedges

BETTY'S TIPS

☺ **Substitution**
If you don't have taco seasoning mix on hand, you can use 1 teaspoon chili powder and ¼ teaspoon salt.

☺ **Success Hint**
A thin serrated knife is a great tool for horizontally slicing large bread rounds. Be sure to hold your hand flat on top of the round and gently press to hold the bread in place while slicing.

☺ **Do-Ahead**
The sandwiches can be made up to 6 hours ahead of time. Cut into wedges just before serving.

☺ **Special Touch**
Top each serving with a whole pitted ripe olive or cherry tomato wedge.

Grilled Italian Panini

Prep: 10 min Grill: 20 min

1   round loaf (1 pound) unsliced French or Italian bread
4   ounces thinly sliced salami
1   jar (7 ounces) roasted red bell peppers, well drained
½   cup olive tapenade
4   ounces sliced provolone cheese
    Olive oil, if desired

1. Heat coals or gas grill for direct heat. Cut a circle ½ inch from edge of bread, cutting 2 inches down into loaf but not all the way through. Remove center of bread loaf and set aside. Arrange salami inside bread loaf; top with peppers, tapenade and cheese. Place center of bread loaf over filling to fit tightly. Wrap tightly in aluminum foil.

2. Cover and grill loaf 4 to 6 inches from low heat 15 to 20 minutes, turning once, until cheese is melted.

3. Brush olive oil over top of loaf. Cut loaf into 4 wedges.

4 servings.

1 Serving: Calories 485 (Calories from Fat 170); Fat 19g (Saturated 8g); Cholesterol 45mg; Sodium 1390mg; Carbohydrate 62g (Dietary Fiber 4g); Protein 21g
% Daily Value: Vitamin A 62%; Vitamin C 70%; Calcium 32%; Iron 24%
Exchanges: 4 Starch, 1½ High-Fat Meat, ½ Fat

BETTY'S TIPS

✿ **Success Hint**
Most any type and flavor of bread will work for grilled panini. A 1-pound loaf is a good size. Shape isn't that important-round, oblong and narrow all work well. Avoid focaccia, which isn't thick enough to cut as directed.

✿ **Variation**
You can use ½ cup basil pesto instead of the tapenade.

BBQ Veggie Joes

Prep: 30 min Cook: 12 hr

1   cup dried lentils (8 ounces), sorted and rinsed
2   cups water
3   medium stalks celery, chopped (1½ cups)
3   medium carrots, chopped (1½ cups)
1   large onion, chopped (1 cup)
¾   cup ketchup
2   tablespoons packed dark brown sugar
2   tablespoons Worcestershire sauce
2   tablespoons cider vinegar
5   pita breads (6 inches in diameter), cut in half to form pockets

1. Heat lentils and water to boiling in 2-quart saucepan; reduce heat. Cover and simmer 10 minutes.

2. Mix celery, carrots, onion, ketchup, brown sugar, Worcestershire sauce and lentils with water in 3½- to 4-quart slow cooker.

3. Cover and cook on low heat setting 10 to 12 hours or until hot. Just before serving, stir in vinegar. Fill each pita bread half with ½ cup lentil mixture.

10 sandwiches

1 Sandwich: Calories 210 (Calories from Fat 25); Fat 3g (Saturated 1g); Cholesterol 0mg; Sodium 510mg; Carbohydrate 45g (Dietary Fiber 8g); Protein 10g
% Daily Value: Vitamin A 76%; Vitamin C 6%; Calcium 8%; Iron 20%
Exchanges: 2 Starch, 3 Vegetable

BETTY'S TIPS

✿ **Substitution**
Whole wheat buns and sesame seed buns are other great ways to serve these meatless sandwiches.

✿ **Success Hint**
You can trim some time by letting your food processor make quick work of the chopping.

✿ **Health Twist**
Lentils are an inexpensive source of protein. They are also high in fiber, complex carbohydrates and vitamins.

Grilled Italian Panini

BBQ Veggie Joes

~ Low Fat ~

Marinara Sauce

Prep: 15 min Cook: 10 hr

1 large onion, chopped (1 cup)
8 cloves garlic, finely chopped
2 cans (28 ounces each) crushed tomatoes with Italian herbs, undrained
1 can (6 ounces) tomato paste
1 tablespoon olive or vegetable oil
2 teaspoons sugar
2 teaspoons dried basil leaves
1 teaspoon dried oregano leaves
1 teaspoon salt
1 teaspoon pepper

1. Mix all ingredients in 3½- to 4-quart slow cooker.

2. Cover and cook on low heat setting 8 to 10 hours (or high heat setting 4 to 5 hours).

12 servings.

1 Serving: Calories 55 (Calories from Fat 10); Fat 1g (Saturated 0g); Cholesterol 0mg; Sodium 510mg; Carbohydrate 11g (Dietary Fiber 2g); Protein 2g
% Daily Value: Vitamin A 14%; Vitamin C 22%; Calcium 4%; Iron 6%
Exchanges: 2 Vegetable

Italian Meatball Sandwiches

Prep: 15 min Bake: 35 min Cook: 7 hr

¾ pound ground beef
¾ pound ground pork
1 small onion, chopped (¼ cup)
2 cloves garlic, finely chopped
2 teaspoons Italian seasoning
¼ cup Italian-style dry bread crumbs
1 egg, slightly beaten
3½ cups Marinara Sauce (page 80) or 1 jar (28 ounces) marinara sauce
8 small rustic sourdough or Italian rolls
8 slices (1 ounce each) provolone cheese
Fresh Italian parsley, if desired

Italian Meatball Sandwiches

1. Heat oven to 375°. Line rectangular pan, 15 × 10 × 1 inch, with aluminum foil; spray with cooking spray. Mix beef, pork, onion, garlic, Italian seasoning, bread crumbs and egg. Shape mixture into twenty-four 1½-inch balls. Place in pan. Bake 30 to 35 minutes or until no longer pink in center.

2. Place meatballs into 3½- to 4-quart slow cooker. Pour Marinara Sauce over meatballs.

3. Cover and cook on low heat setting 6 to 7 hours or until hot.

4. Cut rolls horizontally in half. To serve, place 3 meatballs in each roll, top with cheese and drizzle with sauce. Garnish with parsley.

8 sandwiches.

1 Sandwich: Calories 440 (Calories from Fat 235); Fat 26g (Saturated 11g); Cholesterol 100mg; Sodium 990mg; Carbohydrate 26g (Dietary Fiber 3g); Protein 28g
% Daily Value: Vitamin A 16%; Vitamin C 18%; Calcium 28%; Iron 18%
Exchanges: 1½ Starch, 3 Medium-Fat Meat, 1 Vegetable, 1 Fat

BETTY'S TIPS

✿ **Substitution**
Substitute any flavor of marinara or spaghetti sauce, such as herbed, sun-dried tomato or garlic and onion, to vary the flavor in this recipe.

✿ **Health Twist**
Make these meatballs using 1½ pounds of ground turkey in place of the beef and pork if desired.

Rustic Vegetable Baguette with Smashed Avocado

Prep: 15 min Broil: 3 min
Photo on page 69

1 loaf (1 pound) rustic sourdough baguette bread
⅓ cup Italian dressing
2 small ripe avocados, pitted and peeled
4 small tomatoes, sliced
6 ounces sliced Cheddar cheese

1. Cut bread horizontally in half. Drizzle dressing on cut side of top half of bread. Place both halves on large cookie sheet.

2. Mash avocados until slightly smooth. Spread avocado over bottom half of bread; top with tomato slices and cheese. Broil with tops 4 to 6 inches from heat 2 to 3 minutes or until cheese is melted and bread is slightly golden brown. Top with top half of bread. Cut loaf into 4 pieces.

4 sandwiches.

1 Sandwich: Calories 525 (Calories from Fat 315); Fat 35g (Saturated 12g); Cholesterol 50mg; Sodium 790mg; Carbohydrate 40g (Dietary Fiber 6g); Protein 18g
% Daily Value: Vitamin A 24%; Vitamin C 38%; Calcium 30%; Iron 16%
Exchanges: 2 Starch, 1 High-Fat Meat, 2 Vegetable, 5 Fat

BETTY'S TIPS

❂ **Success Hint**
When buying avocados, choose ones that yield to gentle palm pressure. If the avocados are not ripe, place them in a paper bag with an apple, then pierce the bag in several places and let stand at room temperature a couple of days.

❂ **Serve-With**
Serve with sweet potato chips and crunchy vegetables, such as zucchini, carrot and celery sticks.

Beef Fajita Pitas

Prep: 10 min

¼ cup thick-and-chunky salsa
2 pita breads (6 inches in diameter), cut in half to form pockets
½ pound thinly sliced deli cooked roast beef
1 small red bell pepper, cut into ¼-inch strips
½ cup shredded Monterey Jack cheese (2 ounces)

1. Spoon salsa into pita bread halves.

2. Fill pita breads with beef, bell pepper and cheese. Serve with additional salsa if desired.

4 sandwiches.

1 Sandwich: Calories 225 (Calories from Fat 65); Fat 7g (Saturated 4g); Cholesterol 60mg; Sodium 330mg; Carbohydrate 17g (Dietary Fiber 1g); Protein 24g
% Daily Value: Vitamin A 28%; Vitamin C 62%; Calcium 12%; Iron 14%
Exchanges: 1 Starch, 3 Very Lean Meat, 1 Fat

BETTY'S TIPS

❂ **Substitution**
Use 4 pita bread folds instead of the pita breads.

❂ **Variation**
Add ¼ cup finely chopped red onion.

Beef Fajita Pitas

Cheeseburger Sandwiches

Prep: 20 min Cook: 7 hr

1½ pounds ground beef

½ teaspoon garlic pepper

1 package (8 ounces) process cheese spread loaf, diced (2 cups)

2 tablespoons milk

1 medium green bell pepper, chopped (1 cup)

1 small onion, chopped (¼ cup)

2 cloves garlic, finely chopped

8 sandwich buns, split

1. Cook beef and garlic pepper in 12-inch skillet over medium heat 8 to 10 minutes, stirring occasionally, until brown; drain.

2. Mix beef and remaining ingredients except buns in 3½- to 4-quart slow cooker.

3. Cover and cook on low heat setting 6 to 7 hours or until hot. Fill buns with beef mixture.

8 sandwiches.

1 Sandwich: Calories 395 (Calories from Fat 205); Fat 23g (Saturated 11g); Cholesterol 75mg; Sodium 690mg; Carbohydrate 24g (Dietary Fiber 2g); Protein 26g
% Daily Value: Vitamin A 10%; Vitamin C 12%; Calcium 22%; Iron 16%
Exchanges: 1½ Starch, 3 Medium-Fat Meat, 1 Fat

BETTY'S TIPS

☺ **Substitution**
Ground turkey can be used in place of the ground beef.

☺ **Serve-With**
These sandwiches are great for casual get-togethers. Use sandwich buns as suggested, or for more servings, use smaller dollar buns. Provide a slotted spoon and let guests make their own sandwiches. Serve with chips and a tray of raw veggies and dip. For dessert, provide brownies.

☺ **Did You Know?**
Garlic pepper is a seasoning mix of garlic powder and cracked pepper that can be found in the spice aisle of the supermarket. It adds a double dose of flavor with just a few dashes.

Cheeseburger Sandwiches

Pastrami Deli Folds

Santa Fe Turkey and Hummus Bagel Sandwiches

Pastrami Deli Folds

Prep: 15 min

1 pint (2 cups) deli coleslaw (creamy style)
1 tablespoon prepared horseradish
1 to 2 teaspoons grated lemon peel
1 pound sliced turkey pastrami
2 small red bell peppers, cut into ¼-inch strips
1 bag (15 ounces) pita fold breads

1. Mix coleslaw, horseradish and lemon peel.

2. Arrange pastrami, coleslaw and bell pepper strips on half of each pita fold bread; fold over.

6 servings.

1 Serving: Calories 395 (Calories from Fat 125); Fat 14g (Saturated 3g); Cholesterol 45mg; Sodium 1280mg; Carbohydrate 49g (Dietary Fiber 3g); Protein 21g
% Daily Value: Vitamin A 58%; Vitamin C 100%; Calcium 8%; Iron 20%
Exchanges: 3 Starch, 1½ Medium-Fat Meat, 1 Vegetable

BETTY'S TIPS

⚙ **Variation**
This recipe is easily doubled to please larger crowds or hungry family and friends who can't get enough of these tasty sandwiches.

These sandwiches can be modified for kids who like simpler foods. Omit the coleslaw and bell peppers. Substitute lettuce leaves and perhaps a thin slice of tomato. Spread the pastrami with a favorite sandwich spread.

⚙ **Special Touch**
Wrap these portable sandwiches in regular aluminum foil or foil sandwich squares (precut foil sheets), then refrigerate or keep in a cooler until serving time.

Santa Fe Turkey and Hummus Bagel Sandwiches

Prep: 20 min

6 tablespoons red chili pepper hummus (from 7-ounce container)
6 onion bagels, cut horizontally in half
1½ cups loosely packed shredded romaine
1½ pounds sliced smoked turkey
6 slices peppered bacon, cooked, drained and broken in half

1. Spread hummus over bottom half of each bagel.

2. Fill bagels with romaine, turkey and bacon.

6 sandwiches.

1 Sandwich: Calories 330 (Calories from Fat 80); Fat 9g (Saturated 2g); Cholesterol 60mg; Sodium 1800mg; Carbohydrate 37g (Dietary Fiber 3g); Protein 29g
% Daily Value: Vitamin A 6%; Vitamin C 2%; Calcium 6%; Iron 18%
Exchanges: 2 Starch, 3 Lean Meat, 1 Vegetable

BETTY'S TIPS

⚙ **Substitution**
Microwave-ready regular bacon can be used in place of the peppered bacon. You can use regular hummus if the red chili pepper variety is not available.

⚙ **Serve-With**
Serve these flavorful sandwiches with wedges of cantaloupe and glasses of iced tea.

Barbecue Beef Sandwiches

Prep: 15 min Cook: 8 hr

1½   pounds beef boneless round steak
½   teaspoon salt
¼   teaspoon coarsely ground pepper
2   cups coleslaw mix or shredded cabbage
1   medium onion, coarsely chopped (½ cup)
¼   cup uncooked regular long-grain rice
½   cup barbecue sauce
½   cup water
8   sandwich buns, split
8   slices (1 ounce each) Colby-Monterey Jack cheese, if desired

1. Spray inside of 3½- to 4-quart slow cooker with cooking spray.

2. Remove fat from beef. Cut beef into 3-inch pieces. Sprinkle beef with salt and pepper. Mix coleslaw mix, onion, rice, barbecue sauce and water. Layer beef and coleslaw mixture in slow cooker.

3. Cover and cook on low heat setting about 8 hours or until beef is tender and falls apart when stirred with fork. Fill buns with beef mixture. Top with cheese.

8 sandwiches.

1 Sandwich: Calories 260 (Calories from Fat 45); Fat 5g (Saturated 1g); Cholesterol 45mg; Sodium 580mg; Carbohydrate 34g (Dietary Fiber 2g); Protein 22g
% Daily Value: Vitamin A 2%; Vitamin C 6%; Calcium 8%; Iron 18%
Exchanges: 2 Starch, 2 Very Lean Meat, 1 Vegetable

BETTY'S TIPS

❂ **Substitution**
You can make this filling with tomato sauce instead of barbecue sauce if you want a milder-flavored sauce.

Bone-in round steak can also be used instead of the boneless steak. Cut the steak into 3-inch pieces, leaving the bone attached to one of the pieces. The bone adds great flavor. Be sure to remove the bone before serving.

Barbecue Beef Sandwiches

Taco Burgers

Prep: 10 min Grill: 18 min

1   pound ground beef
1   envelope (about 1¼ ounces) taco seasoning
     mix
4   slices (1 ounce each) Monterey Jack cheese
4   hamburger buns, split
1   avocado, sliced
¼   cup thick-and-chunky salsa

1. Heat coals or gas grill for direct heat. Mix beef and taco seasoning mix. Shape mixture into 4 patties, each about ¾ inch thick.

2. Cover and grill patties 4 to 6 inches from medium heat 14 to 16 minutes, turning once, until beef is no longer pink in center and juice is clear.

3. Top each patty with cheese slice. Grill 1 to 2 minutes or until cheese begins to melt. Serve in buns with avocado and salsa.

4 sandwiches.

1 Sandwich: Calories 550 (Calories from Fat 305); Fat 34g (Saturated 13g); Cholesterol 90mg; Sodium 910mg; Carbohydrate 32g (Dietary Fiber 4g); Protein 33g
% Daily Value: Vitamin A 26%; Vitamin C 8%; Calcium 30%; Iron 24%
Exchanges: 2 Starch, 4 Medium-Fat Meat, 3 Fat

Taco Burgers

BETTY'S TIPS

✪ **Substitution**
Ground turkey can be substituted for the ground beef.

✪ **Variation**
Turn up the heat! Seed and finely chop 2 or 3 jalapeño chilies and add to the ground beef mixture.

✪ **Success Hint**
Use crumpled aluminum foil to scrape cooked-on food bits from the grill rack. This is a great way to recycle slightly used foil!

✪ **Special Touch**
Sprinkle cheese-topped burgers with chopped bell pepper

Betty... ON WHAT'S NEW

The Art of the Party

Whether you're hosting a summer social, casual get-together, family reunion or impromptu guests, organization and planning is key. Let your occasion serve as the blueprint for the party, guiding you in what types of foods to serve, how to serve them and how to pull it all together.

10 Tips to the Perfect Menu

The menu you create and share is an expression of you and your hospitality. These tips will help you show guests how much you care.

1. Begin by considering the time of day, season and weather and your guests' appetites when sketching out menu ideas.

2. Keep the occasion and your guests in mind when outlining a menu. Would an informal buffet or barbecue work best, or does the occasion merit a sit-down dinner? Are there any diet restrictions?

3. Decide the main course and choose other foods that will complement it. A main dish with an assertive flavor works well with milder-flavored side dishes. If your meal is light, consider a decadent dessert.

4. Decide on one or two familiar or favorite recipes and build your menu around those. If you have one new recipe that doesn't work out, you'll still feel confident about the rest of the menu.

5. Plan your menu with a variety of foods. Be sure to have contrasting textures and tastes: crunchy and creamy; salty and sweet; hot and cold. Keep in mind contrasting shapes and colors of foods and dishes as well.

6. Use local bakery breads or desserts to help round out a menu. You'll have great food with less stress, and you'll save time, too!

7. Avoid repeating a type of food in a menu. If you're serving quiche, for example, don't serve pie for dessert.

8. Savor seasonal fresh produce: tomatoes and corn in summer; apples and squash in fall; pears and pomegranates in winter; and asparagus and rhubarb in spring.

9. Choose as many recipes as possible that you can make ahead. Limit last-minute recipes that have lots of detail. Make sure you have enough refrigerator, freezer and oven space to accommodate your recipes.

10. Serve what you love to cook and eat! There's no need to astound your guests with exotic kitchen concoctions. If you serve good food that you like to make, your friends and family are sure to enjoy it, too.

Planning for Impromptu Guests

When unplanned guests stop by, raid your pantry, refrigerator and garden and try some of these ideas for your next "emergency."

APPETIZERS

■ Stir together equal amounts of salsa and sour cream. Serve with fresh vegetables or chips.

■ Arrange chopped tomatoes and fresh basil on thin slices of French bread.

■ Thaw frozen cooked shrimp to use as shrimp cocktail. Or stir shrimp into a purchased sour cream dip for an upscale dip.

SALADS AND SIDES

■ Marinate vegetables in a vinaigrette, Italian dressing or other salad dressing, then grill.

■ Slice fresh tomatoes and add fresh basil, olive oil, salt and pepper for a sensational salad.

MAIN DISHES

■ Toss fully cooked sausage, bacon or pepperoni with cooked pasta and vegetables. Stir in spaghetti or Alfredo sauce and heat through.

■ Fill tortillas with deli meats and cheeses, sloppy joe mix, barbecue pork or beef or leftover meats for presto wraps.

DESSERTS

■ Use store-bought cookies as the base for ice-cream sundaes. Or crush the cookies and sprinkle over ice cream as a topping.

■ Make a fresh-fruit slush by blending fruits and orange juice and/or yogurt. Serve in tall glasses over ice.

Cooking for a Crowd

■ Remember, when you're feeding a large number of people, the number of servings doesn't necessarily equal the number of guests to be served. The amount of food you'll need will depend on who you're feeding (football fans versus ladies' bridge club) and when your party is planned.

■ Kids typically have small appetites and are a bit more finicky. If your party will include many kids or the theme is centered around kids, plan that each child will eat about two-thirds the amount of food that an adult will eat.

■ If you're still unsure whether you need 12 cups or 16 cups of potato salad, err with the greater amount. It's possible you may have one or two unexpected guests, and having leftovers is better than running out of food.

PARTY PLANNING CHECKLIST

The menu

☐ **PLAN** recipes and food selections.

☐ **DECIDE** how to serve the food: buffet, formal, family style, potluck.

☐ **READ** through recipes and create a shopping list.

☐ **OUTLINE** a preparation timetable.

Make lists

☐ **DETERMINE A FINAL GUEST COUNT** so you can figure food and beverage amounts and tableware needs.

☐ **ORGANIZE A LIST** of serving dishes, paperware and decorating needs.

☐ **MAKE A TIMETABLE** for the last several days before the party to lessen the chance of forgetting something.

☐ **CREATE A PARTY-DAY COUNTDOWN.** Make it specific and leave time in it to get yourself ready.

Do-ahead tasks

☐ **BORROW OR BUY** extra serving pieces; organize paperware.

☐ **ORGANIZE DECORATIONS** and centerpieces.

☐ **SET THE TABLE** ahead and cover with a clean tablecloth or sheet.

☐ **PURCHASE OR MAKE** a generous supply of ice cubes for beverages.

Sour Cream and Onion Burgers

Prep: 10 min   Grill: 15 min

2   pounds ground beef
1   envelope (about 1½ ounces) onion soup mix
1   cup sour cream
½   cup dry bread crumbs
⅛   teaspoon pepper
8   sandwich buns, split, or 1 round focaccia bread (about 10 inches in diameter), cut horizontally in half, then cut into 8 wedges
    Leaf lettuce, if desired

1. Heat coals or gas grill for direct heat. Mix all ingredients except buns and lettuce. Shape mixture into 8 patties, about ½ inch thick.

2. Cover and grill patties 4 to 6 inches from medium heat 10 to 15 minutes, turning once, until patties are no longer pink in center and juice is clear. Serve in buns with lettuce.

8 sandwiches.

1 Sandwich: Calories 435 (Calories from Fat 215); Fat 24g (Saturated 10g); Cholesterol 85mg; Sodium 820mg; Carbohydrate 31g (Dietary Fiber 2g); Protein 26g
% Daily Value: Vitamin A 4%; Vitamin C 2%; Calcium 12%; Iron 20%
Exchanges: 2 Starch, 3 Medium-Fat Meat, 1 Fat

BETTY'S TIPS

⊘ **Serve-With**
Try sprinkling burgers with canned French-fried onions for fun, flavor and crunch!

⊘ **Variation**
Instead of shaping patties into the usual round shape, shape them into wedges and serve on wedges of focaccia.

Pizza Turnovers

Prep: 12 min   Bake: 15 min

1   can (10 ounces) refrigerated pizza crust dough
¼   cup pizza sauce
¼   cup finely shredded carrot
24 slices pepperoni (1 to 1¼ inches in diameter)
1   tablespoon grated Parmesan cheese
2   slices mozzarella cheese (1½ ounces), cut in half

1. Heat oven to 400°. Roll pizza crust dough on lightly floured surface into 12-inch square. Cut dough into four 6-inch squares.

2. Spread about 1 tablespoon pizza sauce on each square to within ½ inch of edges. Top half of each square with carrot, pepperoni and cheeses. Fold other half of each square over filling; press edges to seal. Place on ungreased cookie sheet.

3. Bake 12 to 15 minutes or until light golden brown. Serve warm.

4 servings.

1 Serving: Calories 390 (Calories from Fat 180); Fat 20g (Saturated 7g); Cholesterol 30mg; Sodium 1160mg; Carbohydrate 38g (Dietary Fiber 2g); Protein 16g
% Daily Value: Vitamin A 28%; Vitamin C 2%; Calcium 12%; Iron 16%
Exchanges: 2 Starch, 1 High-Fat Meat, 2 Vegetable, 2 Fat

BETTY'S TIPS

⊘ **Health Twist**
For 6 grams of fat and 265 calories per serving, use turkey pepperoni slices, fat-free grated Parmesan cheese topping and fat-free mozzarella cheese.

⊘ **Variation**
Pack these turnovers with more nutrition by adding an additional tablespoon of cooked vegetables to each. It's a great way to use leftovers while adding a nutrition boost.

Sour Cream and Onion Burgers

Pizza Turnovers

Sandwiches, Burgers and Pizza   91

Easy Bagel Pizzas

Prep: 5 min Bake: 10 min

1 cup pizza sauce

8 bagels, split

2 cups shredded mozzarella or Cheddar cheese (8 ounces)

Assorted toppings (sliced pepperoni or Canadian-style bacon, sliced mushrooms, sliced ripe olives, chopped zucchini, chopped bell pepper)

1. Heat oven to 425°. Spread 1 tablespoon pizza sauce over each bagel half. Sprinkle each with 1 tablespoon of the cheese.

2. Arrange toppings on pizzas. Sprinkle with remaining cheese. Place on ungreased cookie sheet. Bake 5 to 10 minutes or until cheese is melted.

8 pizzas.

1 Pizza: Calories 270 (Calories from Fat 70); Fat 8g (Saturated 4g); Cholesterol 25mg; Sodium 840mg; Carbohydrate 34g (Dietary Fiber 2g); Protein 18g
% Daily Value: Vitamin A 6%; Vitamin C 6%; Calcium 26%; Iron 14%
Exchanges: 2 Starch, 1 Medium-Fat Meat, 1 Vegetable

BETTY'S TIPS

⚙ **Substitution**
English muffins can be used instead of the bagels. Toast the muffins before topping.

⚙ **Variation**
To prepare in the microwave, toast the bagel halves first, then arrange toppings and cheese on the bagels. Place 4 bagel halves on a microwavable paper plate. Cover loosely and microwave on High 30 seconds or until cheese is melted. Repeat with remaining bagels.

Easy Bagel Pizzas

Grilled Italian Pesto Pizza

Prep: 15 min Grill: 8 min

1 package (16 ounces) ready-to-serve original Italian pizza crust or other 12-inch ready-to-serve pizza crust

½ cup basil pesto

2 cups shredded mozzarella cheese (8 ounces)

3 large roma (plum) tomatoes, cut into ¼-inch slices

½ cup whole basil leaves

¼ cup shredded Parmesan cheese

4 servings.

1 Serving: Calories 665 (Calories from Fat 295); Fat 33g (Saturated 11g); Cholesterol 40mg; Sodium 1190mg; Carbohydrate 66g (Dietary Fiber 4g); Protein 30g
% Daily Value: Vitamin A 28%; Vitamin C 8%; Calcium 64%; Iron 28%
Exchanges: 4 Starch, 2 High-Fat Meat, 1 Vegetable, 2½ Fat

1. Heat coals or gas grill for direct heat. Brush pizza crust with pesto. Sprinkle 1 cup of the mozzarella cheese over pesto. Arrange tomato slices and basil leaves on cheese. Sprinkle with remaining 1 cup mozzarella cheese and the Parmesan cheese.

2. Cover and grill pizza 4 to 6 inches from medium heat 6 to 8 minutes or until crust is crisp and cheese is melted. (If crust browns too quickly, place a piece of aluminum foil between crust and grill.)

BETTY'S TIPS

✪ **Substitution**
If you have lots of fresh basil, make your own pesto. Place 2 cups firmly packed basil leaves, ¾ cup grated Parmesan cheese, ¼ cup pine nuts, ½ cup olive oil and 3 cloves garlic in a blender or food processor. Cover and blend on medium speed about 3 minutes or until smooth.

Provolone cheese can be used in place of the mozzarella cheese on the pizza.

Grilled Italian Pesto Pizza

Bacon Cheeseburger Pizza

Prep: 10 min Bake: 15 min

1 loaf (1 pound) unsliced French bread
1 pound ground beef
1 medium onion, chopped (½ cup)
1 jar (14 ounces) pizza sauce (any variety)
1 large tomato, seeded and chopped (1 cup)
8 slices bacon, crisply cooked and crumbled
2 cups finely shredded pizza cheese blend (mozzarella and Cheddar cheeses) (8 ounces)

1. Heat oven to 400°. Cut bread loaf horizontally in half. Cut bread halves crosswise in half to make 4 pieces (to fit on cookie sheet). Arrange on large ungreased cookie sheet.

2. Cook beef and onion in 10-inch skillet over medium-high heat, stirring occasionally, until beef is brown; drain. Stir in pizza sauce. Spread beef mixture over bread. Sprinkle with tomato, bacon and cheese.

3. Bake 12 to 15 minutes or until pizza is hot and cheese is melted.

8 servings.

1 Serving: Calories 430 (Calories from Fat 200); Fat 22g (Saturated 10g); Cholesterol 60mg; Sodium 860mg; Carbohydrate 35g (Dietary Fiber 3g); Protein 26g
% Daily Value: Vitamin A 14%; Vitamin C 12%; Calcium 24%; Iron 18%
Exchanges: 2 Starch, 3 Medium-Fat Meat, 1 Vegetable, ½ Fat

BETTY'S TIPS

❂ **Success Hint**
Not all pizza cheese blends are alike. Some brands are mostly mozzarella cheese with just a little Cheddar, and others give you about half mozzarella and half Cheddar. Choose the blend you prefer.

❂ **Time-Saver**
Get the whole family involved to quickly get dinner on the table! Young children can set the table, wash vegetables and load the dishwasher. Older children can cut up vegetables and help assemble recipes. What child wouldn't be proud to have helped make this pizza?

Bacon Cheeseburger Pizza

$\mathcal{B}etty$...
MAKES IT EASY

Double-Cheese Chicken Caesar Pizza

Prep: 10 min Bake: 15 min

Arrange cheese nuggets, ends touching, in circle 1 inch from edge of crust.

1	package (10 ounces) ready-to-serve thin Italian pizza crust (12 inches in diameter)
¼	cup creamy Caesar dressing
1	cup shredded mozzarella cheese (4 ounces)
16 to 18	frozen fully cooked breaded mozzarella cheese nuggets (from 13½-ounce package)
1	package (9 ounces) frozen smoke-flavor fully cooked chicken breast strips
¼	cup sliced ripe olives
1	small red bell pepper, cut into thin strips
⅓	cup grated Parmesan cheese

1. Heat oven to 450°. Place pizza crust on ungreased cookie sheet.

2. Spread dressing evenly on pizza crust; sprinkle with mozzarella cheese. Arrange cheese nuggets, ends touching, in circle 1 inch from edge of crust. Arrange chicken, olives and bell pepper inside circle of cheese nuggets; sprinkle with Parmesan cheese.

3. Bake 12 to 15 minutes or until nuggets are golden brown and edge of crust is deep golden brown.

8 servings.

1 Serving: Calories 355 (Calories from Fat 155); Fat 17g (Saturated 7g); Cholesterol 65mg; Sodium 630mg; Carbohydrate 25g (Dietary Fiber 1g); Protein 27g
% Daily Value: Vitamin A 18%; Vitamin C 14%; Calcium 38%; Iron 12%
Exchanges: 1½ Starch, 3 Medium-Fat Meat, 1 Vegetable

Arrange chicken, olives and bell pepper inside circle of cheese nuggets.

Double-Cheese Chicken Caesar Pizza

Santa Fe Pizza

Prep: 20 min Bake: 28 min

2   cups Original Bisquick mix

¼   cup mild salsa-flavored or jalapeño-flavored process cheese sauce

¼   cup hot water

1   can (16 ounces) Old El Paso® refried beans

½   cup Old El Paso thick 'n chunky salsa (from 16-ounce jar)

4   medium green onions, sliced (¼ cup)

1   cup shredded Colby-Monterey Jack cheese (4 ounces)

1   cup shredded lettuce

1   medium tomato, chopped (¾ cup)

1. Heat oven to 375°. Grease large cookie sheet with shortening.

2. Stir Bisquick mix, cheese sauce and hot water until soft dough forms; beat vigorously 20 strokes. Place dough on surface dusted with Bisquick mix; gently roll in Bisquick mix to coat. Shape into ball; knead about 5 times or until smooth. Roll dough into 14-inch circle; place on cookie sheet.

3. Mix beans and salsa; spread over crust to within 2 inches of edge. Sprinkle with onions. Fold edge over bean mixture. Sprinkle with cheese.

4. Bake 25 to 28 minutes or until crust is golden brown and cheese is melted. Garnish with lettuce and tomato.

8 servings.

High Altitude (3500-6500 ft): No changes.

1 Serving: Calories 260 (Calories from Fat 100); Fat 11g (Saturated 5g); Cholesterol 25mg; Sodium 790mg; Carbohydrate 30g (Dietary Fiber 4g); Protein 10g
% Daily Value: Vitamin A 10%; Vitamin C 8%; Calcium 16%; Iron 12%
Exchanges: 2 Starch, 1 High-Fat Meat

BETTY'S TIPS

☺ **Time-Saver**
If you're stopping at the grocery store, swing by the salad bar and pick up shredded greens, sliced green onions and chopped tomato to save prep time.

☺ **Special Touch**
Boost the vitamin C and the color by adding chopped bell pepper with the onions. Use green bell pepper or chop a variety of colors of bell peppers.

☺ **Did You Know?**
Canned refried beans come in a variety of types. Look for traditional, fat-free and vegetarian.

Santa Fe Pizza

Soups, Stews and Chilis

Satisfying Meals for Family and Friends

Cajun Beef Stew (page 112)

Turkey and Brown Rice Chili (page 114)

French Onion Soup

Prep: 15 min   Cook: 35 min + 9 hr

3   large onions, sliced

3   tablespoons butter or margarine, melted

3   tablespoons Gold Medal all-purpose flour

1   tablespoon Worcestershire sauce

1   teaspoon sugar

¼   teaspoon pepper

4   cans (14 ounces each) beef broth
    Cheesy Broiled French Bread (below)

1. Mix onions and butter in 3½- to 4-quart slow cooker.

2. Cover and cook on high heat setting 30 to 35 minutes or until onions begin to brown slightly around edges.

3. Mix flour, Worcestershire sauce, sugar and pepper. Stir flour mixture and broth into onions. Cover and cook on low heat setting 7 to 9 hours or until onions are very tender.

4. Make Cheesy Broiled French Bread. Place 1 slice bread on each bowl of soup.

8 servings.

Cheesy Broiled French Bread

8   slices French bread, 1 inch thick

¾   cup shredded mozzarella cheese (3 ounces)

2   tablespoons grated or shredded Parmesan cheese

Set oven control to broil. Place bread slices on rack in broiler pan. Sprinkle with cheeses. Broil with tops 5 to 6 inches from heat about 3 minutes or until cheese is melted.

1 Serving: Calories 190 (Calories from Fat 70); Fat 8g (Saturated 3g); Cholesterol 10mg; Sodium 1190mg; Carbohydrate 21g (Dietary Fiber 2g); Protein 10g
% Daily Value: Vitamin A 6%; Vitamin C 2%; Calcium 14%; Iron 8%
Exchanges: 1 Starch, 2 Vegetable, 1½ Fat

BETTY'S TIPS

☺ **Substitution**
Substitute large sweet onions, such as Bermuda, Maui or Spanish, for the large onions in this recipe for a slightly sweeter onion flavor.

☺ **Time-Saver**
Top this soup with large crouton cubes instead of making the cheesy bread. Simply sprinkle soup with shredded Parmesan or mozzarella cheese before serving.

French Onion Soup

Creamy Split Pea Soup

Prep: 20 min Cook: 11 hr + 30 min

2 cups dried green split peas (1 pound), sorted and rinsed

6 cups water

½ cup dry sherry, if desired

1 large dark orange sweet potato, peeled and chopped (2 cups)

1 large onion, chopped (1 cup)

4 cloves garlic, finely chopped

1 tablespoon salt

3 cups firmly packed chopped fresh spinach leaves

1 cup half-and-half

2 tablespoons chopped fresh dill weed

Freshly ground pepper to taste

8 servings.

1 Serving: Calories 235 (Calories from Fat 90); Fat 10g (Saturated 6g); Cholesterol 35mg; Sodium 910mg; Carbohydrate 35g (Dietary Fiber 11g); Protein 12g
% Daily Value: Vitamin A 98%; Vitamin C 8%; Calcium 6%; Iron 10%
Exchanges: 2 Starch, 1 Vegetable, 1 Fruit

1. Mix split peas, water, sherry, sweet potato, onion, garlic and salt in 3½- to 4-quart slow cooker.

2. Cover and cook on low heat setting 10 to 11 hours or until peas and vegetables are tender.

3. Stir in spinach, half-and-half and dill weed. Cover and cook on low heat setting about 30 minutes or until spinach is wilted. Season with pepper.

BETTY'S TIPS

✿ **Substitution**
If you are looking for a meatless but not vegetarian recipe, use a 48-ounce can of chicken broth and 2 cups of water instead of 6 cups water.

✿ **Substitution**
Substitute 2 cups peeled and chopped butternut squash for the sweet potato.

✿ **Variation**
Add 1 cup diced fully cooked smoked ham with the peas for a traditional split pea soup.

Creamy Split Pea Soup

Chicken and Wild Rice Soup

Prep: 5 min Cook: 8 hr + 30 min

- 1 pound boneless, skinless chicken thighs, cut into 1-inch pieces
- ½ cup uncooked wild rice
- ¼ cup frozen chopped onions (from 12-ounce bag)
- 2 cans (10¾ ounces each) condensed cream of potato soup
- 1 can (14 ounces) chicken broth with roasted garlic
- 2 cups frozen sliced carrots (from 1-pound bag)
- 1 cup half-and-half

1. Place chicken in 3½- to 4-quart slow cooker. Mix wild rice, onions, soup, broth and carrots; pour over chicken.

2. Cover and cook on low heat setting 7 to 8 hours or until juice of chicken is no longer pink when centers of thickest pieces are cut.

3. Stir in half-and-half. Cover and cook on high heat setting 15 to 30 minutes or until hot.

8 servings.

1 Serving: Calories 240 (Calories from Fat 90); Fat 10g (Saturated 4g); Cholesterol 50mg; Sodium 840mg; Carbohydrate 24g (Dietary Fiber 3g); Protein 17g
% Daily Value: Vitamin A 100%; Vitamin C 2%; Calcium 8%; Iron 10%
Exchanges: 1 Starch, 1½ Medium-Fat Meat, 2 Vegetable

BETTY'S TIPS

❂ Success Hint
To reheat the soup, cook over low heat and stir frequently to avoid curdling.

❂ Health Twist
To reduce the calories to 230 and the fat to 7 grams per serving, use a 12-ounce can of evaporated low-fat milk instead of half-and-half.

— Quick & Low-Fat —

After-Work Chicken Noodle Soup

Prep: 10 min Cook: 20 min

- 4 cans (14½ ounces each) reduced-sodium chicken broth
- 2 cups cut-up cooked chicken
- 1 cup frozen green peas
- 1 tablespoon chopped fresh parsley or 1 teaspoon parsley flakes
- 1 teaspoon dried thyme leaves
- ¼ teaspoon pepper
- 2 medium stalks celery, chopped (1 cup)
- 2 medium carrots, sliced (1 cup)
- 1 medium onion, chopped (½ cup)
- 2 cloves garlic, finely chopped
- 1 cup uncooked wide egg noodles (2 ounces)

1. Heat all ingredients except noodles to boiling in 3-quart saucepan. Stir in noodles. Heat to boiling; reduce heat.

2. Simmer uncovered 10 to 15 minutes, stirring occasionally, until noodles and vegetables are tender.

6 servings.

1 Serving: Calories 180 (Calories from Fat 45); Fat 5g (Saturated 1g); Cholesterol 50mg; Sodium 1030mg; Carbohydrate 14g (Dietary Fiber 3g); Protein 23g
% Daily Value: Vitamin A 34%; Vitamin C 6%; Calcium 4%; Iron 12%
Exchanges: 1 Starch, 3 Very Lean Meat

BETTY'S TIPS

❂ Substitution
Orzo or rosamarina pasta can be used instead of the noodles. You can also use 1 cup of your favorite pasta.

❂ Time-Saver
Freeze this soup in individual portions to reheat on busy weeknights.

❂ Did You Know?
There's nothing like a bowl of soothing chicken noodle soup when you have a cold. Chicken soup eases stuffed nasal passages more effectively than other types of hot beverages.

Chicken and Wild Rice Soup

After-Work Chicken Noodle Soup

Chicken-Broccoli Tortellini Soup

Prep: 10 min   Cook: 11 min

1 tablespoon olive or vegetable oil

1 small onion, chopped (¼ cup)

1 can (14½ ounces) chicken broth

½ cup water

½ teaspoon Italian seasoning

1 package (10 ounces) frozen cut broccoli in cheese-flavored sauce

1 package (9 ounces) refrigerated cheese-filled tortellini

1 cup cubed cooked chicken

1 large roma (plum) tomato, chopped (½ cup)

¼ cup shredded Parmesan cheese

1. Heat oil in 2-quart saucepan over medium-high heat. Cook onion in oil about 2 minutes, stirring frequently, until crisp-tender.

2. Stir in broth, water, Italian seasoning, broccoli in cheese sauce and tortellini. Heat to boiling, stirring occasionally and breaking up broccoli.

3. Stir in chicken. Cook about 4 minutes, stirring occasionally, until tortellini is tender. Stir in tomato. Top each serving with 1 tablespoon cheese.

4 servings.

1 Serving: Calories 320 (Calories from Fat 160); Fat 18g (Saturated 7g); Cholesterol 100mg; Sodium 920mg; Carbohydrate 18g (Dietary Fiber 2g); Protein 24g
% Daily Value: Vitamin A 26%; Vitamin C 16%; Calcium 24%; Iron 10%
Exchanges: 1 Starch, 2 Medium-Fat Meat, 1 Vegetable

BETTY'S TIPS

❂ **Health Twist**
If sodium is a concern, look for reduced-sodium canned chicken broth. Also, if you poach your own chicken breasts in reduced-sodium chicken broth instead of using packaged cooked cubed chicken, you'll reduce the overall sodium in this recipe.

❂ **Serve-With**
Quickly complete this easy soup meal with warmed purchased focaccia bread and fresh pears or clusters of red grapes.

Chicken-Broccoli Tortellini Soup

Black-Eyed Pea and Sausage Soup

Black-Eyed Pea and Sausage Soup

Prep: 15 min Cook: 9 hr + 15 min

2 cans (15 to 16 ounces each) black-eyed peas, rinsed and drained
1 package (16 ounces) smoked turkey kielbasa sausage, cut lengthwise in half and then sliced
4 medium carrots, chopped (2 cups)
4 cloves garlic, finely chopped
½ cup uncooked wheat berries
1 cup water
3 cans (14 ounces each) beef broth
2 cups shredded fresh spinach
1 teaspoon dried marjoram leaves

1. Mix all ingredients except spinach and marjoram in 3½- to 4-quart slow cooker.

2. Cover and cook on low heat setting 8 to 9 hours or until wheat berries are tender.

3. Stir in spinach and marjoram. Cover and cook about 15 minutes or until spinach is tender.

6 servings.

1 Serving: Calories 270 (Calories from Fat 70); Fat 8g (Saturated 2g); Cholesterol 40mg; Sodium 1400mg; Carbohydrate 37g (Dietary Fiber 11g); Protein 24g
% Daily Value: Vitamin A 100%; Vitamin C 6%; Calcium 6%; Iron 30%
Exchanges: 2 Starch, 2½ Very Lean Meat, 1 Vegetable

BETTY'S TIPS

✪ **Substitution**
For those who enjoy other greens as well, use the greens solo or in combination with the spinach. Swiss chard, mustard greens and turnip greens are all good choices. Also, andouille sausage, a Cajun favorite, would give this soup more of a kick.

✪ **Serve-With**
Here's a soup with a southern flair. To spike it with even more flavor, offer diners Dijon mustard and horseradish to stir into their soup.

Chill-Chasing Chili

Prep: 15 min Cook: 7 hr + 15 min

1 pound beef boneless round steak, cut into ½-inch pieces

1 large onion, chopped (1 cup)

2 medium stalks celery, cut into ½-inch pieces (1 cup)

1 tablespoon chili powder

2 teaspoons ground cumin

¼ teaspoon dried oregano leaves

¼ teaspoon ground cinnamon

2 cans (14½ ounces each) diced tomatoes, undrained

1 can (15 ounces) tomato sauce

1 medium bell pepper, cut into 1-inch pieces (1 cup)

1 can (15 to 16 ounces) kidney beans, rinsed and drained

   Shredded Cheddar cheese, if desired

1. Mix all ingredients except bell pepper, beans and cheese in 3½- to 4-quart slow cooker.

2. Cover and cook on low heat setting 6 to 7 hours or until beef and vegetables are tender.

3. Stir in bell pepper and beans. Cook uncovered on high heat setting about 15 minutes or until slightly thickened. Serve with cheese.

8 servings.

1 Serving: Calories 170 (Calories from Fat 25); Fat 3g (Saturated 1g); Cholesterol 30mg; Sodium 640mg; Carbohydrate 24g (Dietary Fiber 6g); Protein 18g
% Daily Value: Vitamin A 24%; Vitamin C 32%; Calcium 6%; Iron 22%
Exchanges: 1 Starch, 1 Lean Meat, 2 Vegetable

BETTY'S TIPS

⊙ **Substitution**
You can also use one 28-ounce can of whole tomatoes instead of the diced tomatoes. Use a spoon to break up the whole tomatoes in the slow cooker.

⊙ **Variation**
If you like chili with a little kick, stir in ¼ teaspoon ground red pepper (cayenne) with the cinnamon.

⊙ **Special Touch**
Add some zip to your serving bowls by brushing the edges of the bowls with butter or shortening and then sprinkling with chili powder.

Chill-Chasing Chili

Ham and Lentil Stew

Prep: 20 min Cook: 9 hr

3 cups diced fully cooked ham

2 cups dried lentils (1 pound), sorted and rinsed

4 medium stalks celery, chopped (2 cups)

4 medium carrots, chopped (2 cups)

1 large onion, chopped (1 cup)

2 cans (10½ ounces each) condensed chicken broth

4 cups water

1. Mix all ingredients in 3½- to 4-quart slow cooker.

2. Cover and cook on low heat setting 7 to 9 hours or until lentils are tender.

8 servings.

1 Serving: Calories 245 (Calories from Fat 55); Fat 6g (Saturated 2g); Cholesterol 30mg; Sodium 1260mg; Carbohydrate 33g (Dietary Fiber 12g); Protein 27g
% Daily Value: Vitamin A 100%; Vitamin C 6%; Calcium 6%; Iron 32%
Exchanges: 2 Starch, 2 Very Lean Meat, 1 Vegetable

BETTY'S TIPS

⊙ **Health Twist**
The lentils in this stew provide a good amount of fiber, 12 grams per serving!

⊙ **Special Touch**
A swirl of pesto is a great way to jazz up this down-home stew. Let diners serve themselves.

⊙ **Did You Know?**
Lentils come in a variety of colors. Regular brown lentils are commonly found in the grocery store. Smaller red and yellow lentils can be found in food co-ops and Middle Eastern stores.

Ham and Lentil Stew

Betty... ON BASICS

Beef and Broth

Prep: 30 min Cook: 10 hr Cool: 10 min

- 2 tablespoons vegetable oil
- 2 pounds beef shank cross-cuts or soup bones
- 5 cups cold water
- 1¼ teaspoons salt
- ¼ teaspoon dried thyme leaves
- 1 medium carrot, cut up
- 1 medium stalk celery with leaves, cut up
- 1 small onion, cut up
- 5 peppercorns
- 3 whole cloves
- 3 sprigs parsley
- 1 dried bay leaf

Cook beef in oil until brown on both sides. Precooking the meat helps add color and flavor to the broth.

1. Heat oil in 10-inch skillet over medium heat. Cook beef in oil until brown on both sides.

2. Mix remaining ingredients in 3½- to 4-quart slow cooker. Add beef.

3. Cover and cook on low heat setting 8 to 10 hours or until beef is tender.

4. Remove beef from broth. Cool beef about 10 minutes or just until cool enough to handle. Strain broth through cheesecloth-lined sieve; discard vegetables and seasonings.

5. Remove beef from bones. Cut beef into ½-inch pieces. Skim fat from broth. Use immediately or cover and refrigerate broth and beef in separate containers up to 24 hours (or freeze for future use).

4 servings.

1 Serving: Calories 160 (Calories from Fat 45); Fat 5g (Saturated 1g); Cholesterol 45mg; Sodium 160mg; Carbohydrate 0g (Dietary Fiber 0g); Protein 17g
% Daily Value: Vitamin A 12%; Vitamin C 0%; Calcium 0%; Iron 8%
Exchanges: 2½ Lean Meat

Strain broth through cheesecloth-lined sieve; discard vegetables and seasonings.

Fresh Vegetable Beef Soup

Prep: 20 min Cook: 9 hr

1½ pounds beef stew meat

1 small bell pepper, chopped (½ cup)

¾ cup 1-inch pieces fresh green beans

¾ cup chopped onion

¾ cup sliced carrots

⅔ cup fresh whole kernel corn

2 medium unpeeled potatoes, cut into 1-inch pieces (about 2 cups)

1½ cups water

1 teaspoon salt

1 teaspoon chopped fresh or ½ teaspoon dried thyme leaves

¼ teaspoon pepper

3½ cups Beef Broth (opposite) or 2 cans (14 ounces each) beef broth

2 cans (14½ ounces each) diced tomatoes with garlic, undrained

1 can (8 ounces) tomato sauce

1. Mix all ingredients in 3½- to 4-quart slow cooker.

2. Cover and cook on low heat setting 8 to 9 hours (or high heat setting 4 to 5 hours) or until vegetables are tender.

10 servings.

1 Serving: Calories 190 (Calories from Fat 70); Fat 8g (Saturated 3g); Cholesterol 40mg; Sodium 920mg; Carbohydrate 15g (Dietary Fiber 3g); Protein 17g
% Daily Value: Vitamin A 12%; Vitamin C 18%; Calcium 4%; Iron 16%
Exchanges: 1 Starch, 1½ Medium-Fat Meat, 1 Vegetable

BETTY'S TIPS

☻ **Substitution**
If you can't find the canned diced tomatoes with garlic, use 2 cans of plain diced tomatoes and add ½ teaspoon garlic powder.

☻ **Success Hint**
If you like, you can omit the beef stew meat and use the beef from the Beef and Broth recipe (page 110) in this stew. Cook the soup as directed, except do not add the cooked beef. Stir the cooked beef in the last 15 to 30 minutes of cooking.

Fresh Vegetable Beef Soup

Cajun Beef Stew

Prep: 15 min Stand: 15 min Cook: 8 hr + 30 min
Photo on page 99

¼ cup Caribbean jerk marinade

1½ pounds beef stew meat

4 medium red potatoes (about ¾ pound), cut into fourths

⅓ cup Gold Medal all-purpose flour

1 tablespoon spicy Cajun seasoning

1 can (14½ ounces) diced tomatoes, undrained

3 cups frozen stir-fry bell peppers and onions (from 1-pound bag)

1. Pour marinade over beef in resealable plastic food-storage bag or glass or plastic dish; coat beef with marinade. Let stand 15 minutes.

2. Spray inside of 3½- to 4-quart slow cooker with cooking spray. Place potatoes in slow cooker. Mix flour and Cajun seasoning; toss with beef and marinade, coating well. Place beef and marinade on potatoes. Add tomatoes.

3. Cover and cook on low heat setting 7 to 8 hours or until beef is tender.

4. Stir in vegetables. Cover and cook on low heat setting 15 to 30 minutes or until vegetables are tender.

4 to 6 servings.

1 Serving: Calories 550 (Calories from Fat 180); Fat 20g (Saturated 8g); Cholesterol 100mg; Sodium 320mg; Carbohydrate 52g (Dietary Fiber 6g); Protein 41g
% Daily Value: Vitamin A 26%; Vitamin C 60%; Calcium 8%; Iron 38%
Exchanges: 3 Starch, 4 Medium-Fat Meat, 1 Vegetable

BETTY'S TIPS

✿ **Variation**
If you like your food hot and spicy, you may want to increase the Cajun seasoning to 2 tablespoons.

✿ **Did You Know?**
Cajun cooks like rice! A regional specialty is Dirty Rice, which has a brownish or "dirty" appearance from the chicken livers that are cooked and ground and then added to the rice mixture. With bits of bell pepper, onion, garlic and pepper, this rice has a distinct spiciness and unique flavor. For milder palates, simply serve this southern-inspired stew with hot cooked white or brown rice.

Scottish Lamb Stew

Prep: 20 min   Cook: 10 hr + 15 min

2   pounds boneless lamb shoulder or stew meat

⅓   cup Gold Medal all-purpose flour

½   teaspoon ground mustard

½   teaspoon seasoned salt

1   tablespoon vegetable oil

3   medium potatoes, cut into 1-inch pieces

2   medium carrots or parsnips, peeled and cut into ½-inch pieces

1   cup frozen small whole onions (from 1-pound bag)

1   teaspoon seasoned salt

2¼   cups chicken broth

1½   cups frozen green peas

Hot cooked barley or rice, if desired

Apple mint jelly, if desired

1. Cut lamb into 1½-inch pieces. Toss together lamb, flour, mustard and ½ teaspoon seasoned salt. Heat oil in 12-inch skillet over medium-high heat. Cook lamb in oil, stirring occasionally, until brown.

2. Place potatoes, carrots and onions in 3½- to 4-quart slow cooker. Sprinkle with 1 teaspoon seasoned salt. Place lamb on top of vegetables. Pour broth over lamb.

3. Cover and cook on low heat setting 9 to 10 hours or until lamb is tender.

4. Stir in peas. Cover and cook 15 minutes. Serve with barley and jelly.

6 servings.

1 Serving: Calories 320 (Calories from Fat 100); Fat 11g (Saturated 3g); Cholesterol 85mg; Sodium 760mg; Carbohydrate 28g (Dietary Fiber 5g); Protein 32g
% Daily Value: Vitamin A 100%; Vitamin C 10%; Calcium 4%; Iron 18%
Exchanges: 1½ Starch, 3½ Lean Meat, 1 Vegetable

BETTY'S TIPS

☻ Substitution

For a heartier taste with a subtle ale flavor, use 1 cup of ale or dark beer in place of 1 cup of the chicken broth.

Beef or pork can also be used in place of the lamb in this stew. When choosing the meat, take into consideration personal preference, availability of lamb and the cost.

☻ Serve-With

Quick-cooking barley cooks up fast and can be made when the peas are stirred in. Common in Scottish cooking, barley complements this lamb stew nicely.

Scottish Lamb Stew

Turkey and Brown Rice Chili

Prep: 15 min Cook: 10 hr + 15 min
Photo on page 99

1	tablespoon vegetable oil
¾	pound ground turkey breast
1	large onion, chopped (1 cup)
2	cans (14½ ounces each) diced tomatoes, undrained
1	can (15 to 16 ounces) chili beans in sauce, undrained
1	can (4 ounces) chopped green chilies, drained
½	cup water
1	tablespoon sugar
2	teaspoons chili powder
1	teaspoon ground cumin
½	teaspoon salt
2	cups cooked brown rice

BETTY'S TIPS

◎ **Substitution**
Do you have ground beef in the freezer? Use it instead of the turkey, plus you won't need to use oil when you cook it. Stir in either brown or white rice at the end.

◎ **Success Hint**
This is a low-fat chili because it is made with ground turkey breast. Check that you are buying ground turkey breast and not regular ground turkey, which includes both light and dark meat and will be higher in fat.

◎ **Special Touch**
Enjoy this chili topped with your favorite salsa and corn chips.

1. Heat oil in 12-inch skillet over medium heat. Cook turkey and onion in oil about 5 minutes, stirring frequently, until turkey is no longer pink; drain.

2. Mix turkey mixture and remaining ingredients except rice in 3½- to 4-quart slow cooker.

3. Cover and cook on low heat setting 8 to 10 hours (or high heat setting 4 to 5 hours).

4. Stir in rice. Cover and cook on high heat setting about 15 minutes longer or until rice is hot.

6 servings.

1 Serving: Calories 240 (Calories from Fat 35); Fat 4g (Saturated 1g); Cholesterol 40mg; Sodium 1270mg; Carbohydrate 38g (Dietary Fiber 7g); Protein 20g
% Daily Value: Vitamin A 26%; Vitamin C 24%; Calcium 8%; Iron 20%
Exchanges: 2 Starch, 2 Very Lean Meat, 1 Vegetable

Main Dish Seafood & Vegetables

Fresh, Light and Fabulous

Seafaring Packets (page 123)

Caribbean Salmon Packets (page 122)

Grilled Halibut with Tomato-Avocado Salsa

Prep: 20 min Marinate: 30 min Grill: 15 min

1½ pounds halibut, tuna or swordfish steaks, ¾ to 1 inch thick
2 tablespoons olive or vegetable oil
2 tablespoons lemon or lime juice
¼ teaspoon salt
¼ teaspoon ground cumin
⅛ teaspoon ground red pepper (cayenne)
1 clove garlic, finely chopped
Tomato-Avocado Salsa (below)

1. If fish steaks are large, cut into 6 serving pieces. Mix remaining ingredients except Tomato-Avocado Salsa in shallow glass or plastic dish. Add fish; turn to coat with marinade. Cover and refrigerate at least 30 minutes but no longer than 2 hours.

2. Heat coals or gas grill for direct heat. Remove fish from marinade; reserve marinade. Cover and grill fish 4 to 5 inches from medium heat 10 to 15 minutes, brushing 2 or 3 times with marinade and turning once, until fish flakes easily with fork. Discard any remaining marinade.

3. While fish is grilling, make Tomato-Avocado Salsa. Serve salsa with fish.

6 servings.

Tomato-Avocado Salsa

2 medium tomatoes, chopped (1½ cups)
1 medium avocado, coarsely chopped
1 small jalapeño chili, seeded and finely chopped
¼ cup chopped fresh cilantro
2 teaspoons lemon or lime juice

Mix all ingredients.

1 Serving: Calories 200 (Calories from Fat 90); Fat 10g (Saturated 2g); Cholesterol 50mg; Sodium 200mg; Carbohydrate 5g (Dietary Fiber 2g); Protein 22g
% Daily Value: Vitamin A 10%; Vitamin C 24%; Calcium 2%; Iron 4%
Exchanges: 1½ Lean Meat, 1 Vegetable, 1 Fat

BETTY'S TIPS

☻ **Serve-With**
If you have any of this yummy salsa left over, serve it with tortilla chips the next day!

☻ **Variation**
If you like salsa with a little more kick, leave the seeds in the jalapeño pepper.

☻ **Do-Ahead**
You can prepare the salsa up to 1 hour ahead of time. Toss the avocado with the lemon juice before mixing with the remaining ingredients. Cover and refrigerate.

Grilled Halibut with Tomato-Avocado Salsa

Grilled Sea Bass with Citrus-Olive Butter

Prep: 10 min Chill: 30 min Grill: 13 min

Citrus-Olive Butter (below)
1 sea bass fillet, about 1 inch thick (1 pound)
1 tablespoon olive or vegetable oil
¼ teaspoon salt
⅛ teaspoon pepper

1. Make Citrus-Olive Butter. Heat coals or gas grill for direct heat. Brush all surfaces of fish with oil; sprinkle with salt and pepper.

2. Cover and grill fish 4 to 5 inches from medium heat 10 to 13 minutes, turning fish after 5 minutes, until fish flakes easily with fork. Serve with Citrus-Olive Butter.

4 servings.

Citrus-Olive Butter
2 tablespoons butter or margarine, softened
1 tablespoon finely chopped Kalamata olives
2 teaspoons chopped fresh parsley
½ teaspoon balsamic vinegar
¼ teaspoon grated orange peel

Mix all ingredients. Refrigerate 30 minutes or until firm.

1 Serving: Calories 185 (Calories from Fat 100); Fat 11g (Saturated 4g); Cholesterol 75mg; Sodium 300mg; Carbohydrate 0g (Dietary Fiber 0g); Protein 21g
% Daily Value: Vitamin A 6%; Vitamin C 0%; Calcium 2%; Iron 2%
Exchanges: 3 Lean Meat, ½ Fat

BETTY'S TIPS

✪ **Substitution**
You could use another fish such as tuna or halibut instead of the sea bass.

✪ **Serve-With**
Serve the grilled fish with wild rice salad from the deli and a sliced fresh tomato drizzled with Italian dressing.

✪ **Did You Know?**
Sea bass describes several varieties of saltwater fish of the drum or grouper family. Sea bass has firm, lean to moderately fat flesh that can be baked, grilled, poached or fried. If there is skin on the fish, it can be removed with a very sharp knife.

Grilled Sea Bass with Citrus-Olive Butter

Asian Grilled Tuna with Wasabi Aioli

Prep: 10 min Marinate: 2 hr Grill: 15 min

Wasabi Aioli (right)
2 pounds tuna steaks, ¾ to 1 inch thick
½ cup vegetable oil
⅓ cup soy sauce
2 tablespoons packed brown sugar
2 teaspoons sesame oil
2 teaspoons grated gingerroot
2 cloves garlic, finely chopped
2 teaspoons sesame seed, toasted if desired

Asian Grilled Tuna with Wasabi Aioli

1. Make Wasabi Aioli. If tuna steaks are large, cut into 8 serving pieces. Mix vegetable oil, soy sauce, brown sugar, sesame oil, gingerroot and garlic in shallow glass or plastic dish or resealable plastic food-storage bag. Add tuna; turn to coat with marinade. Cover dish or seal bag and refrigerate, turning once, at least 2 hours but no longer than 4 hours.

2. Heat coals or gas grill for direct heat. Remove tuna from marinade; reserve marinade. Cover and grill tuna about 4 inches from medium heat 10 to 15 minutes, brushing 2 to 3 times with marinade and turning once, until tuna flakes easily with fork. Discard any remaining marinade. Sprinkle tuna with sesame seed. Serve with Wasabi Aioli.

8 servings.

Wasabi Aioli
½ cup mayonnaise or salad dressing
1 teaspoon wasabi powder or prepared horseradish

Mix ingredients. Cover and refrigerate until serving.

1 Serving: Calories 415 (Calories from Fat 290); Fat 32g (Saturated 5g); Cholesterol 50mg; Sodium 730mg; Carbohydrate 5g (Dietary Fiber 0g); Protein 27g
% Daily Value: Vitamin A 2%; Vitamin C 0%; Calcium 2%; Iron 8%
Exchanges: 4 Medium-Fat Meat, 2½ Fat

BETTY'S TIPS

✿ **Success Hint**
To toast sesame seed, bake uncovered in ungreased shallow pan in 350° oven 8 to 10 minutes, stirring occasionally, until golden brown. Or cook in ungreased heavy skillet over medium heat about 2 minutes, stirring frequently until browning begins, then stirring constantly until golden brown.

✿ **Variation**
The Wasabi Aioli also makes a super sandwich spread. Spread on bread or buns instead of mayo and top with your favorite deli meat or a juicy grilled burger.

Betty... ON HEALTH

4 Tips for Safe Grilling

DON'T LET BACTERIA SPOIL YOUR BARBECUE

Approximately one out of every four people gets food poisoning each year. The risk can go up as the mercury climbs. Warmer temperatures and a more casual approach to cooking in the summer give bacteria plenty of opportunity to get acquainted with the meals you serve. Keep your barbecue safe. Here's how.

1. CLEAN

Clean everything, starting with your hands. Experts say half of all cases of food poisoning could be avoided if people washed their hands more often. Wash before you start cooking and between steps in food preparation. It is one of the best ways to keep bacteria out.

Clean cooking surfaces as well, including the grill. Heat the grill for several minutes to kill lingering bacteria before placing food on the rack.

2. SEPARATE

Separate uncooked foods from each other and from cooked foods. Different foods can carry different bacteria. Divide and conquer!

- Always place cooked meat on a clean plate, not on the plate that previously held raw meat.

- Wash utensils and surfaces between uses.

- Use paper towels, not sponges, to wipe up drippings.

- Replace used dish towels frequently.

3. COOK

Make sure foods on the grill reach the correct temperature before you serve them (see chart at right and the one on page 124). Use a meat thermometer to check doneness.

Food	Internal Temperature
Beef: steaks, roasts, kabobs	145°-160° (medium-rare, medium)
Ground Beef	160°
Poultry: cut-up bone-in and boneless pieces and whole breasts	170°
Whole Birds and Rock Cornish Hens	180°

Food	Internal Temperature
Ground Turkey or Chicken Burgers	170°
Bratwurst (uncooked)	160°
Hot Dogs	165°
Pork	160° (medium)

4. CHILL

Keep cold foods cold. Ice baths and coolers work well. If foods have been handled safely, they can be out at room temperature up to 2 hours before needing to be discarded. Cut that time in half, however, if the temperature is above 85°.

Marinade Reminders

- Always marinate meat, poultry and fish in the refrigerator. Keep foods cold until ready to cook.

- Boil the marinade from raw meat, poultry and fish before serving with cooked food.

Grilled Swordfish Steaks

Salmon with Honey-Mustard Glaze

Salmon with Honey-Mustard Glaze

Prep: 5 min Marinate: 15 min Grill: 15 min

Honey-Mustard Marinade (below)
1 salmon fillet (1 pound)

1. Make Honey-Mustard Marinade. Place salmon in shallow glass or plastic dish. Pour marinade over salmon. Cover and refrigerate at least 15 minutes but no longer than 1 hour.

2. Heat coals or gas grill for direct heat. Remove salmon from marinade; reserve marinade. Place salmon, skin side down, on grill. Cover and grill 4 to 6 inches from medium heat 10 to 15 minutes, brushing 2 or 3 times with marinade, until salmon flakes easily with fork. Discard any remaining marinade.

4 servings.

Honey-Mustard Marinade
1 tablespoon packed brown sugar
1 tablespoon butter or margarine, melted
1 tablespoon olive or vegetable oil
1 tablespoon honey
1 tablespoon soy sauce
1 tablespoon Dijon mustard
1 clove garlic, finely chopped

Mix all ingredients.

1 Serving: Calories 220 (Calories from Fat 100); Fat 11g (Saturated 3g); Cholesterol 80mg; Sodium 290mg; Carbohydrate 6g (Dietary Fiber 0g); Protein 24g
% Daily Value: Vitamin A 4%; Vitamin C 0%; Calcium 2%; Iron 4%
Exchanges: ½ Starch, 3 Lean Meat

BETTY'S TIPS

✪ **Success Hint**
Fish generally takes about 10 minutes to grill for each inch of thickness. Add more time if the fillet is thicker; if you are grilling 2 thinner pieces, grill the fish for slightly less time.

✪ **Variation**
The salmon can also be broiled instead of grilled. It will cook in about the same amount of time.

Grilled Swordfish Steaks

Prep: 15 min Marinate: 15 min Grill: 15 min

¼ cup olive or vegetable oil
2 tablespoons capers
1½ tablespoons lemon juice
1 tablespoon chopped fresh parsley
½ teaspoon pepper
2 flat anchovy fillets in oil
2 cloves garlic
4 swordfish steaks, about 1 inch thick (about 2 pounds)

1. Place all ingredients except swordfish in food processor or blender. Cover and process until smooth.

2. Place swordfish in ungreased rectangular baking dish, 11 × 7 × 1½ inches. Pour marinade over swordfish. Cover and refrigerate at least 15 minutes but no longer than 1 hour, turning swordfish occasionally.

3. Heat coals or gas grill for direct heat. Remove swordfish from marinade; reserve marinade. Grill swordfish uncovered about 4 inches from medium-high heat 5 minutes, brushing frequently with marinade. Turn carefully; brush generously with marinade. Grill 5 to 10 minutes longer or until swordfish flakes easily with fork. Discard any remaining marinade.

4 servings.

1 Serving: Calories 325 (Calories from Fat 180); Fat 20g (Saturated 4g); Cholesterol 110mg; Sodium 260mg; Carbohydrate 1g (Dietary Fiber 0g); Protein 35g
% Daily Value: Vitamin A 4%; Vitamin C 4%; Calcium 2%; Iron 6%
Exchanges: 5 Lean Meat, 1 Fat

BETTY'S TIPS

✪ **Substitution**
Tuna or salmon steaks can be used instead of the swordfish. The grilling times will be the same.

Caribbean Salmon Packets

Prep: 20 min Grill: 18 min

2 cups uncooked instant rice
1 can (14 ounces) chicken broth
1 small red bell pepper, chopped (½ cup)
2 medium green onions, sliced (2 tablespoons)
4 salmon fillets (6 ounces each), skin removed
1 teaspoon salt
½ cup chutney
1 cup pineapple chunks

1. Heat coals or gas grill for direct heat. Spray half of one side of four 18 X 12-inch sheets of heavy-duty aluminum foil with cooking spray.

2. Mix rice and broth in large bowl; let stand about 7 minutes or until broth is almost absorbed. Stir in bell pepper and onions. Place ¾ cup rice mixture on center of each sprayed foil sheet.

3. Top rice with salmon. Sprinkle each salmon fillet with ¼ teaspoon salt; top with 2 tablespoons chutney and ¼ cup pineapple chunks. Fold foil over salmon and rice mixture so edges meet. Seal edges, making tight ½-inch fold; fold again. Allow space on sides for heat circulation and expansion.

4. Grill packets 4 to 6 inches from medium heat 12 to 18 minutes or until salmon flakes easily with fork. Place packets on plates. Cut large X across top of each packet; fold back foil.

4 servings.

1 Serving: Calories 525 (Calories from Fat 100); Fat 11g (Saturated 3g); Cholesterol 110mg; Sodium 1180mg; Carbohydrate 65g (Dietary Fiber 3g); Protein 43g
% Daily Value: Vitamin A 28%; Vitamin C 40%; Calcium 4%; Iron 20%
Exchanges: 3 Starch, 4½ Very Lean Meat, 1 Vegetable, 1 Fruit, 1 Fat

BETTY'S TIPS

☺ **Success Hint**
Soaking the rice in broth before grilling the packet ensures the rice will be done at the same time as the salmon.

Open the foil packets very carefully, keeping the opening pointed away from you. Very hot steam collects inside the packets during cooking and could result in burns.

☺ **Substitution**
You can use either fresh or canned pineapple chunks in these easy fish packets.

Caribbean Salmon Packets

Seafaring Packets

Prep: 20 min Grill: 20 min
Photo on page 115

Lemon Butter or Chive Butter (right)

32 littleneck or cherrystone shell clams (about 2½ pounds)

32 uncooked medium shrimp in shells (about 1¼ pounds), thawed if frozen

32 sea scallops (about 2½ pounds)

8 ears corn, husked and cut into fourths

32 large cherry tomatoes

Fresh chive stems or chopped fresh chives, if desired

1. Make Lemon Butter or Chive Butter. Heat coals or gas grill for direct heat. Divide clams, shrimp, scallops, corn and tomatoes on one side of eight 18 × 12-inch sheets of heavy-duty aluminum foil. Drizzle 1 tablespoon of Lemon Butter or Chive Butter over seafood and vegetables on each sheet.

2. Fold foil over seafood and vegetables so edges meet. Seal edges, making tight ½-inch fold; fold again. Allow space on sides for heat circulation and expansion.

3. Cover and grill packets 4 to 5 inches from medium heat 15 to 20 minutes or until clams open, shrimp are pink and firm and vegetables are tender.* Place packets on plates. Cut large X across top of each packet; fold back foil. Top with chives.

8 servings.

Lemon Butter

½ cup butter or margarine, melted

1 tablespoon grated lemon peel

Mix ingredients.

Chive Butter

½ cup butter or margarine, melted

1 tablespoon chopped fresh or 1 teaspoon freeze-dried chives

Mix ingredients.

*Cooking time may vary depending on ingredients selected.

1 Serving: Calories 300 (Calories from Fat 125); Fat 14g (Saturated 8g); Cholesterol 90mg; Sodium 230mg; Carbohydrate 30g (Dietary Fiber 4g); Protein 18g
% Daily Value: Vitamin A 26%; Vitamin C 20%; Calcium 6%; Iron 40%
Exchanges: 1 Starch, 1½ Lean Meat, 3 Vegetable, 1 Fat

BETTY'S TIPS

⊗ **Substitution**
Mussels can be substituted for the clams. If your guests don't care for either clams or mussels, you may double the amount of shrimp or scallops instead.

⊗ **The Finishing Touch**
For a more elegant presentation, make the packets with parchment paper, then wrap in foil. The foil keeps the parchment from burning and slips off easily for serving.

Betty... MAKES IT EASY

Handy ... Grill ... Chart

If You're Grilling	Use This Method	Grill over This Heat	For This Long	Or Until Done
Pork loin roast (boneless) (3 pounds)	Indirect	Medium-Low	1 hour	Meat thermometer reads 160°
Pork tenderloin (1 pound)	Direct	Medium	20 to 25 minutes	Meat thermometer reads 160°
Hot dogs or bratwurst (cooked)	Direct	Medium	5 to 10 minutes	Hot
Bratwurst (uncooked)	Indirect	Medium	20 to 25 minutes	Meat thermometer reads 160°
Hamburger patties (¾ inch thick)	Direct	Medium	10 to 15 minutes	Meat thermometer reads 160°
Beef T-bone, sirloin, rib-eye, top loin or tenderloin steaks (1 inch thick)	Direct	Medium	12 to 15 minutes	Meat thermometer reads 145-160°
Beef T-bone, sirloin, rib-eye, top loin or tenderloin steaks (¾ inch thick)	Direct	Medium	8 to 12 minutes	Meat thermometer reads 145-160°
Beef flank steak (1½ pounds)	Direct	Medium	12 to 15 minutes	Meat thermometer reads 145-160°
Chicken breast halves (bone-in) (1 pound)	Direct	Medium	20 to 25 minutes	Meat thermometer reads 170° and juice is no longer pink
Chicken breast halves or thighs (boneless) (1¼ pounds)	Direct	Medium	15 to 20 minutes	Meat thermometer reads 170° and juice is no longer pink
Chicken legs or thighs (bone-in) (2 pounds)	Direct	Medium	20 to 25 minutes	Meat thermometer reads 170° and juice is no longer pink
Chicken wings (2 to 2½ pounds)	Direct	Medium	12 to 18 minutes	Meat thermometer reads 170° and juice is no longer pink
Whole broiler-fryer chicken (3 to 3½ pounds)	Indirect	Medium	1½ to 2¼ hours	Meat thermometer reads 180° and juice is no longer pink
Whole turkey breast (bone-in) (3½ to 4 pounds)	Indirect	Medium	1¼ to 1½ hours	Meat thermometer reads 170° and juice is no longer pink
Whole turkey (8 to 10 pounds)	Indirect	Medium	2¾ to 3 hours	Meat thermometer reads 180° and juice is no longer pink
Fish fillets or steaks (¾ to 1 inch thick)	Direct	Medium	10 to 15 minutes	Fish flakes easily with fork
Whole fish (1½ pounds)	Indirect	Medium	20 to 25 minutes	Fish flakes easily with fork
Shrimp (1 pound large)	Direct	Medium	5 to 7 minutes	Pink and firm
Corn on the cob (with husk)	Direct	Medium	20 to 30 minutes	Tender
Corn on the cob (without husk)	Direct	Medium	10 to 12 minutes	Tender
New potatoes (halves or quartered)	Direct	Medium	15 to 20 minutes	Tender
Russet potatoes (quartered lengthwise)	Direct	Medium	20 to 25 minutes	Tender
Russet potatoes (whole), in foil	Direct	Medium	45 to 60 minutes	Tender

Mexican Fish in Foil

Prep: 15 min Grill: 15 min

1½ pounds halibut fillets, ½ to ¾ inch thick

¼ cup sliced pimiento-stuffed olives

2 teaspoons capers

1 medium tomato, seeded and coarsely chopped (¾ cup)

3 medium green onions, thinly sliced (3 tablespoons)

1 clove garlic, finely chopped

2 tablespoons lemon juice

¼ teaspoon salt

⅛ teaspoon pepper

Lemon wedges

1. Heat coals or gas grill for direct heat. If fish fillets are large, cut into 6 serving pieces. Place fish in heavy-duty aluminum foil bag. Mix olives, capers, tomato, onions and garlic; spoon over fish. Drizzle with lemon juice. Sprinkle with salt and pepper. Double-fold open end of bag.

2. Cover and grill bag 5 to 6 inches from medium heat about 15 minutes or until fish flakes easily with fork.

Place bag on serving plate. Cut large X across top of packet; fold back foil. Serve fish with lemon wedges.

6 servings.

1 Serving: Calories 115 (Calories from Fat 20); Fat 2g (Saturated 0g); Cholesterol 60mg; Sodium 380mg; Carbohydrate 2g (Dietary Fiber 1g); Protein 22g
% Daily Value: Vitamin A 4%; Vitamin C 4%; Calcium 2%; Iron 2%
Exchanges: 3 Very Lean Meat

BETTY'S TIPS

✪ **Substitution**
If halibut is not available, use cod or red snapper.

✪ **Success Hint**
To test fish for doneness, place a fork in the thickest part and gently twist. The fish will flake easily when done.

✪ **Did You Know?**
You can make your own foil packet by placing food on half of an 18 × 12-inch piece of heavy-duty aluminum foil. Fold other half of foil so edges meet. Seal edges, making a tight ½-inch fold; fold again. Allow space on sides for heat circulation and expansion.

Mexican Fish in Foil

Betty ... MAKES IT EASY

Quick

Lemon- and Parmesan-Crusted Salmon

Prep: 10 min Bake: 20 min

1 salmon fillet (1¼ pounds)
2 tablespoons butter or margarine, melted
¼ teaspoon salt
¾ cup fresh white bread crumbs (about 1 slice bread)
¼ cup grated Parmesan cheese
2 tablespoons thinly sliced green onions
2 teaspoons grated lemon peel
¼ teaspoon dried thyme leaves

1. Heat oven to 375°. Spray shallow baking pan with cooking spray. Pat salmon dry with paper towel. Place salmon, skin side down, in pan; brush with 1 tablespoon of the butter. Sprinkle with salt.

2. Mix bread crumbs, cheese, onions, lemon peel and thyme in small bowl. Stir in remaining 1 tablespoon butter. Press bread crumb mixture evenly on salmon.

3. Bake uncovered 15 to 25 minutes or until salmon flakes easily with fork. Serve immediately.

4 servings.

1 Serving: Calories 290 (Calories from Fat 145); Fat 16g (Saturated 7g); Cholesterol 115mg; Sodium 420mg; Carbohydrate 4g (Dietary Fiber 0g); Protein 33g
% Daily Value: Vitamin A 8%; Vitamin C 2%; Calcium 10%; Iron 6%
Exchanges: 5 Lean Meat

Pat salmon dry with paper towel.

Press bread crumb mixture evenly on salmon.

Lemon- and Parmesan-Crusted Salmon

Crispy Baked Fish with Tropical Fruit Salsa

Prep: 20 min Bake: 25 min

3 tablespoons butter or margarine
²/₃ cup Original Bisquick mix
¼ cup yellow cornmeal
1 teaspoon chili powder
1¼ teaspoons salt
1 pound orange roughy or other white fish fillets
1 egg, slightly beaten
Tropical Fruit Salsa (below)

1. Heat oven to 425°. Melt butter in rectangular baking dish, 13 × 9 × 2 inches, in oven.

2. Mix Bisquick mix, cornmeal, chili powder and salt. Dip fish fillets into egg, then coat with Bisquick mixture. Place in baking dish.

3. Bake uncovered 10 minutes; turn fish. Bake about 15 minutes longer or until fish flakes easily with fork.

4. While fish is baking, make Tropical Fruit Salsa. Serve salsa with fish.

4 servings.

Tropical Fruit Salsa

1 can (8 ounces) pineapple chunks, drained
1 tablespoon finely chopped red onion
1 tablespoon chopped fresh cilantro
1 tablespoon lime juice
1 kiwifruit, peeled and chopped
1 mango or papaya, cut lengthwise in half, pitted and chopped
1 jalapeño chili, seeded and finely chopped

Mix all ingredients in glass or plastic bowl.

1 Serving: Calories 395 (Calories from Fat 125); Fat 14g (Saturated 7g); Cholesterol 125mg; Sodium 1200mg; Carbohydrate 40g (Dietary Fiber 3g); Protein 27g
% Daily Value: Vitamin A 22%; Vitamin C 34%; Calcium 8%; Iron 10%
Exchanges: 1 Starch, 3½ Lean Meat, 1½ Fruit, 1 Fat

BETTY'S TIPS

⚙ **Success Hint**
The fruit salsa is perfect for making ahead. Mix ingredients and then cover and refrigerate at least 1 hour for the maximum flavor.

Crispy Baked Fish with Tropical Fruit Salsa

Lemony Fish over Vegetables and Rice

Prep: 10 min Cook: 23 min

- 1 package (6.1 ounces) fried rice (rice and vermicelli mix with almonds and Oriental seasonings)
- 2 tablespoons butter or margarine
- 2 cups water
- ½ teaspoon grated lemon peel
- 1 bag (1 pound) frozen corn, broccoli and red peppers
- 1 pound mild-flavored fish fillets, about ½ inch thick
- ½ teaspoon lemon pepper
- 1 tablespoon lemon juice
- 2 tablespoons chopped fresh parsley

1. Cook rice and butter in 12-inch nonstick skillet over medium heat 2 to 3 minutes, stirring occasionally, until rice is golden brown. Stir in water, seasoning packet from rice mix and lemon peel. Heat to boiling; reduce heat. Cover and simmer 10 minutes.

2. Stir in vegetables. Heat to boiling, stirring occasionally. Cut fish into 4 serving pieces; arrange on rice mixture. Sprinkle fish with lemon pepper; drizzle with lemon juice. Reduce heat. Cover and simmer 8 to 10 minutes or until fish flakes easily with fork and vegetables are tender. Sprinkle with parsley.

4 servings.

1 Serving: Calories 230 (Calories from Fat 65); Fat 7g (Saturated 1g); Cholesterol 55mg; Sodium 330mg; Carbohydrate 22g (Dietary Fiber 3g); Protein 23g
% Daily Value: Vitamin A 38%; Vitamin C 72%; Calcium 4%; Iron 6%
Exchanges: 1 Starch, 2½ Lean Meat, 1 Vegetable

BETTY'S TIPS

☺ **Substitution**
No lemon pepper on hand? Just add ⅛ teaspoon of pepper instead.

☺ **Success Hint**
Good choices of mild-flavored fish include cod, flounder, haddock, halibut, orange roughy and sole.

Lemony Fish over Vegetables and Rice

Champagne Shrimp Risotto

Prep: 10 min Cook: 40 min

1 pound uncooked medium shrimp in shells, thawed if frozen

2 tablespoons butter or margarine

1 medium onion, thinly sliced

½ cup brut champagne, dry white wine or chicken broth

1½ cups uncooked Arborio or other short-grain white rice

2 cups chicken broth, warmed

1 cup clam juice or water, warmed

2 cups chopped arugula, watercress or spinach

⅓ cup grated Parmesan cheese

½ teaspoon pepper

Chopped fresh parsley, if desired

1. Peel shrimp. Make a shallow cut lengthwise down back of each shrimp; wash out vein.

2. Melt butter in 12-inch skillet or 4-quart Dutch oven over medium-high heat. Cook onion in butter, stirring frequently, until tender. Reduce heat to medium. Add shrimp. Cook uncovered about 8 minutes, turning once, until shrimp are pink and firm. Remove shrimp from skillet; keep warm.

3. Add champagne to onion in skillet; cook until liquid has evaporated. Stir in rice. Cook uncovered over medium heat about 5 minutes, stirring frequently, until edges of rice kernels are translucent. Mix chicken broth and clam juice; pour ½ cup mixture over rice. Cook uncovered, stirring occasionally, until liquid is absorbed. Repeat with remaining broth mixture, ½ cup at a time, until rice is tender and creamy.

4. About 5 minutes before risotto is done, stir in shrimp, arugula, cheese and pepper. Sprinkle with parsley before serving.

6 servings.

1 Serving: Calories 295 (Calories from Fat 65); Fat 7g (Saturated 4g); Cholesterol 85mg; Sodium 730mg; Carbohydrate 43g (Dietary Fiber 1g); Protein 16g
% Daily Value: Vitamin A 24%; Vitamin C 4%; Calcium 12%; Iron 20%
Exchanges: 3 Starch, 1 Very Lean Meat, 1 Vegetable

BETTY'S TIPS

✪ Success Hint
Even though you may be tempted, don't rush the process! When making risotto, adding the broth a little at a time ensures that the dish will be creamy while allowing the grains to remain separate.

✪ Variation
Leave out the shrimp and serve this as a lovely main course for your vegetarian friends.

Champagne Shrimp Risotto

Seafood à la King

Prep: 15 min Bake: 10 min

2¼ cups Reduced Fat Bisquick mix
¾ cup fat-free (skim) milk
1 can (18.5 ounces) Progresso® New England clam chowder
1 cup Green Giant frozen mixed vegetables (from 1-pound bag)
1 package (5 ounces) frozen cooked salad shrimp, rinsed and thawed
1 tablespoon Reduced Fat Bisquick mix
1 teaspoon dried dill weed
⅛ teaspoon pepper

6 servings.

1 Serving: Calories 445 (Calories from Fat 115); Fat 13g (Saturated 3g); Cholesterol 70mg; Sodium 1380mg; Carbohydrate 64g (Dietary Fiber 3g); Protein 18g
% Daily Value: Vitamin A 100%; Vitamin C 6%; Calcium 16%; Iron 36%
Exchanges: 4 Starch, 1 Medium-Fat Meat, 1 Fat

1. Heat oven to 450°. Stir 2¼ cups Bisquick mix and the milk until soft dough forms. Drop by 6 spoonfuls onto ungreased cookie sheet. Bake 10 minutes or until golden brown.

2. While biscuits are baking, mix remaining ingredients in 2-quart saucepan. Heat to boiling over medium heat, stirring occasionally.

3. To serve, split biscuits in half. Spoon generous ¼ cup hot chowder mixture over bottom of each biscuit. Top with remaining biscuit halves. Spoon ¼ cup chowder mixture over top of each biscuit.

BETTY'S TIPS

☼ **Substitution**
These quick biscuits and sauce make a great Lenten meal. If you don't like shrimp, you can use a 6-ounce can of skinless boneless salmon or tuna, drained.

☼ **Do-Ahead**
You can make both the biscuits and the seafood sauce ahead. Refrigerate seafood sauce until serving time, then re-heat. Store baked biscuits at room temperature, then warm in the oven or microwave.

Seafood à la King

Ramen Shrimp and Vegetables

Prep: 5 min Cook: 17 min

1   pound uncooked peeled deveined medium shrimp, thawed if frozen
2   cups water
1   package (3 ounces) Oriental-flavor ramen soup mix
1   bag (1 pound) fresh stir-fry vegetables
¼   cup stir-fry sauce

1. Spray 12-inch nonstick skillet with cooking spray; heat over medium-high heat. Cook shrimp in skillet 3 to 5 minutes, stirring occasionally, until pink and firm. Remove shrimp from skillet; keep warm.

2. Heat water to boiling in same skillet. Break up noodles from soup mix into water; stir until slightly softened. Stir in vegetables.

3. Heat to boiling. Boil 5 to 7 minutes, stirring occasionally, until vegetables are crisp-tender. Stir in seasoning packet from soup mix and stir-fry sauce. Cook 3 to 5 minutes, stirring frequently, until hot. Stir in shrimp.

4 servings.

1 Serving: Calories 205 (Calories from Fat 55); Fat 6g (Saturated 2g); Cholesterol 160mg; Sodium 1000mg; Carbohydrate 20g (Dietary Fiber 4g); Protein 22g
% Daily Value: Vitamin A 34%; Vitamin C 32%; Calcium 8%; Iron 24%
Exchanges: 1 Starch, 2½ Very Lean Meat, 1 Vegetable

BETTY'S TIPS

☺ **Substitution**
One pound beef boneless sirloin, cut into thin strips, can be substituted for the shrimp. Cook the beef in the skillet until no longer pink.

Replace 2 tablespoons of the water with dry sherry for a nutty, delicate flavor.

Easy Salmon Puff

Prep: 15 min Bake: 40 min

1   cup Original Bisquick mix
1   cup milk
½   cup sour cream
1   teaspoon dried dill weed
4   eggs
2   cans (6 ounces each) skinless boneless salmon, drained and flaked
1   cup shredded Havarti or Swiss cheese (4 ounces)

1. Heat oven to 375°. Spray pie plate, 9 × 1¼ inches, with cooking spray. Stir Bisquick mix, milk, sour cream, dill weed and eggs with wire whisk until blended. Gently stir in salmon and cheese. Pour into pie plate.

2. Bake uncovered 35 to 40 minutes or until knife inserted in center comes out clean.

6 servings.

1 Serving: Calories 340 (Calories from Fat 190); Fat 21g (Saturated 9g); Cholesterol 210mg; Sodium 780mg; Carbohydrate 15g (Dietary Fiber 0g); Protein 23g
% Daily Value: Vitamin A 12%; Vitamin C 0%; Calcium 34%; Iron 10%
Exchanges: 1 Starch, 3 Medium-Fat Meat, 1 Fat

BETTY'S TIPS

☺ **Substitution**
Red salmon will make a more attractive pie. You may not be able to find skinless boneless red salmon, so purchase a 14-ounce can and remove the skin and bones yourself. Flake before adding to this savory pie.

☺ **Health Twist**
Give this rich quiche-like pie a leaner look by using fat-free (skim) milk, reduced-fat sour cream and Reduced Fat Bisquick mix. You'll save 6 grams of fat and 25 calories per serving.

☺ **Did You Know?**
Havarti cheese, a rich Danish cheese, comes in a variety of flavors, including dill. If you like, you can use dill Havarti in this recipe.

Ramen Shrimp and Vegetables

Easy Salmon Puff

Bayou Gumbo

Prep: 25 min Cook: 9 hr + 20 min

3 tablespoons vegetable oil

3 tablespoons Gold Medal all-purpose flour

½ pound smoked pork sausage, cut into ½-inch slices

2 cups frozen cut okra

1 large onion, chopped (1 cup)

1 large green bell pepper, chopped (1½ cups)

3 cloves garlic, finely chopped

¼ teaspoon ground red pepper (cayenne)

¼ teaspoon pepper

1 can (14½ ounces) diced tomatoes, undrained

1½ cups uncooked regular long-grain rice

3 cups water

1 package (12 ounces) frozen cooked peeled and deveined medium shrimp, rinsed and drained

1. Heat oil in 1-quart saucepan over medium-high heat. Stir in flour. Cook 5 minutes, stirring constantly; reduce heat to medium. Cook about 10 minutes, stirring constantly, until mixture turns reddish brown.

2. Place flour-oil mixture in 3½- to 4-quart slow cooker. Stir in remaining ingredients except rice, water and shrimp.

3. Cover and cook on low heat setting 7 to 9 hours.

4. Cook rice in water as directed on package. While rice is cooking, stir shrimp into gumbo mixture in slow cooker. Cover and cook on low heat setting 20 minutes. Serve gumbo over rice.

6 servings.

1 Serving: Calories 490 (Calories from Fat 180); Fat 20g (Saturated 5g); Cholesterol 140mg; Sodium 720mg; Carbohydrate 54g (Dietary Fiber 4g); Protein 26g
% Daily Value: Vitamin A 12%; Vitamin C 32%; Calcium 14%; Iron 28%
Exchanges: 3 Starch, 2 Medium-Fat Meat, 1 Vegetable, 2 Fat

BETTY'S TIPS

☺ **Substitution**
Fresh shrimp can be used, too. Stir in the fresh shrimp at the same time you would the frozen.

☺ **Did You Know?**
Gumbo is a Creole specialty that is standard fare in New Orleans cuisine. There are as many different types of gumbo as there are cooks, but all good gumbos start with a rich roux (flour and oil base) and use okra or filé powder as a thickener.

Okra is typically known as a southern vegetable. This pod-shaped vegetable has a mild flavor when cooked, and it has a slippery characteristic that thickens liquids, like in gumbo.

Bayou Gumbo

Angel Hair Pasta with Shrimp

Prep: 15 min   Cook: 15 min

1 package (16 ounces) capellini (angel hair) pasta
¼ cup olive or vegetable oil
2 tablespoons chopped fresh parsley
2 cloves garlic, finely chopped
1 red jalapeño chili, seeded and finely chopped
⅓ cup dry white wine or chicken broth
½ teaspoon ground nutmeg
¾ pound uncooked fresh or frozen (thawed) peeled deveined small shrimp

1. Cook and drain pasta as directed on package.

2. While pasta is cooking, heat oil in 12-inch skillet or 4-quart Dutch oven over medium-high heat. Cook parsley, garlic and chili in oil about 3 minutes, stirring frequently, until garlic is soft.

3. Stir in wine, nutmeg and shrimp; reduce heat. Cover and simmer about 5 minutes or until shrimp are pink and firm.

4. Add pasta to shrimp mixture in skillet; toss gently until pasta is evenly coated.

6 servings.

1 Serving: Calories 425 (Calories from Fat 100); Fat 11g (Saturated 2g); Cholesterol 80mg; Sodium 150mg; Carbohydrate 61g (Dietary Fiber 3g); Protein 19g
% Daily Value: Vitamin A 6%; Vitamin C 2%; Calcium 2%; Iron 24%
Exchanges: 4 Starch, 1 Very Lean Meat, 2 Fat

BETTY'S TIPS

✿ **Special Touch**
Spectacular garnishes can be very easy to make. Pepper-stuffed ripe olives would add pizzazz to each serving plate or the serving platter for this pasta. To make, drain and pat dry desired number of canned pitted colossal ripe olives. Cut a red or green bell pepper into 2½- to 3-inch julienne strips. Thread pepper strips through each olive so the strips poke out both ends of the olives.

✿ **Did You Know?**
The Italian word capellini means "thin hair," and this pasta is one of the thinnest-cut spaghetti noodles. Legend has it that Parmesan cheese clings to this pasta like gold clings to angels' hair.

Angel Hair Pasta with Shrimp

Creamy Seafood Lasagna

Creamy Seafood Lasagna

Prep: 20 min Bake: 40 min Stand: 15 min

¼ cup butter or margarine

2 cloves garlic, finely chopped

⅔ cup Gold Medal all-purpose flour

2 cups milk

1½ cups chicken broth

¼ cup dry sherry or chicken broth

2 cups shredded mozzarella cheese (8 ounces)

8 medium green onions, sliced (½ cup)

1 tablespoon chopped fresh or 1 teaspoon dried basil leaves

¼ teaspoon pepper

12 uncooked lasagna noodles (12 ounces)

1 package (8 ounces) frozen salad-style imitation crabmeat, thawed, drained and chopped

1 package (4 ounces) frozen cooked salad shrimp, thawed and drained

1 cup ricotta cheese

½ cup grated Parmesan cheese

1. Heat oven to 350°. Melt butter in 3-quart saucepan over low heat. Stir in garlic and flour. Cook and stir 1 minute; remove from heat. Stir in milk, broth and sherry. Heat to boiling, stirring constantly. Boil and stir 1 minute.

2. Stir mozzarella cheese, onions, basil and pepper into sauce. Cook over low heat, stirring constantly, until cheese is melted.

3. Spread 1 cup of the cheese sauce in ungreased rectangular baking dish, 13 × 9 × 2 inches. Top with 4 uncooked noodles. Spread half of the crabmeat and shrimp over noodles; spread with 1 cup of the cheese sauce. Top with 4 noodles. Spread ricotta cheese over noodles; spread with 1 cup of the cheese sauce. Top with 4 noodles. Spread with remaining crabmeat, shrimp and cheese sauce.

4. Bake uncovered 35 to 40 minutes or until hot in center. Sprinkle with Parmesan cheese. Let stand 15 minutes before cutting.

8 servings.

1 Serving: Calories 425 (Calories from Fat 155); Fat 17g (Saturated 10g); Cholesterol 85mg; Sodium 880mg; Carbohydrate 40g (Dietary Fiber 2g); Protein 30g
% Daily Value: Vitamin A 18%; Vitamin C 2%; Calcium 48%; Iron 16%
Exchanges: 2½ Starch, 3 Lean Meat, 1 Fat

BETTY'S TIPS

❂ Success Hint
When choosing cheese for this lasagna, it's best to select regular or part-skim ricotta. Creamed cottage cheese, which is not as dry as ricotta, will thin the cheese sauce and make the lasagna a bit soupy.

❂ Serve-With
Serve the lasagna with a crisp Caesar salad and soft breadsticks brushed with garlic butter for a simple yet elegant meal.

Garden-Fresh Linguine and Vegetables

Prep: 15 min Cook: 10 min

8 ounces uncooked linguine

1 cup broccoli flowerets

1 cup ¼-inch slices mushrooms (3 ounces)

1 medium tomato, cut into 1-inch pieces

1 medium carrot, cut into ¼-inch diagonal slices (½ cup)

½ medium bell pepper, cut into 2 × ¼-inch pieces

1 bottle (8 ounces) roasted garlic vinaigrette

Freshly cracked pepper, if desired

1. Cook linguine as directed on package, adding broccoli during last 3 minutes of cooking; drain. Rinse with cold water; drain.

2. Toss linguine, broccoli and remaining ingredients except pepper. Serve immediately or cover and refrigerate 1 to 2 hours to blend flavors. Serve with pepper.

4 servings.

1 Serving: Calories 470 (Calories from Fat 225); Fat 25g (Saturated 2g); Cholesterol 10mg; Sodium 530mg; Carbohydrate 58g (Dietary Fiber 4g); Protein 10g
% Daily Value: Vitamin A 64%; Vitamin C 18%; Calcium 10%; Iron 16%
Exchanges: 3 Starch, 3 Vegetable, 3½ Fat

BETTY'S TIPS

✿ **Success Hint**
Select bell peppers that are firm, have a richly colored, shiny skin and are heavy for their size.

✿ **Serve-With**
A loaf of French bread is all that is needed to complete this perfect summer meal.

Vermicelli with Fresh Herbs

Prep: 10 min Cook: 15 min

1 package (16 ounces) vermicelli

¼ cup olive or vegetable oil

¼ cup pine nuts

1 tablespoon chopped fresh parsley

1 tablespoon capers, chopped

2 teaspoons chopped fresh rosemary leaves

2 teaspoons chopped fresh sage leaves

1 teaspoon chopped fresh basil leaves

1 pint (2 cups) cherry tomatoes, cut into fourths

Freshly ground pepper

1. Cook and drain vermicelli as directed on package.

2. While vermicelli is cooking, mix remaining ingredients except tomatoes and pepper in large bowl. Mix in tomatoes.

3. Add vermicelli to tomato mixture; toss gently until vermicelli is evenly coated. Serve with pepper.

6 servings.

1 Serving: Calories 415 (Calories from Fat 125); Fat 14g (Saturated 2g); Cholesterol 0mg; Sodium 50mg; Carbohydrate 65g (Dietary Fiber 4g); Protein 11g
% Daily Value: Vitamin A 12%; Vitamin C 10%; Calcium 2%; Iron 20%
Exchanges: 4 Starch, 1 Vegetable, 2 Fat

BETTY'S TIPS

✿ **Substitution**
Vermicelli is a very thin pasta that cooks quickly, making it ideal for summertime meals. Spaghetti is a good substitute.

Use a variety of fresh herbs as suggested in the recipe or use 3 tablespoons chopped fresh parsley or basil.

Garden-Fresh Linguine and Vegetables

Vermicelli with Fresh Herbs

Niçoise Skillet Supper

Prep: 15 min Cook: 27 min

2 tablespoons olive or vegetable oil

½ small red onion, coarsely chopped (½ cup)

4 or 5 small red potatoes, sliced (2 cups)

1½ cups 1-inch pieces green beans (4 ounces)

½ teaspoon Italian seasoning

½ teaspoon garlic salt

2 roma (plum) tomatoes, thinly sliced

2 hard-cooked eggs, chopped

1. Heat oil in 12-inch skillet over medium-high heat. Cook onion in oil 2 minutes, stirring frequently. Stir in potatoes; reduce heat to medium-low. Cover and cook 10 to 12 minutes, stirring occasionally, until potatoes are tender.

2. Stir in green beans, Italian seasoning and garlic salt. Cover and cook 6 to 8 minutes, stirring occasionally, until beans are tender and potatoes are light golden brown.

3. Stir in tomatoes. Cook 3 to 5 minutes, stirring occasionally and gently, just until hot. Sprinkle each serving with eggs.

4 servings.

1 Serving: Calories 170 (Calories from Fat 70); Fat 8g (Saturated 2g); Cholesterol 105mg; Sodium 160mg; Carbohydrate 22g (Dietary Fiber 3g); Protein 6g
% Daily Value: Vitamin A 12%; Vitamin C 14%; Calcium 4%; Iron 8%
Exchanges: 1 Starch, 1 Vegetable, 1½ Fat

BETTY'S TIPS

☺ Success Hint

Choose slender green beans that are crisp, brightly colored and free of blemishes. Store in the refrigerator, tightly wrapped in a plastic bag, for up to 5 days.

To hard-cook eggs, place in saucepan and cover with cold water. Heat to boiling, then remove from heat, cover and let stand 18 minutes. Immediately cool in cold water.

Niçoise Skillet Supper

Impossibly Easy Vegetable Pie

Prep: 20 min Bake: 35 min Stand: 5 min

2 cups chopped broccoli or sliced cauliflowerets
⅓ cup chopped onion
⅓ cup chopped yellow or red bell pepper
1 cup shredded Cheddar cheese (4 ounces)
½ cup Original Bisquick mix
1 cup milk
½ teaspoon salt
¼ teaspoon pepper
2 eggs

1. Heat oven to 400°. Spray pie plate, 9 × 1¼ inches, with cooking spray. Heat 1 inch water (salted if desired) to boiling in 2-quart saucepan. Add broccoli; cover and heat to boiling. Cook about 5 minutes or until almost tender; drain thoroughly.

2. Mix broccoli, onion, bell pepper and cheese in pie plate. Stir remaining ingredients until blended. Pour into pie plate.

3. Bake uncovered 30 to 35 minutes or until golden brown and knife inserted in center comes out clean. Let stand 5 minutes before cutting.

6 servings.

1 Serving: Calories 170 (Calories from Fat 90); Fat 10g (Saturated 5g); Cholesterol 95mg; Sodium 500mg; Carbohydrate 11g (Dietary Fiber 1g); Protein 10g
% Daily Value: Vitamin A 16%; Vitamin C 14%; Calcium 18%; Iron 4%
Exchanges: ½ Starch, 1 Medium-Fat Meat, 1 Vegetable, 1 Fat

BETTY'S TIPS

☺ Substitution

Grab a 9-ounce package of Green Giant broccoli cuts from the freezer to use instead of the fresh broccoli. It doesn't need to be boiled; just thaw, drain and add to the pie.

☺ Variation

For an **Impossibly Easy Spinach Pie**, use a 9-ounce package of Green Giant frozen spinach, thawed and squeezed to drain, for the broccoli; do not cook. Omit bell pepper. Substitute Swiss cheese for the Cheddar cheese. Add ¼ teaspoon ground nutmeg with the pepper. Bake about 30 minutes.

Impossibly Easy Vegetable Pie

Asparagus and Swiss Bake

Prep: 20 min Bake: 40 min

   2 cups 1-inch pieces asparagus
 ½ cup chopped red bell pepper
   8 medium green onions, sliced (½ cup)
   2 cups shredded Swiss cheese (8 ounces)
 ¾ cup Original Bisquick mix
1½ cups milk
   1 teaspoon lemon pepper seasoning salt
   3 eggs

1. Heat oven to 350°. Spray square baking dish, 8 × 8 × 2 inches, with cooking spray.

2. Heat 1 inch water to boiling in 1-quart saucepan. Add asparagus. Cook 2 minutes; drain thoroughly. Mix asparagus, bell pepper and onions in baking dish. Stir 1½ cups of the cheese and the remaining ingredients until blended; pour into baking dish.

3. Bake uncovered 35 to 40 minutes, sprinkling with remaining ½ cup cheese for last 5 minutes of baking, until knife inserted between center and edge comes out clean.

6 servings.

1 Serving: Calories 290 (Calories from Fat 145); Fat 16g (Saturated 9g); Cholesterol 145mg; Sodium 600mg; Carbohydrate 18g (Dietary Fiber 2g); Protein 18g
% Daily Value: Vitamin A 36%; Vitamin C 30%; Calcium 48%; Iron 8%
Exchanges: 1 Starch, 3 Medium-Fat Meat

BETTY'S TIPS

⊘ **Substitution**
If you don't have fresh asparagus on hand, use a 9-ounce package of Green Giant frozen asparagus cuts, thawed and drained. Don't cook the asparagus in boiling water; just add to the casserole.

⊘ **Serve-With**
Serve this savory brunch dish with a bowl of fresh berries and biscuits with butter, jam or honey.

Asparagus and Swiss Bake

Black Bean- and Rice-Stuffed Peppers

Prep: 10 min   Grill: 20 min

1 can (15 to 16 ounces) black beans, rinsed and drained
¾ cup cooked white rice
4 medium green onions, sliced (¼ cup)
¼ cup chopped fresh cilantro
2 tablespoons vegetable oil
2 tablespoons lime juice
1 clove garlic, finely chopped
¼ teaspoon salt
3 large bell peppers, cut lengthwise in half and seeds removed
1 roma (plum) tomato, diced
   Additional chopped fresh cilantro, if desired

1. Heat coals or gas grill for direct heat. Cut three 18 × 12-inch pieces of heavy-duty aluminum foil. Spray with cooking spray. Mix beans, rice, onions, cilantro, oil, lime juice, garlic and salt. Place 2 bell pepper halves on one side of each foil piece. Fill with bean mixture.

2. Fold foil over peppers so edges meet. Seal edges, making tight ½-inch fold; fold again. Allow space on sides for heat circulation and expansion.

3. Cover and grill packets 4 to 5 inches from medium heat 15 to 20 minutes or until peppers are tender. Place packets on serving platter. Cut large X across top of each packet; fold back foil. Sprinkle with tomato and additional cilantro.

6 servings.

1 Serving: Calories 175 (Calories from Fat 45); Fat 5g (Saturated 1g); Cholesterol 0mg; Sodium 380mg; Carbohydrate 31g (Dietary Fiber 6g); Protein 8g
% Daily Value: Vitamin A 8%; Vitamin C 66%; Calcium 6%; Iron 14%
Exchanges: 1½ Starch, 1 Vegetable, 1 Fat

BETTY'S TIPS

✿ **Substitution**
If you like, sprinkle the cooked peppers with shredded Cheddar or Monterey Jack cheese.

✿ **Success Hint**
Any color of bell peppers can be used for this recipe. For fiesta flair, try using a variety of colors.

✿ **Serve-With**
These meatless stuffed bell peppers can be served as a main dish with a salad and bread, or they make a nice side dish with pork chops or chicken.

Black Bean- and Rice-Stuffed Peppers

Mexican Corn Cakes

Prep: 30 min Cook: 6 min

1½ cups Reduced Fat Bisquick mix

½ cup cornmeal

1 cup fat-free (skim) milk

3 egg whites

1 jar (16 ounces) Old El Paso thick 'n chunky salsa

½ cup canned Green Giant whole kernel sweet corn

2 tablespoons chopped ripe olives

1 cup Old El Paso fat-free refried beans (from 16-ounce can)

½ cup shredded reduced-fat Cheddar cheese (2 ounces)

Additional salsa, if desired

Sour cream, if desired

1. Heat nonstick griddle to 375° or heat skillet over medium heat; grease with shortening if necessary (or spray with cooking spray before heating). Stir Bisquick mix, cornmeal, milk and egg whites in large bowl until blended. Pour batter by ¼ cupfuls onto hot griddle. Cook until edges are dry. Turn; cook other sides until golden.

2. Mix salsa, corn and olives. Place 1 corn cake on each of 6 microwavable serving plates; spread each cake with generous 2 tablespoons beans. Top each with additional corn cake. Spread ⅓ cup salsa mixture over top of each cake stack. Sprinkle each serving with generous 1 tablespoon cheese.

3. Microwave each serving uncovered on High about 1 minute or until heated through and cheese is melted. Serve with additional salsa and sour cream.

6 servings.

1 Serving: Calories 265 (Calories from Fat 35); Fat 4g (Saturated 1g); Cholesterol 5mg; Sodium 980mg; Carbohydrate 45g (Dietary Fiber 5g); Protein 12g
% Daily Value: Vitamin A 14%; Vitamin C 10%; Calcium 16%; Iron 18%
Exchanges: 3 Starch, ½ Lean Meat

BETTY'S TIPS

⊙ **Success Hint**
Yellow cornmeal will give these corn cakes a buttery golden color, but white cornmeal can also be used.

⊙ **Special Touch**
If you like cilantro, sprinkle chopped cilantro or place whole cilantro leaves on top of each stack.

Mexican Corn Cakes

Main Dish Poultry

Roasted, Grilled and Great

Ham- and Swiss-Stuffed Chicken Breasts (page 162)

Teriyaki Chicken (page 147)

Chicken with Chipotle Peach Glaze

Prep: 10 min Grill: 20 min

½ cup peach preserves

¼ cup lime juice

1 canned chipotle chili in adobo sauce, seeded and chopped

1 teaspoon adobo sauce (from can of chilies)

2 tablespoons chopped fresh cilantro

8 boneless, skinless chicken breast halves (about 2½ pounds)

1 teaspoon garlic pepper

½ teaspoon ground cumin

½ teaspoon salt

4 peaches, cut in half and pitted, if desired
Cilantro sprigs

BETTY'S TIPS

❂ Substitution
You can use ½ teaspoon garlic powder and ½ teaspoon coarsely ground black pepper instead of the 1 teaspoon garlic pepper.

❂ The Finishing Touch
Serve this in a heated large cast-iron skillet to keep the food warm. Wrap a napkin with a southwestern theme around the handle and garnish around the edges with fruit branches or a lemon leaf.

1. Heat coals or gas grill for direct heat. Mix preserves, lime juice, chili and adobo sauce in 1-quart saucepan. Heat over low heat, stirring occasionally, until preserves are melted. Stir in chopped cilantro; set aside. Sprinkle chicken with garlic pepper, cumin and salt.

2. Cover and grill chicken 4 to 6 inches from medium heat 15 to 20 minutes, turning once or twice and brushing with preserves mixture during last 2 minutes of grilling, until juice of chicken is no longer pink when centers of thickest pieces are cut. Add peach halves to grill for last 2 to 3 minutes of grilling just until heated.

3. Heat any remaining preserves mixture to boiling; boil and stir 1 minute. Serve with chicken and peaches. Garnish with cilantro sprigs.

8 servings.

1 Serving: Calories 225 (Calories from Fat 35); Fat 4g (Saturated 1g); Cholesterol 75mg; Sodium 270mg; Carbohydrate 20g (Dietary Fiber 1g); Protein 27g
% Daily Value: Vitamin A 4%; Vitamin C 6%; Calcium 2%; Iron 6%
Exchanges: 4 Very Lean Meat, 1 Vegetable, 1 Fruit

Chicken with Chipotle Peach Glaze

Teriyaki Chicken

Prep: 10 min Marinate: 1 hr Grill: 35 min

Teriyaki Marinade (below)

8   bone-in chicken breast halves (about 3 pounds)

1. Make Teriyaki Marinade in shallow glass or plastic dish or heavy-duty resealable plastic food-storage bag. Add chicken; turn to coat with marinade. Cover dish or seal bag and refrigerate, turning chicken occasionally, at least 1 hour but no longer than 24 hours.

2. Heat coals or gas grill for direct heat. Remove chicken from marinade; reserve marinade. Cover and grill chicken, skin sides up, 5 to 6 inches from medium heat 15 minutes. Turn chicken. Cover and grill 10 to 20 minutes longer, turning and brushing 2 or 3 times with marinade, until juice of chicken is no longer pink when centers of thickest pieces are cut. Discard any remaining marinade.

8 servings.

Teriyaki Marinade

½   cup soy sauce

½   cup dry sherry or orange juice

2   tablespoons sugar

2   tablespoons vegetable oil

2   teaspoons grated gingerroot or ½ teaspoon ground ginger

2   cloves garlic, crushed

Mix all ingredients.

1 Serving: Calories 220 (Calories from Fat 90); Fat 10g (Saturated 2g); Cholesterol 75mg; Sodium 790mg; Carbohydrate 4g (Dietary Fiber 0g); Protein 28g
% Daily Value: Vitamin A 2%; Vitamin C 0%; Calcium 2%; Iron 6%
Exchanges: 4 Lean Meat

BETTY'S TIPS

✺ **Variation**
For a handheld style of this favorite dish, cut the grilled chicken into thin strips, then wrap 'em up in flour tortillas. Add some chopped fresh cilantro or shredded lettuce if you like.

✺ **Serve-With**
Baby carrots, grilled pineapple and hot cooked rice turn this easy entrée into a fabulous meal.

Teriyaki Chicken

Betty... ON BASICS

Lime-Cilantro Marinade

Prep: 5 min Marinate: 30 min

2	teaspoons grated lime peel
¼	cup lime juice
¼	cup olive or vegetable oil
2	tablespoons chopped fresh cilantro
½	teaspoon sugar
½	teaspoon salt
1	small jalapeño chili, seeded and finely chopped
1	clove garlic, finely chopped

1. Mix all ingredients in shallow glass or plastic dish or resealable plastic food-storage bag. Add 1 to 1½ pounds boneless chicken, pork, fish or seafood; turn to coat with marinade. Cover dish or seal bag and refrigerate at least 30 minutes but no longer than 4 hours.

2. Remove meat from marinade; discard marinade. Grill meat as desired.

About ⅔ cup marinade.

2 Tablespoons: Calories 105 (Calories from Fat 100); Fat 11g (Saturated 1g); Cholesterol 0mg; Sodium 240mg; Carbohydrate 2g (Dietary Fiber 0g); Protein 0g
% Daily Value: Vitamin A 0%; Vitamin C 8%; Calcium 0%; Iron 0%
Exchanges: 2 Fat

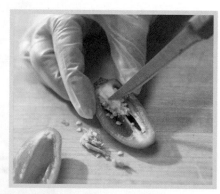

Wearing plastic gloves, use a knife to remove the seeds from the chili.

Lime Grilled Chicken

Prep: 5 min Marinate: 30 min Grill: 10 min

Lime-Cilantro Marinade (opposite) or purchased tequila lime marinade

4 boneless, skinless chicken breast halves (about 1¼ pounds)

1. Make Tequila Lime Marinade. Flatten each chicken breast half to ¼-inch thickness between sheets of plastic wrap or waxed paper. Add chicken to marinade; turn to coat with marinade. Cover dish or seal bag and refrigerate at least 30 minutes but no longer than 4 hours.

2. Heat coals or gas grill for direct heat. Remove chicken from marinade; discard marinade. Cover and grill chicken 8 to 10 minutes, turning once, until juice of chicken is no longer pink when centers of thickest pieces are cut.

4 servings.

1 Serving: Calories 270 (Calories from Fat 155); Fat 17g (Saturated 3g); Cholesterol 75mg; Sodium 360mg; Carbohydrate 2g (Dietary Fiber 0g); Protein 27g
% Daily Value: Vitamin A 2%; Vitamin C 4%; Calcium 2%; Iron 6%
Exchanges: 4 Lean Meat, 1 Fat

BETTY'S TIPS

⊕ **Substitution**

If you don't care for the taste of cilantro in the marinade, try using chopped fresh parsley instead.

⊕ **Success Hint**

To use the leftover marinade as a sauce, boil it for 1 minute to destroy any bacteria that may have been transferred to it from the chicken.

Lime Grilled Chicken

Caribbean Chicken Kabobs

Chicken with Green Herb Sauce

Caribbean Chicken Kabobs

Prep: 15 min Grill: 20 min

1¾ pounds boneless, skinless chicken breasts, cut into 1½-inch pieces

¼ cup vegetable oil

3 tablespoons Garlic-Lime Seasoning (page 76) or Key West-style coarsely ground seasoning blend

1 small pineapple, peeled and cut into 1-inch cubes

1 medium red bell pepper, cut into 1-inch pieces

1 small red onion, cut into 1-inch pieces

1. Brush grill rack with vegetable oil. Heat coals or gas grill for direct heat.

2. Brush chicken with 2 tablespoons of the oil. Place chicken and Garlic-Lime Seasoning in resealable plastic food-storage bag. Shake bag to coat chicken with seasoning. Thread chicken, pineapple, bell pepper and onion alternately on each of eight 12-inch metal skewers, leaving ¼-inch space between pieces. Brush kabobs with remaining 2 tablespoons oil.

3. Cover and grill kabobs 4 to 5 inches from medium heat 15 to 20 minutes, turning once, until juice of chicken is no longer pink when centers of thickest pieces are cut.

8 servings.

1 Serving: Calories 180 (Calories from Fat 65); Fat 7g (Saturated 1g); Cholesterol 60mg; Sodium 120mg; Carbohydrate 7g (Dietary Fiber 1g); Protein 22g
% Daily Value: Vitamin A 0%; Vitamin C 14%; Calcium 2%; Iron 4%
Exchanges: 3 Lean Meat, ½ Fruit

BETTY'S TIPS

✪ **Special Touch**
For a pretty presentation, place romaine leaves on a large serving platter and arrange kabobs on top.

Quick

Green Herb Sauce

Prep: 10 min

1 cup lightly packed fresh cilantro

¼ cup lightly packed fresh parsley

2 tablespoons lightly packed fresh basil leaves

2 tablespoons coarsely chopped fresh chives

¼ cup chicken broth

2 tablespoons olive or vegetable oil

1 clove garlic, chopped

½ to 1 jalapeño chili, seeded and chopped

¼ cup grated Parmesan cheese

¼ teaspoon salt

1. Place all ingredients in food processor or blender. Cover and process, stopping to scrape sides if necessary, until smooth.

2. Serve sauce with grilled pork, poultry or fish.

½ cup sauce.

2 Tablespoons: Calories 50 (Calories from Fat 35); Fat 4g (Saturated 1g); Cholesterol 0mg; Sodium 170mg; Carbohydrate 1g (Dietary Fiber 0g); Protein 2g
% Daily Value: Vitamin A 8%; Vitamin C 18%; Calcium 4%; Iron 2%
Exchanges: 1 Fat

BETTY'S TIPS

✪ **Success Hint**
This pretty sauce can be stored in a covered container in the refrigerator for up to 7 days.

✪ **Did You Know?**
You'll find cilantro in bunches in the produce area next to the parsley. Cilantro can be refrigerated for several days wrapped tightly in a plastic bag or with the stems in a container of water. If you store it in water, be sure to change the water every 2 or 3 days.

Betty... MAKES IT EASY

Beer Can Chicken

Prep: 10 min   Grill: 1 hr 45 min   Stand: 15 min

Basic Barbecue Rub (opposite)
1   whole broiler-fryer chicken (4 to 4½ pounds)
1   can (12 ounces) beer or lemon-lime soda pop

1. If using charcoal grill, place drip pan directly under grilling area and arrange coals around edge of firebox. Heat coals or gas grill for indirect heat.

2. Make Basic Barbecue Rub. Fold wings of chicken across back with tips touching. Sprinkle the rub inside cavity and all over outside of chicken; rub with fingers.

3. Pour ½ cup of beer from can. Hold chicken upright, with opening of body cavity down; insert beer can into cavity. Insert barbecue meat thermometer so tip is in thickest part of inside thigh muscle and does not touch bone.

4. Cover and grill chicken upright over drip pan or over unheated side of gas grill and 4 to 6 inches from medium heat 1 hour 15 minutes to 1 hour 45 minutes or until thermometer reads 180° and juice is no longer pink when center of thigh is cut.

5. Using tongs, carefully lift chicken to rectangular pan, 13 × 9 × 2 inches, holding large metal spatula under beer can for support. Let stand 15 minutes before carving. Remove beer can; discard.

6 servings.

1 Serving: Calories 315 (Calories from Fat 160); Fat 18g (Saturated 5g); Cholesterol 115mg; Sodium 890mg; Carbohydrate 3g (Dietary Fiber 0g); Protein 35g
% Daily Value: Vitamin A 2%; Vitamin C 0%; Calcium 2%; Iron 8%
Exchanges: 5 Lean Meat, 1 Fat

Insert beer can into cavity of chicken.

Cover and grill chicken over indirect heat until thermometer reads 180°.

Using tongs, carefully lift chicken to pan, holding metal spatula under beer can for support.

Basic Barbecue Rub

1 tablespoon paprika
2 teaspoons salt
½ teaspoon garlic powder
½ teaspoon onion powder
½ teaspoon pepper

Mix all ingredients.

Beer Can Chicken

— Low-Fat —

Baked Oregano Chicken

Prep: 10 min Bake: 25 min

¼ cup dry bread crumbs

2 tablespoons grated Parmesan cheese

¼ teaspoon dried oregano leaves

⅛ teaspoon garlic salt

⅛ teaspoon pepper

¼ cup Dijon mustard

6 boneless, skinless chicken breast halves (1¾ to 2 pounds)

1. Heat oven to 425°. Spray rectangular pan, 15 × 10 × 1 inches, with cooking spray.

2. Mix bread crumbs, cheese, oregano, garlic salt and pepper. Spread mustard on all sides of 4 chicken breasts. Cover mustard-coated chicken breasts with bread crumb mixture. Place all 6 chicken breasts in pan.

3. Bake uncovered about 25 minutes or until juice of chicken is no longer pink when centers of thickest pieces are cut. Cover and refrigerate the 2 uncoated chicken breasts.

4 servings (plus 2 chicken breasts for another meal).

1 Serving: Calories 200 (Calories from Fat 55); Fat 6g (Saturated 2g); Cholesterol 75mg; Sodium 580mg; Carbohydrate 6g (Dietary Fiber 0g); Protein 32g
% Daily Value: Vitamin A 0%; Vitamin C 0%; Calcium 8%; Iron 8%
Exchanges: 1 Starch, 3½ Very Lean Meat

BETTY'S TIPS

⊛ **Do-Ahead**

Baking extra chicken to use in recipes for other meals is an easy do-ahead hint. A quick rule of thumb is that one chicken breast will yield 1 cup of cut-up cooked chicken. Cut up the 2 uncoated chicken breasts to use in Chicken and Corn Bread Stuffing Casserole (opposite).

⊛ **Serve-With**

A side of spaghetti—perhaps leftover spaghetti—along with Italian green beans, fresh pears and breadsticks is an easy way to finish off this meal.

Baked Oregano Chicken

Chicken and Corn Bread Stuffing Casserole

Prep: 15 min Bake: 15 min

1 can (10¾ ounces) condensed cream of chicken or celery soup
¾ cup milk
1 package (10 ounces) frozen mixed vegetables, thawed and drained
1 medium onion, finely chopped (½ cup)
½ teaspoon ground sage or poultry seasoning
2 cooked chicken breasts from Baked Oregano Chicken (opposite), cut up (2 cups)
1½ cups corn bread stuffing mix
⅛ teaspoon pepper
Paprika, if desired

1. Heat oven to 400°. Spray 3-quart casserole with cooking spray.

2. Heat soup and milk to boiling in 3-quart saucepan over high heat, stirring frequently. Stir in mixed vegetables, onion and sage. Heat to boiling, stirring frequently; remove from heat.

3. Stir in chicken and stuffing mix. Spoon into casserole. Sprinkle with pepper and paprika. Bake uncovered about 15 minutes or until hot in center.

4 servings.

1 Serving: Calories 285 (Calories from Fat 55); Fat 7g (Saturated 2g); Cholesterol 60mg; Sodium 1060mg; Carbohydrate 34g (Dietary Fiber 4g); Protein 28g
% Daily Value: Vitamin A 46%; Vitamin C 22%; Calcium 16%; Iron 10%
Exchanges: 2 Starch, 2½ Very Lean Meat, 1 Vegetable

BETTY'S TIPS

☺ **Substitution**
You can substitute cut-up leftover turkey for the chicken.

☺ **Health Twist**
For 5 grams of fat and 250 calories per serving, use condensed 98% fat-free cream of chicken soup and fat-free (skim) milk. You could also use condensed reduced-fat cream of mushroom or cream of celery soup.

☺ **Serve-With**
This comfy casserole is a wonderful reminder of an old-fashioned chicken dinner, without all the work! Try serving with a side of cranberry sauce spiked with a little orange-flavored liqueur or orange juice and grated orange peel.

Chicken and Corn Bread Stuffing Casserole

Provençal Roast Chicken

Provençal Roast Chicken

Prep: 15 min Bake: 2 hr

1 whole broiler-fryer chicken (3 to 3½ pounds)
1 lemon
1 teaspoon olive or vegetable oil
1 tablespoon dried herbes de Provence
¼ teaspoon pepper
8 new potatoes (1½ pounds), cut into fourths
2 medium zucchini, cut into 1½-inch pieces
1 can (14½ ounces) diced tomatoes with basil, garlic and oregano, drained
½ cup chopped pitted Kalamata olives

1. Heat oven to 400°. Place chicken, breast side up, in shallow roasting pan.

2. Grate peel from lemon; squeeze juice. Mix lemon peel, lemon juice and oil in small bowl. Drizzle half of lemon mixture over chicken; pat herbes de Provence and pepper on skin of chicken. Place squeezed lemon halves inside chicken cavity.

3. Toss potatoes, zucchini, tomatoes, olives and remaining lemon mixture in large bowl. Arrange vegetables around chicken in roasting pan. Insert meat thermometer in chicken so tip is in thickest part of inside thigh muscle and does not touch bone.

4. Bake uncovered 1 hour 45 minutes to 2 hours or until thermometer reads 180°, juice of chicken is no longer pink when center of thigh is cut and vegetables are tender.

6 servings.

1 Serving: Calories 420 (Calories from Fat 160); Fat 18g (Saturated 4g); Cholesterol 85mg; Sodium 530mg; Carbohydrate 38g (Dietary Fiber 4g); Protein 30g
% Daily Value: Vitamin A 20%; Vitamin C 24%; Calcium 6%; Iron 20%
Exchanges: 2 Starch, 3 Medium-Fat Meat, 2 Vegetable

BETTY'S TIPS

✪ Success Hint

The peel, or zest, of citrus fruits comes from the outermost layer of skin. It contains pungent, aromatic oils that add intense flavor to foods. Remove the colored outer peel (not the white) by using a citrus zester, paring knife or vegetable peeler.

✪ Did You Know?

Herbes de Provence combines favorite herbs from the Provence region in southern France. It commonly contains basil, fennel seed, lavender, marjoram, rosemary, sage, summer savory and thyme.

One-Pan Potatoes and Chicken

Prep: 10 min Cook: 20 min

2 tablespoons vegetable oil
8 medium red potatoes, thinly sliced
1 pound boneless, skinless chicken breast halves, cut into thin strips
1 medium red bell pepper, cut into thin strips
1 teaspoon garlic salt

1. Heat oil in 12-inch nonstick skillet over medium heat. Add potatoes, chicken and bell pepper to skillet. Sprinkle with garlic salt.

2. Cook 15 to 20 minutes, stirring frequently, until juice of chicken is no longer pink when centers of thickest pieces are cut and potatoes are tender.

4 servings.

1 Serving: Calories 410 (Calories from Fat 80); Fat 9g (Saturated 2g); Cholesterol 70mg; Sodium 320mg; Carbohydrate 59g (Dietary Fiber 6g); Protein 30g
% Daily Value: Vitamin A 34%; Vitamin C 70%; Calcium 4%; Iron 22%
Exchanges: 3 Starch, 3 Lean Meat

BETTY'S TIPS

✿ Substitution
Let your imagination run wild by trying different potatoes for new flavors and colors. Choose Yukon gold, purple, yellow Finnish or Texas finger potatoes.

✿ Variation
Sprinkle this dish with sliced green onion to add a little color. Chopped fresh basil or parsley would also add great eye and flavor appeal.

Apple- and Ginger-Glazed Chicken Breasts

Prep: 10 min Grill: 20 min

¼ cup teriyaki baste and glaze (from 12-ounce bottle)
¼ cup apple jelly
1 teaspoon grated gingerroot
1 tablespoon chopped fresh cilantro
4 boneless, skinless chicken breast halves (about 1¼ pounds)

1. Heat coals or gas grill for direct heat. Mix teriyaki glaze, apple jelly and gingerroot in 1-quart saucepan. Heat to boiling, stirring constantly, until jelly is melted. Spoon half of the mixture into small bowl or custard cup; stir in cilantro. Set aside to serve with chicken.

2. Cover and grill chicken 4 to 6 inches from medium heat 15 to 20 minutes, turning and brushing with teriyaki mixture during last 10 minutes of grilling, until juice of chicken is no longer pink when centers of thickest pieces are cut. Serve with reserved teriyaki-cilantro mixture.

4 servings.

1 Serving: Calories 210 (Calories from Fat 35); Fat 4g (Saturated 1g); Cholesterol 75mg; Sodium 760mg; Carbohydrate 16g (Dietary Fiber 0g); Protein 28g
% Daily Value: Vitamin A 0%; Vitamin C 0%; Calcium 2%; Iron 6%
Exchanges: 4 Very Lean Meat, 1 Fruit

BETTY'S TIPS

✿ Variation
This glaze is also good to use with boneless pork chops.

✿ Serve-With
Rice pilaf or white rice and an Asian salad from the deli are nice accompaniments to this flavorful chicken dish. For an appetizer, serve miniature egg rolls that are available in the frozen foods department.

✿ Did You Know?
For a more intense flavor, marinate the chicken breasts in the teriyaki mixture for up to 4 hours before cooking.

Apple- and Ginger-Glazed Chicken Breasts

One-Pan Potatoes and Chicken

$\mathcal{B}etty$...
MAKES IT EASY

—— Quick & Low Fat ——

Sweet-and-Sour Chicken Packets

Prep: 10 min Grill: 22 min

- 4 boneless, skinless chicken breast halves (about 1¼ pounds)
- ½ cup sweet-and-sour sauce
- 1 can (8 ounces) pineapple chunks, drained
- 1 medium bell pepper, cut into strips
- ¼ small onion, cut into small wedges
- ½ cup chow mein noodles, if desired

1. Heat coals or gas grill for direct heat. Cut four 18 × 12-inch pieces of heavy-duty aluminum foil. Spray with cooking spray. Place 1 chicken breast half on one side of each foil piece. Top each with 1 tablespoon sweet-and-sour sauce and one-fourth of the pineapple, bell pepper and onion. Top with remaining sauce.

2. Fold foil over chicken and vegetables so edges meet. Seal edges, making tight ½-inch fold; fold again. Allow space on sides for heat circulation and expansion.

3. Cover and grill packets 4 to 5 inches from medium heat 18 to 22 minutes or until juice of chicken is no longer pink when centers are cut. Place packets on plates. Cut large X across top of each packet; fold back foil. Top with chow mein noodles.

4 servings.

1 Serving: Calories 230 (Calories from Fat 45); Fat 5g (Saturated 1g); Cholesterol 75mg; Sodium 180mg; Carbohydrate 19g (Dietary Fiber 1g); Protein 27g
% Daily Value: Vitamin A 4%; Vitamin C 26%; Calcium 2%; Iron 8%
Exchanges: 4 Very Lean Meat, 1 Fruit, ½ Fat

Fold foil over chicken and vegetables so edges meet.

Seal edges, making tight ½-inch fold; fold again.

Cut large X across top of packet; fold back foil.

Sweet-and-Sour Chicken Packets

Ham- and Swiss-Stuffed Chicken Breasts

Prep: 15 min Grill: 20 min
(Photo on page 145)

4 boneless, skinless chicken breast halves (about 1¼ pounds)
4 slices (½ ounce each) Swiss cheese, 3 × 1½ inches
4 slices (½ ounce each) cooked ham, 3 × 1½ inches
½ teaspoon seasoned salt
¼ teaspoon pepper
½ cup honey-mustard dressing

1. Heat coals or gas grill for direct heat. Flatten each chicken breast half to ¼-inch thickness between sheets of plastic wrap or waxed paper.

2. Place cheese slice and ham slice on center of each chicken breast; roll up. Secure with small metal skewers. Sprinkle with seasoned salt and pepper.

3. Reserve ¼ cup of the dressing. Cover and grill chicken rolls 4 to 6 inches from medium heat 15 to 20 minutes, brushing with remaining ¼ cup dressing during last 10 minutes of grilling, until juice of chicken is no longer pink when centers of thickest pieces are cut. Serve chicken rolls with reserved dressing.

4 servings.

1 Serving: Calories 325 (Calories from Fat 170); Fat 19g (Saturated 6g); Cholesterol 95mg; Sodium 680mg; Carbohydrate 4g (Dietary Fiber 0g); Protein 34g
% Daily Value: Vitamin A 2%; Vitamin C 0%; Calcium 14%; Iron 6%
Exchanges: 5 Lean Meat, 1 Fat

BETTY'S TIPS

⊕ **Substitution**
For a gourmet touch, substitute Havarti or Gruyère cheese for the Swiss.

⊕ **Do-Ahead**
Stuff the chicken breasts up to 24 hours in advance. Cover tightly and refrigerate until it's time to cook.

⊕ **Serve-With**
Serve the chicken breasts with wild rice and fresh asparagus spears.

Home-Style Chicken Dinner

Prep: 5 min Cook: 29 min

1 tablespoon butter or margarine

4 boneless, skinless chicken breast halves (about 1¼ pounds)

½ teaspoon salt

¼ teaspoon pepper, if desired

¾ cup water

1 envelope (0.87 ounce) chicken gravy mix

1 bag (14 ounces) frozen baby whole potatoes, broccoli, carrots, baby corn and red pepper strips

1 jar (4½ ounces) sliced mushrooms, drained
Chopped fresh chives or parsley, if desired

1. Melt butter in 10-inch nonstick skillet over medium heat. Sprinkle chicken with salt and pepper. Cook chicken in butter 15 to 20 minutes, turning once, until juice is no longer pink when centers of thickest pieces are cut. Remove chicken from skillet; keep warm.

2. Mix water and gravy mix (dry) in small bowl; pour into same skillet. Stir in vegetable mixture and mushrooms. Heat to boiling; reduce heat. Simmer uncovered about 5 minutes, stirring occasionally, until largest pieces of potato are hot. Add chicken; cover and simmer about 2 minutes or until chicken is heated through.

3. Serve vegetable and gravy mixture over chicken. Sprinkle with chives.

4 servings.

1 Serving: Calories 265 (Calories from Fat 70); Fat 8g (Saturated 3g); Cholesterol 95mg; Sodium 590mg; Carbohydrate 17g (Dietary Fiber 3g); Protein 34g
% Daily Value: Vitamin A 100%; Vitamin C 10%; Calcium 4%; Iron 10%
Exchanges: 1 Starch, 4½ Very Lean Meat, ½ Fat

BETTY'S TIPS

☺ **Substitution**

Love potatoes but can't find the frozen vegetable blend in this recipe? Try using one of your favorite frozen vegetable blends and a 15- or 16-ounce can of whole potatoes, drained, instead.

☺ **Serve-With**

Finish off this quick meal with a colorful coleslaw made by stirring cubed unpeeled red apple into purchased coleslaw. Add crusty hard rolls for hearty appetites.

Home-Style Chicken Dinner

Mediterranean Chicken and Orzo

Mediterranean Chicken and Orzo

Prep: 10 min Cook: 23 min

1 tablespoon olive or vegetable oil

4 boneless, skinless chicken breast halves (about 1¼ pounds)

2 cloves garlic, finely chopped

1⅓ cups uncooked orzo or rosamarina pasta

1 can (14½ ounces) fat-free chicken broth

½ cup water

1 tablespoon chopped fresh or 1 teaspoon dried rosemary leaves

½ teaspoon salt

2 medium zucchini, cut lengthwise into fourths, then cut crosswise into slices (1½ cups)

3 roma (plum) tomatoes, cut into fourths and sliced (1½ cups)

1 medium green bell pepper, chopped (1 cup)

¼ cup crumbled feta cheese (2 ounces), if desired

Sliced ripe olives, if desired

1. Heat oil in 10-inch skillet over medium-high heat. Cook chicken in oil about 10 minutes, turning once, until brown. Remove chicken from skillet; keep warm.

2. Mix garlic, pasta, broth and water in skillet. Heat to boiling; reduce heat. Cover and simmer about 8 minutes, stirring occasionally, until most of the liquid is absorbed.

3. Stir in remaining ingredients except cheese and olives. Add chicken. Heat to boiling; reduce heat. Cover and simmer about 5 minutes, stirring once, until bell pepper is crisp-tender and pasta is tender. Sprinkle with cheese and olives.

4 servings.

1 Serving: Calories 380 (Calories from Fat 80); Fat 9g (Saturated 2g); Cholesterol 75mg; Sodium 830mg; Carbohydrate 42g (Dietary Fiber 4g); Protein 37g
% Daily Value: Vitamin A 28%; Vitamin C 40%; Calcium 6%; Iron 20%
Exchanges: 2 Starch, 4 Very Lean Meat, 2 Vegetable, 1 Fat

BETTY'S TIPS

✪ **Substitution**
If your family prefers, sprinkle Parmesan cheese over this skillet instead of using feta cheese and omit the olives.

✪ **Special Touch**
Quickly complete this meal with warmed purchased focaccia bread and fresh pears or clusters of red grapes.

Betty... MAKES IT EASY

Mediterranean Chicken Packets

Prep: 20 min Grill: 25 min

1 package (4 ounces) crumbled basil-and-tomato feta cheese or plain feta cheese

2 tablespoons grated lemon peel

1 teaspoon dried oregano leaves

4 boneless, skinless chicken breast halves (about 1¼ pounds)

4 roma (plum) tomatoes, each cut into 3 slices

1 small red onion, finely chopped (1 cup)

20 pitted Kalamata olives

1. Heat coals or gas grill for direct heat. Mix cheese, lemon peel and oregano. Place 1 chicken breast half, 3 tomato slices, ¼ cup onion and 5 olives on one side of each of four 18 × 12-inch sheets of heavy-duty aluminum foil. Spoon one-fourth of cheese mixture over chicken and vegetables on each sheet.

2. Fold foil over chicken and vegetables so edges meet. Seal edges, making tight ½-inch fold; fold again. Allow space on sides for heat circulation and expansion.

3. Cover and grill packets 4 to 5 inches from medium heat 20 to 25 minutes or until juice of chicken is no longer pink when centers of thickest pieces are cut. Place packets on plates. Cut large X across top of each packet; fold back foil.

4 servings.

1 Serving: Calories 250 (Calories from Fat 110); Fat 12g (Saturated 6g); Cholesterol 100mg; Sodium 560mg; Carbohydrate 7g (Dietary Fiber 2g); Protein 31g
% Daily Value: Vitamin A 12%; Vitamin C 10%; Calcium 18%; Iron 10%
Exchanges: 4 Lean Meat, 1 Vegetable

Fold foil over chicken and vegetables so edges meet.

Seal edges, making tight ½-inch fold; fold again.

Cut large X across top of packet; fold back foil.

Mediterranean Chicken Packets

Chicken and Ravioli Carbonara

Prep: 10 min Cook: 20 min

2 tablespoons Italian dressing

1 pound boneless, skinless chicken breasts, cut into ½-inch strips

¾ cup chicken broth

1 package (9 ounces) refrigerated cheese-filled ravioli

½ cup half-and-half

4 slices bacon, crisply cooked and crumbled

Shredded Parmesan cheese, if desired

Chopped fresh parsley, if desired

1. Heat dressing in 10-inch skillet over high heat. Cook chicken in dressing 2 to 4 minutes, turning occasionally, until brown.

2. Add broth and ravioli to skillet. Heat to boiling; reduce heat to medium. Cook uncovered about 4 minutes or until ravioli are tender and almost all broth has evaporated. Stir in half-and-half; reduce heat. Simmer uncovered 3 to 5 minutes or until sauce is hot and desired consistency (see Success Hint). Sprinkle with bacon, cheese and parsley.

4 servings.

1 Serving: Calories 265 (Calories from Fat 170); Fat 19g (Saturated 7g); Cholesterol 150mg; Sodium 960mg; Carbohydrate 13g (Dietary Fiber 0g); Protein 36g
% Daily Value: Vitamin A 6%; Vitamin C 0%; Calcium 18%; Iron 10%
Exchanges: 1 Starch, 5 Lean Meat

BETTY'S TIPS

✿ **Success Hint**
After adding the half-and-half to the ravioli and chicken mixture, you can determine how saucy the finished dish will be. The less time it is cooked, the thinner the sauce will be; if cooked longer, the sauce will become thick and coat the ravioli.

✿ **Health Twist**
To reduce fat in this recipe, use fat-free Italian dressing, fat-free half-and-half and ¼ cup Bac-Os bacon flavor bits instead of the 4 slices bacon.

✿ **Special Touch**
For a splash of vibrant color, cut one orange or red bell pepper into ¼-inch strips and add to the skillet with the broth and ravioli.

Chicken and Ravioli Carbonara

Cheesy Southwest Chicken Casserole

Prep: 15 min   Bake: 55 min

3 cups uncooked mafalda (mini-lasagna noodle) pasta (6 ounces)

1 cup frozen whole kernel corn

¼ cup sliced ripe olives

¼ cup chopped fresh cilantro

⅓ cup milk

8 medium green onions, sliced (½ cup)

1 large roma (plum) tomato, chopped (½ cup)

1 jar (16 ounces) double Cheddar cheese pasta sauce

1 package (9 ounces) frozen smoke-flavor fully cooked chicken breast strips

1 cup shredded Colby-Monterey Jack cheese (4 ounces)

1. Heat oven to 350°. Spray rectangular baking dish, 11 × 7 × 1½ inches, with cooking spray. Cook and drain pasta as directed on package.

2. Mix pasta and remaining ingredients except cheese in large bowl. Spoon into baking dish.

3. Cover and bake 45 minutes. Sprinkle with cheese.

Bake uncovered 5 to 10 minutes or until cheese is melted and casserole is bubbly.

5 servings.

1 Serving: Calories 490 (Calories from Fat 215); Fat 24g (Saturated 11g); Cholesterol 100mg; Sodium 1110mg; Carbohydrate 40g (Dietary Fiber 3g); Protein 31g
% Daily Value: Vitamin A 18%; Vitamin C 6%; Calcium 20%; Iron 14%
Exchanges: 2½ Starch, 3½ Medium-Fat Meat, 1 Fat

BETTY'S TIPS

⊕ **Do-Ahead**
To make ahead, omit the milk and mix uncooked pasta, 1¼ cups water and the remaining ingredients (except cheese) in the sprayed dish. Cover tightly and refrigerate at least 8 hours but no longer than 24 hours. Increase the first bake time to 1 hour, then add cheese and bake 5 to 10 minutes longer.

⊕ **Did You Know?**
Mafalda looks like mini-lasagna noodles and can come in long ribbons or short pieces. Use the short variety for this recipe. If you don't have mafalda on hand, you can use another pasta of a similar size, such as gemelli, rotini or mostaccioli.

Cheesy Southwest Chicken Casserole

Mandarin Chicken Stir-Fry

Prep: 20 min Cook: 8 min

2 tablespoons rice vinegar

2 tablespoons soy sauce

1 tablespoon honey

1 tablespoon cornstarch

⅛ teaspoon ground red pepper (cayenne)

1 can (11 ounces) mandarin orange segments, drained and 2 tablespoons syrup reserved

1 can (8 ounces) pineapple chunks, drained and juice reserved

1 tablespoon vegetable oil

1 pound boneless, skinless chicken breasts, cut into 1-inch pieces

1 teaspoon finely chopped gingerroot

1 clove garlic, finely chopped

1 package (6 ounces) frozen snow (Chinese) pea pods, thawed and drained

2 medium green onions, sliced (2 tablespoons)

Hot cooked Chinese noodles or rice, if desired

1. Mix vinegar, soy sauce, honey, cornstarch, red pepper, reserved orange syrup and pineapple juice in small bowl; set aside.

2. Heat oil in 10-inch skillet over medium-high heat. Add chicken, gingerroot and garlic; stir-fry 3 to 4 minutes or until chicken is no longer pink in center. Stir in soy sauce mixture. Heat to boiling. Boil 1 minute, stirring constantly.

3. Stir in pea pods, onions and pineapple; heat through. Fold in orange segments. Serve over noodles.

4 servings.

1 Serving: Calories 315 (Calories from Fat 65); Fat 7g (Saturated 2g); Cholesterol 70mg; Sodium 530mg; Carbohydrate 38g (Dietary Fiber 2g); Protein 27g
% Daily Value: Vitamin A 10%; Vitamin C 32%; Calcium 4%; Iron 14%
Exchanges: 3½ Very Lean Meat, 1 Vegetable, 2 Fruit, 1 Fat

BETTY'S TIPS

✪ **Substitution**
One pound of boneless pork loin, shoulder or tenderloin can be substituted for the chicken.

✪ **Did You Know?**
Rice vinegar is made from fermented rice and has a slightly sweet, mild flavor. Look for it with the other vinegars or with the Asian ingredients. Don't confuse rice vinegar with seasoned rice vinegar. Rice vinegar is plain, and seasoned rice vinegar contains other ingredients, as its name suggests.

Mandarin Chicken Stir-Fry

Betty . . . MAKES IT EASY

Quick

Sweet-and-Sour Chicken Crepes

Prep: 20 min Cook: 6 min

Crepes (below)
2 cups frozen stir-fry bell peppers and onions (from 1-pound bag), thawed and drained
1 cup cut-up cooked chicken
1 can (8 ounces) pineapple tidbits or chunks, drained
⅔ cup sweet-and-sour sauce

1. Make Crepes.

2. Heat stir-fry vegetables, chicken, pineapple and ⅓ cup of the sweet-and-sour sauce in 2-quart saucepan over medium-high heat, stirring constantly, until hot.

3. Spoon about 2 tablespoons filling onto each crepe. Fold sides over filling. Heat remaining ⅓ cup sweet-and-sour sauce until hot. Serve over crepes.

4 servings (2 crepes each).

Crepes
1 cup Original Bisquick mix
¾ cup milk
1 teaspoon soy sauce
1 egg

Stir all ingredients until blended. Grease 6- or 7-inch skillet lightly with shortening; heat over medium-high heat. For each crepe, pour 2 tablespoons batter into hot skillet; rotate skillet until batter covers bottom. Cook until golden brown. Gently loosen edge with metal spatula; turn and cook other side until golden brown. Stack crepes as you remove them from skillet, placing waxed paper over each. Keep crepes covered to prevent them from drying out.

Pour 2 tablespoons batter into hot skillet; rotate skillet until batter covers bottom. The crepe will be very thin.

Spoon about 2 tablespoons filling down center of each crepe. Fold sides over filling.

1 Serving: Calories 325 (Calories from Fat 90); Fat 10g (Saturated 3g); Cholesterol 85mg; Sodium 730mg; Carbohydrate 43g (Dietary Fiber 2g); Protein 16g
% Daily Value: Vitamin A 32%; Vitamin C 58%; Calcium 14%; Iron 12%
Exchanges: 2 Starch, 1 Medium-Fat Meat, 1 Vegetable, ½ Fruit, 1 Fat

Sweet-and-Sour Chicken Crepes

Slow-Cooked Turkey Wild Rice Casserole

Prep: 25 min   Cook: 6 hr

4 slices bacon, cut into $\frac{1}{2}$-inch pieces

1 pound turkey breast tenderloins, cut into $\frac{1}{2}$- to 1-inch pieces

2 medium carrots, coarsely chopped (1 cup)

1 medium onion, coarsely chopped ($\frac{1}{2}$ cup)

1 medium stalk celery, sliced ($\frac{1}{2}$ cup)

1 cup uncooked wild rice

1 can ($10\frac{3}{4}$ ounces) condensed cream of chicken soup

$2\frac{1}{2}$ cups water

2 tablespoons soy sauce

$\frac{1}{4}$ to $\frac{1}{2}$ teaspoon dried marjoram leaves

$\frac{1}{8}$ teaspoon pepper

1. Cook bacon in 12-inch skillet over medium heat, stirring occasionally, until almost crisp. Stir in turkey, carrots, onion and celery. Cook about 2 minutes, stirring frequently, until turkey is brown.

2. Spoon turkey mixture into $3\frac{1}{2}$- to 4-quart slow cooker. Stir in remaining ingredients.

3. Cover and cook on low heat setting 5 to 6 hours or until wild rice is tender, turkey is no longer pink in center and liquid is absorbed.

5 servings.

1 Serving: Calories 325 (Calories from Fat 70); Fat 8g (Saturated 2g); Cholesterol 70mg; Sodium 950mg; Carbohydrate 37g (Dietary Fiber 4g); Protein 30g
% Daily Value: Vitamin A 94%; Vitamin C 2%; Calcium 2%; Iron 14%
Exchanges: 2 Starch, 3 Lean Meat, 1 Vegetable

BETTY'S TIPS

⚙ **Substitution**
Chicken breasts can be used in place of the turkey in this casserole.

⚙ **Success Hint**
When using a slow cooker, don't lift the lid unnecessarily. Removing the lid releases the steam that's vital to the slow cooking process.

⚙ **Did You Know?**
Wild rice is not actually rice but a long-grain marsh grass native to the northern Great Lakes region. In addition to being harvested in this area, wild rice is grown commercially in several Midwestern states and in California. Wild rice has a wonderful nutty flavor and chewy texture that enhances casseroles, soups, stuffings and salads.

Slow-Cooked Turkey Wild Rice Casserole

Turkey Smothered with Maple Sweet Potatoes

Prep: 10 min Cook: 20 min

1	pound turkey breast tenderloins
⅓	cup dried cranberries
¼	cup orange juice
⅓	cup maple-flavored syrup
1	tablespoon butter or margarine
¼	teaspoon ground cinnamon
1	can (23 ounces) sweet potatoes in light syrup, drained

1 Serving: Calories 415 (Calories from Fat 35); Fat 4g (Saturated 2g); Cholesterol 80mg; Sodium 160mg; Carbohydrate 71g (Dietary Fiber 5g); Protein 29g
% Daily Value: Vitamin A 100%; Vitamin C 2%; Calcium 4%; Iron 16%
Exchanges: 2 Starch, 3 Very Lean Meat, 2½ Fruit

1. Spray 10-inch nonstick skillet with cooking spray; heat over medium heat. Cook turkey in skillet about 5 minutes, turning once, until brown.

2. While turkey is cooking, heat cranberries, orange juice, maple syrup, butter and cinnamon to boiling in 1-quart saucepan. Arrange sweet potatoes around turkey. Pour orange juice mixture over turkey and potatoes.

3. Cover and cook over low heat 10 minutes. Uncover and cook about 5 minutes longer or until juice of turkey is no longer pink when centers of thickest pieces are cut and sauce is slightly thickened.

4 servings.

BETTY'S TIPS

❂ **Substitution**
Dried cherries, raisins or currants can be substituted for the dried cranberries.

Not a sweet potato fan? Omit them and serve the turkey with mashed potatoes or rice instead.

❂ **Did You Know?**
Turkey tenderloins are very lean and should be prepared using a sauce or glaze so they don't become too dry during cooking.

Turkey Smothered with Maple Sweet Potatoes

Quick

Slow Cooker Turkey Breast with Wild Rice Stuffing

Prep: 15 min Cook: 9 hr

4	cups cooked wild rice
¾	cup finely chopped onion
½	cup dried cranberries
⅓	cup slivered almonds
2	medium peeled or unpeeled cooking apples, coarsely chopped (2 cups)
1	boneless whole turkey breast (4 to 5 pounds), thawed if frozen

1. Mix all ingredients except turkey.

2. Place turkey in 3½- to 4-quart slow cooker. Place wild rice mixture around edge of cooker.

3. Cover and cook on low heat setting 8 to 9 hours or until turkey is no longer pink in center.

8 servings (plus about 2 cups turkey and wild rice for another recipe).

1 Serving: Calories 370 (Calories from Fat 115); Fat 13g (Saturated 3g); Cholesterol 100mg; Sodium 80mg; Carbohydrate 26g (Dietary Fiber 3g); Protein 41g
% Daily Value: Vitamin A 2%; Vitamin C 2%; Calcium 2%; Iron 10%
Exchanges: 1 Starch, 5 Very Lean Meat, 2 Vegetable, 1½ Fat

Turkey Stuffing Burgers

Prep: 10 min Cook: 12 min

1	container (2 cups) Slow Cooker Turkey Breast with Wild Rice Stuffing (left), thawed if frozen
1	egg, slightly beaten
½	cup saltine cracker crumbs
2	tablespoons butter or margarine
4	hamburger buns, split
1	cup shredded lettuce
2	medium tomatoes, sliced
	Whole berry cranberry sauce, if desired

1. Mix turkey mixture and egg; shape into 4 patties. Coat with cracker crumbs.

2. Melt butter in 12-inch skillet over medium heat. Cook patties in butter 4 to 5 minutes on each side or until hot and golden brown.

3. Serve patties on buns topped with lettuce, tomatoes and cranberry sauce.

4 servings.

1 Serving: Calories 375 (Calories from Fat 115); Fat 13g (Saturated 3g); Cholesterol 100mg; Sodium 460mg; Carbohydrate 43g (Dietary Fiber 5g); Protein 26g
% Daily Value: Vitamin A 14%; Vitamin C 14%; Calcium 8%; Iron 18%
Exchanges: 2 Starch, 2 Medium-Fat Meat, 3 Vegetable

BETTY'S TIPS

⚙ **Do-Ahead**
   Turkey Stuffing Burgers (recipe right) is a yummy recipe for using that extra cooked turkey and rice stuffing. Your family will welcome having "leftovers"!
   Chop turkey and mix with rice stuffing (about 1¼ cups turkey and about ¾ cup rice). Place in freezer or refrigerator container. Cover and refrigerate up to 4 days or freeze up to 4 months. To thaw frozen turkey mixture, place container in refrigerator about 8 hours.

BETTY'S TIPS

⚙ **Serve-With**
   Sweet Potato Fries taste great with these sandwiches. To make, cut 4 medium sweet potatoes into ½-inch wedges and toss with 2 tablespoons vegetable oil. Sprinkle with ½ teaspoon salt and ¼ teaspoon pepper. Place potatoes in single layer in greased jelly roll pan. Bake uncovered in 450° oven for 25 to 30 minutes, turning occasionally, until potatoes are golden brown and tender when pierced with a fork.

Slow Cooker Turkey Breast with Wild Rice Stuffing

Turkey Stuffing Burgers

Chicken Stroganoff

Prep: 20 min Cook: 4 hr + 70 min

1 envelope (0.87 to 1.2 ounces) chicken gravy mix

1 can (10½ ounces) condensed chicken broth

1 pound boneless, skinless chicken breast halves, cut into 1-inch pieces

1 bag (1 pound) frozen stew vegetables, thawed and drained

1 jar (4½ ounces) sliced mushrooms, drained

1 cup frozen green peas, thawed and drained

½ cup sour cream

1 tablespoon Gold Medal all-purpose flour

1½ cups Original or Reduced Fat Bisquick

4 medium green onions, chopped (¼ cup)

½ cup milk

1. Mix gravy mix and broth in 3½- to 4-quart slow cooker until smooth. Stir in chicken, stew vegetables and mushrooms.

2. Cover and cook on low heat setting about 4 hours or until juice of chicken is no longer pink when centers of thickest pieces are cut.

3. Stir peas into chicken mixture. Mix sour cream and flour; stir into chicken mixture. Cover and cook on high heat setting 20 minutes.

4. Mix Bisquick and onions; stir in milk just until moistened. Drop dough by rounded tablespoonfuls onto chicken mixture.

5. Cover and cook on high heat setting 45 to 50 minutes or until toothpick inserted in center of dumplings comes out clean. Serve immediately.

4 servings.

1 Serving: Calories 500 (Calories from Fat 135); Fat 15g (Saturated 6g); Cholesterol 90mg; Sodium 1700mg; Carbohydrate 60g (Dietary Fiber 5g); Protein 38g
% Daily Value: Vitamin A 100%; Vitamin C 24%; Calcium 26%; Iron 22%
Exchanges: 4 Starch, 4 Very Lean Meat, 1 Fat

BETTY'S TIPS

✷ **Success Hint**
Thaw vegetables before using or rinse them under cold running water to separate before adding them to the slow cooker.

✷ **Time-Saver**
Cut the chicken into pieces and chop the green onions the night before. Package each separately and store covered in the refrigerator.

Chicken Stroganoff

Main Dish Pork

Casseroles, Ribs and More

Harvest Time Pork Roast (page 180)

Pork Lo Mein (page 189)

Harvest Time Pork Roast

Prep: 15 min Bake: 1 hr 15 min Stand: 15 min
(Photo on page 179)

1   pork boneless loin roast (3 to 3½ pounds)
½   cup orange marmalade
3   tablespoons orange juice
2   teaspoons fennel seed, crushed
1   teaspoon dried thyme leaves
1   teaspoon dried sage leaves, crumbled
2   medium sweet potatoes, peeled and cut into
    1½-inch pieces
1   pound Brussels sprouts, cut in half if large
2   teaspoons olive or vegetable oil
½   teaspoon salt
¼   teaspoon pepper

1. Heat oven to 375°. Place pork in shallow roasting pan. Mix marmalade, orange juice, fennel, thyme and sage in small bowl. Brush pork with half of the marmalade mixture.

2. Toss sweet potatoes and Brussels sprouts with oil, salt and pepper. Arrange vegetables around pork. Insert meat thermometer so tip is in thickest part of pork.

3. Bake uncovered 1 hour. Brush pork with remaining marmalade mixture; gently stir vegetables to coat with pan juices. Bake about 15 minutes longer or until thermometer reads 155° and vegetables are tender. Cover pork with aluminum foil and let stand 10 to 15 minutes until thermometer reads 160°.

6 servings.

1 Serving: Calories 515 (Calories from Fat 180); Fat 20g (Saturated 6g); Cholesterol 145mg; Sodium 320mg; Carbohydrate 35g (Dietary Fiber 5g); Protein 54g
% Daily Value: Vitamin A 100%; Vitamin C 42%; Calcium 4%; Iron 14%
Exchanges: 2 Starch, 6 Lean Meat, 1 Vegetable

BETTY'S TIPS

⊙ **Substitution**
One pound of whole fresh green beans can be substituted for the Brussels sprouts. Toss with the oil, salt and pepper but wait to add to the pork until the last 20 to 30 minutes of baking.

⊙ **Did You Know?**
Two varieties of sweet potato are found most often in our supermarkets: the light-skinned variety with pale yellow flesh and the dark orange-skinned potato with vivid orange flesh. The pale variety has the same dry and fluffy texture and starchy flavor as a white baking potato. The dark orange potato has a sweet flavor and moist cooked texture and may be labeled "red garnet."

Pork with Apples and Squash

Prep: 15 min Cook: 21 min

- 4 lean pork loin or rib chops, about $\frac{1}{2}$ inch thick (about 1 pound)
- 1 teaspoon dried sage leaves
- $\frac{1}{2}$ teaspoon salt
- $\frac{1}{4}$ teaspoon pepper
- 2 cloves garlic, finely chopped
- 1 medium onion, cut into $\frac{1}{4}$-inch slices
- $\frac{1}{2}$ cup chicken broth
- 1 acorn squash (about $1\frac{1}{2}$ pounds)
- 1 medium unpeeled cooking apple, cored and cut into eighths
- $\frac{1}{4}$ teaspoon salt
- $\frac{1}{4}$ teaspoon pepper

1. Trim fat from pork. Mix sage, $\frac{1}{2}$ teaspoon salt, $\frac{1}{4}$ teaspoon pepper and the garlic; rub on both sides of pork.

2. Cook pork in 10-inch nonstick skillet over medium heat about 3 minutes on each side until brown. Place onion on pork. Pour broth around pork. Heat to boiling; reduce heat.

3. Cut squash crosswise into 1-inch slices; remove seeds and fibers. Cut each slice into fourths. Place squash

and apple on pork; sprinkle with $\frac{1}{4}$ teaspoon salt and $\frac{1}{4}$ teaspoon pepper. Cover and simmer about 15 minutes or until pork is slightly pink when cut near bone and squash is tender.

4 servings.

1 Serving: Calories 255 (Calories from Fat 80); Fat 9g (Saturated 3g); Cholesterol 65mg; Sodium 590mg; Carbohydrate 25g (Dietary Fiber 3g); Protein 25g
% Daily Value: Vitamin A 8%; Vitamin C 12%; Calcium 6%; Iron 10%
Exchanges: 1 Starch, 2 Lean Meat, 2 Vegetable

BETTY'S TIPS

☺ **Time-Saver**
Cut time by omitting the fresh acorn squash and instead microwaving frozen cooked squash as directed on the package to serve alongside the pork, onion and apple.

☺ **Serve-With**
This skillet is a complete meal by itself. Just add some crusty hard rolls for hearty appetites and perhaps fudgy brownies for dessert.

Pork with Apples and Squash

Spinach- and Mushroom-Stuffed Pork Roast

Prep: 40 min Cook: 7 hr

1   pork boneless loin roast (2 to 2½ pounds)
2   tablespoons olive or vegetable oil
3   cloves garlic, finely chopped
1   package (6 ounces) fresh baby portabella mushrooms, chopped
1   package (9 ounces) frozen chopped spinach, thawed and squeezed to drain
½   cup soft bread crumbs (1 slice bread)
⅓   cup grated Parmesan cheese
½   teaspoon salt

1. To cut pork roast so that it can be filled and rolled, cut horizontally down length of pork about ½ inch from top of pork to within ¾ inch of opposite side; open flat. Turn pork so you can cut other side. Repeat with other side of pork, cutting from the inside edge to the outer edge; open flat. If pork is thicker than ¾ inch, cover pork with plastic wrap and pound until about ¾-inch thickness. Remove plastic wrap.

2. Heat 1 tablespoon of the oil in 12-inch nonstick skillet over medium-high heat. Cook garlic and mushrooms in oil, stirring frequently, until mushrooms are tender and liquid has evaporated. Stir in spinach, bread crumbs and cheese.

3. Spread mushroom mixture on inside surfaces of pork. Roll up pork; tie with kitchen twine. Heat remaining 1 tablespoon oil in 12-inch nonstick skillet over medium-high heat. Cook pork in oil until brown on all sides. Place pork in 3½- to 4-quart slow cooker. Sprinkle with salt.

4. Cover and cook on low heat setting 6 to 7 hours or until pork is tender.

6 servings.

1 Serving: Calories 360 (Calories from Fat 170); Fat 19g (Saturated 6g); Cholesterol 100mg; Sodium 460mg; Carbohydrate 10g (Dietary Fiber 2g); Protein 39g
% Daily Value: Vitamin A 54%; Vitamin C 4%; Calcium 14%; Iron 14%
Exchanges: 5 Lean Meat, 2 Vegetable, 1 Fat

Cut horizontally down length of pork roast; open flat.

Roll stuffed roast and tie with kitchen twine to hold roast together.

Turn pork. Repeat with other side of pork, cutting from the inside edge to the outer edge.

Spinach- and Mushroom-Stuffed Pork Roast

— Low Fat —

Spicy Barbecued Pork Tenderloin with Green Beans

Prep: 15 min Bake: 30 min Stand: 15 min

Spicy Barbecue Sauce (below)
2 pork tenderloins (about ¾ pound each)
1 bag (14 ounces) frozen whole green beans
⅓ cup sliced almonds

1. Heat oven to 450°. Line shallow roasting pan with aluminum foil. Make Spicy Barbecue Sauce.

2. Place pork in pan; tucking small ends under for even cooking. Insert meat thermometer so tip is in thickest part of pork. Brush pork with about ¼ cup sauce.

3. Bake uncovered 15 minutes. Remove from oven. Arrange green beans around pork; drizzle green beans with ¼ cup sauce. Sprinkle beans with almonds. Bake 10 to 15 minutes, brushing pork occasionally with drippings, until thermometer reads 155° and beans are almost tender. Cover pork with aluminum foil and let stand 10 to 15 minutes or until thermometer reads 160°. (Temperature will continue to rise about 5°, and pork will be easier to carve.)

4. Serve 1 tenderloin with green beans. Cover and refrigerate second tenderloin up to 2 days.

4 servings (plus 1 tenderloin for another meal).

Spicy Barbecue Sauce

⅓ cup stir-fry sauce
⅓ cup regular (not spicy) barbecue sauce
⅓ cup honey
½ teaspoon crushed red pepper

Mix all ingredients in small bowl until well blended. Reserve ½ cup sauce for Easy Pork Fried Rice (opposite); cover and refrigerate up to 2 days.

1 Serving: Calories 210 (Calories from Fat 55); Fat 6g (Saturated 1g); Cholesterol 55mg; Sodium 180mg; Carbohydrate 20g (Dietary Fiber 1g); Protein 20g
% Daily Value: Vitamin A 4%; Vitamin C 0%; Calcium 2%; Iron 8%
Exchanges: ½ Starch, 2 Lean Meat, 2 Vegetable

BETTY'S TIPS

✿ **Do-Ahead**
Enjoy this easy yet elegant dish on Saturday night, then use the remaining pork tenderloin in Easy Pork Fried Rice (opposite page) on Monday, when you'll appreciate a speedy meal!

✿ **Serve-With**
Serve the pork and green beans with hot cooked rice or Asian noodles. Make extra sauce to serve on the side if you like.

✿ **Variation**
Adjust the crushed red pepper to the tongue-tingling level your family enjoys. Check out the variety of stir-fry sauces, too; some are hot, some are sweeter, and some are traditional in flavor.

Spicy Barbecued Pork Tenderloin with Green Beans

Quick

Easy Pork Fried Rice

Prep: 10 min   Cook: 5 min   Stand: 5 min

1   tablespoon vegetable oil
8   medium green onions, sliced (½ cup)
1   clove garlic, finely chopped
1½ cups water
½   cup Spicy Barbecue Sauce (opposite)
1   tablespoon soy sauce
1   cup frozen mixed vegetables
2   cups uncooked instant rice
1   Spicy Barbecued Pork Tenderloin (opposite), cubed

1. Heat oil in 10-inch skillet over medium-high heat. Cook onions and garlic in oil about 2 minutes, stirring occasionally, until onions are crisp-tender.

2. Stir in water, Spicy Barbecue Sauce, soy sauce and vegetables. Heat to boiling; remove from heat. Stir in rice and pork. Cover and let stand about 5 minutes or until liquid is absorbed.

4 servings.

1 Serving: Calories 430 (Calories from Fat 65); Fat 7g (Saturated 2g); Cholesterol 55mg; Sodium 420mg; Carbohydrate 69g (Dietary Fiber 2g); Protein 25g
% Daily Value: Vitamin A 18%; Vitamin C 12%; Calcium 6%; Iron 22%
Exchanges: 4 Starch, 1 Lean Meat, 2 Vegetable

BETTY'S TIPS

⊗ **Success Hint**
Unlike the traditional take-out version of fried rice, ours is moist and less chewy but every bit as delicious.

⊗ **Variation**
To have lima beans or not to have lima beans, that is the decision when selecting a brand of frozen mixed vegetables. Most mixtures include green beans, carrots, peas and corn, and some also include lima beans. The photo on the bag will show the veggie combination inside. Choose your family favorite!

Easy Pork Fried Rice

Mexican Pork

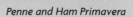

Penne and Ham Primavera

Mexican Pork

Prep: 5 min Cook: 8 hr + 5 min

1 pound pork boneless loin roast, cut into 1-inch pieces
1 jar (20 ounces) salsa
1 can (4 ounces) chopped green chilies, drained
1 can (15 to 16 ounces) pinto beans, rinsed and drained
1 cup shredded Cheddar cheese (4 ounces), if desired

1. Mix pork, salsa and chilies in 3½- to 4-quart slow cooker.

2. Cover and cook on low heat setting 6 to 8 hours or until pork is tender.

3. Stir in beans. Cover and cook about 5 minutes or until hot. Sprinkle with cheese.

4 servings.

1 Serving: Calories 345 (Calories from Fat 90); Fat 10g (Saturated 3g); Cholesterol 70mg; Sodium 1160mg; Carbohydrate 37g (Dietary Fiber 10g); Protein 37g
% Daily Value: Vitamin A 34%; Vitamin C 34%; Calcium 10%; Iron 28%
Exchanges: 2 Starch, 4 Very Lean Meat, 1 Vegetable, ½ Fat

BETTY'S TIPS

⚙ **Substitution**
Vary the taste by using black beans instead of pinto beans and Monterey Jack cheese instead of Cheddar cheese.

⚙ **Special Touch**
Serve with hot cooked rice, Spanish rice or tortilla chips. Serve with any of the traditional condiments of Mexican cuisine, such as guacamole or chopped avocado, sour cream, chopped tomato or chopped cilantro.

Quick

Penne and Ham Primavera

Prep: 10 min Cook: 15 min

2 cups uncooked penne or mostaccioli pasta (6 ounces)
1 cup sliced zucchini
1 cup sliced yellow summer squash
2 cups cubed fully cooked ham
½ cup reduced-fat Italian dressing
¼ cup chopped fresh basil leaves
⅓ cup shredded Parmesan cheese
Coarsely ground pepper, if desired

1. Cook pasta as directed on package, adding zucchini and yellow squash during last 3 to 4 minutes of cooking; drain.

2. Return pasta mixture to saucepan; add ham and dressing. Cook over medium heat, stirring occasionally, until hot. Sprinkle with basil, cheese and pepper.

4 servings.

1 Serving: Calories 390 (Calories from Fat 125); Fat 14g (Saturated 4g); Cholesterol 45mg; Sodium 1360mg; Carbohydrate 43g (Dietary Fiber 3g); Protein 26g
% Daily Value: Vitamin A 10%; Vitamin C 6%; Calcium 14%; Iron 1%
Exchanges: 2 Starch, 2 Lean Meat, 3 Vegetable, 1 Fat

Country-Style Ribs with Hoisin Glaze

Prep: 10 min Bake: 1 hr 30 min Grill: 15 min

4 pounds pork country-style ribs
½ teaspoon onion powder
1 tablespoon liquid smoke
  Hoisin Glaze (below)

1. Heat oven to 350°. Place ribs in rectangular pan, 13 × 9 × 2 inches. Sprinkle with onion powder; brush with liquid smoke. Add ¼ cup water to pan. Cover with aluminum foil and bake 1 hour 30 minutes. While ribs are baking, make Hoisin Glaze.

2. Meanwhile, heat coals or gas grill for direct heat. Remove ribs from pan; place on grill. Cover and grill 4 to 6 inches from medium heat 10 to 15 minutes, turning and brushing with glaze occasionally, until tender. Heat remaining glaze to boiling; boil 1 minute. Serve ribs with remaining glaze.

6 servings.

Hoisin Glaze

½ cup chili sauce
¼ cup hoisin sauce
2 tablespoons honey
⅛ teaspoon ground red pepper (cayenne)

Heat all ingredients to boiling in 1-quart saucepan; reduce heat. Simmer uncovered 10 minutes, stirring occasionally.

1 Serving: Calories 390 (Calories from Fat 180); Fat 20g (Saturated 7g); Cholesterol 105mg; Sodium 500mg; Carbohydrate 16g (Dietary Fiber 1g); Protein 36g
% Daily Value: Vitamin A 8%; Vitamin C 4%; Calcium 2%; Iron 8%
Exchanges: 1 Starch, 4½ Lean Meat, 1 Fat

BETTY'S TIPS

☺ **Substitution**
This glaze is also wonderful to use on chicken.

☺ **Serve-With**
Serve these hearty ribs with creamy coleslaw and grilled new potatoes. Try raspberry or orange sherbet for a perfect ending.

☺ **Did You Know?**
Hoisin is a rich, reddish brown sauce with a sweet and spicy flavor. Also called Peking sauce, it is a mixture of soybeans, garlic, chilies and spices. You'll find it with the Asian foods at the grocery store.

Country-Style Ribs with Hoisin Glaze

Pork Lo Mein

Prep: 20 min Cook: 5 min

½ pound pork boneless loin

2 cups snap pea pods

1 cup baby-cut carrots, cut lengthwise into ¼-inch sticks

½ package (9-ounce size) refrigerated linguine, cut into 2-inch pieces

⅓ cup chicken broth

1 tablespoon soy sauce

2 teaspoons cornstarch

1 teaspoon sugar

2 to 4 cloves garlic, finely chopped

2 teaspoons finely chopped gingerroot

½ cup thinly sliced red onion

Toasted sesame seed, if desired

1. Trim fat from pork. Cut pork with grain into 2 X 1-inch strips; cut strips across grain into ⅛-inch slices (pork is easier to cut if partially frozen, about 1½ hours). Remove strings from pea pods.

2. Heat 2 quarts water to boiling in 3-quart saucepan. Add pea pods, carrots and linguine; heat to boiling. Boil 2 to 3 minutes or until linguine is just tender; drain.

3. Mix broth, soy sauce, cornstarch, sugar, garlic and gingerroot.

4. Spray nonstick wok or 12-inch skillet with cooking spray; heat over medium-high heat until cooking spray starts to bubble. Add pork and onion; stir-fry about 2 minutes or until pork is no longer pink. Stir broth mixture; stir into pork mixture. Stir in pea pods, carrots and linguine. Cook 2 minutes, stirring occasionally. Sprinkle with sesame seed.

6 servings.

1 Serving: Calories 250 (Calories from Fat 35); Fat 4g (Saturated 1g); Cholesterol 25mg; Sodium 230mg; Carbohydrate 41g (Dietary Fiber 3g); Protein 16g
% Daily Value: Vitamin A 96%; Vitamin C 10%; Calcium 2%; Iron 14%
Exchanges: 2 Starch, 1 Lean Meat, 2 Vegetable

BETTY'S TIPS

☺ **Substitution**
Use a 10-ounce package of frozen snap pea pods, thawed and drained, if fresh pea pods are not available.

☺ **Did You Know?**
To toast sesame seed, sprinkle in ungreased heavy skillet and cook over medium-low heat 5 to 6 minutes, stirring frequently until browning begins, then stirring constantly until golden brown.

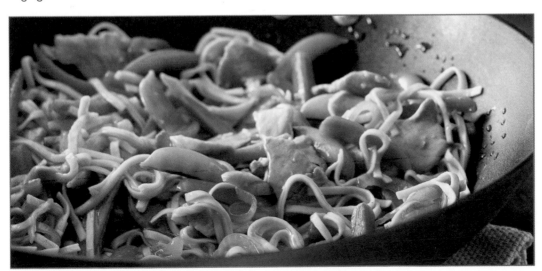

Pork Lo Mein

Pasta Duo

Prep: 10 min Cook: 15 min

Bolognese Sauce (right) and/or Roasted-Vegetable Alfredo Sauce (right)

Serve with One or More of These Pastas (to equal 12 cups cooked pasta for eight 1½-cup servings):

Fettuccine, linguine, spaghetti or other long, thin pasta

Penne, mostaccioli, rigatoni, rotini or other tubular or spiral pasta

Tortellini, ravioli or other filled pasta

Serve with One or More of These Toppings:

1 cup shredded or grated Parmesan cheese
1 cup chopped tomatoes
1 cup chopped fresh basil leaves or parsley
½ cup sliced ripe olives
¼ cup capers, drained
Crushed red pepper
Freshly ground pepper

1. Make Bolognese Sauce and/or Roasted-Vegetable Alfredo Sauce.

2. Cook and drain desired Pastas as directed on packages. Serve with sauces and desired Toppings.

8 servings.

BETTY'S TIPS

○ **Do-Ahead**

To make the pasta ahead of time and keep hot, spray the inside of a slow cooker with cooking spray. Add pasta to the slow cooker and toss with 2 to 4 tablespoons of olive or vegetable oil; cover and keep warm on low heat up to 3 hours, stirring occasionally.

○ **The Finishing Touch**

For a fun centerpiece, make a garlic bouquet. Skewer heads of garlic and small tomatoes on long wooden skewers; place in vase of water. Add long stems of greenery such as herbs.

Bolognese Sauce

Prep: 10 min Cook: 55 min

1 tablespoon olive or vegetable oil
1 teaspoon butter or margarine
2 medium carrots, finely chopped (1 cup)
1 medium onion, chopped (½ cup)
½ pound bulk Italian sausage
½ pound ground beef
½ cup dry red wine or beef broth
3 cans (28 ounces each) whole Italian-style plum tomatoes, drained
1 teaspoon dried oregano leaves
½ teaspoon pepper

1. Heat oil and butter in 12-inch skillet over medium-high heat. Cook carrots and onion in oil mixture, stirring frequently, until crisp-tender. Stir in sausage and beef. Cook, stirring occasionally, until beef is brown and sausage is no longer pink; drain.

2. Stir in wine. Heat to boiling; reduce heat. Simmer uncovered until wine has evaporated. Stir in remaining ingredients, breaking up tomatoes. Heat to boiling; reduce heat. Cover and simmer 45 minutes, stirring occasionally. Use sauce immediately or cover and refrigerate up to 48 hours or freeze up to 2 months.

6 cups sauce.

Roasted-Vegetable Alfredo Sauce

Prep: 20 min Bake: 40 min Cook: 5 min

1 pound asparagus, cut into 1-inch pieces (2 cups)
2 cups halved mushrooms
2 small yellow, red or green bell peppers, cut into ½-inch pieces
2 tablespoons olive or vegetable oil
½ teaspoon salt
2 cups halved cherry tomatoes
1 jar (16 ounces) Alfredo pasta sauce
¼ teaspoon white pepper
½ cup chopped fresh or 1 teaspoon dried basil leaves

Pasta Duo

1. Heat oven to 425°. Spray rectangular pan, 15 × 10 × 1 inches, with cooking spray. Place asparagus, mushrooms and bell peppers in large bowl. Toss with oil and salt until coated. Spread half of mixture in pan; transfer remaining vegetables to a plate and set aside. Add tomatoes to same bowl; toss with oil remaining in bowl until coated and set aside.

2. Bake vegetables in pan uncovered 10 minutes. Stir vegetables; add tomatoes to one end of pan. Bake 8 to 10 minutes longer or until tender. Place roasted vegetables in 4-quart saucepan or Dutch oven. Repeat to bake remaining vegetables.

3. Stir Alfredo sauce and white pepper into vegetables in saucepan. Cook over medium heat 3 to 5 minutes, stirring occasionally, until hot but not boiling. Stir in basil.

Makes about 4¾ cups sauce.

Nutrition information is not provided for this recipe because of the variety of food options.

Basil and Lemon Pepper Rub

Prep: 5 min Marinate: 15 min

1 tablespoon packed brown sugar
1 teaspoon lemon pepper
1 teaspoon dried basil leaves
½ teaspoon garlic powder
½ teaspoon seasoning salt

1. Mix all ingredients.

2. Spread rub evenly on 1 pound boneless meat (fish, chicken or pork). Cover and refrigerate 15 minutes. Grill meat as desired.

About 2 tablespoons rub mixture.

2 Teaspoons: Calories 10 (Calories from Fat 0); Fat 0g (Saturated 0g); Cholesterol 0mg; Sodium 170mg; Carbohydrate 3g (Dietary Fiber 0g); Protein 0g
% Daily Value: Vitamin A 0%; Vitamin C 0%; Calcium 0%; Iron 0%
Exchanges: 1 Serving is a Free Food

BETTY'S TIPS

⚙ **Success Hint**
Each 4-ounce fish fillet, chicken breast half or pork chop will use about 2 teaspoons of the rub. Sprinkle evenly over meat, then rub gently with fingers. Although the meat can be grilled right after the rub is added, letting it stand for a short time to marinate will add flavor.

⚙ **Do-Ahead**
Prepare a double or triple recipe of this rub and store tightly covered at room temperature until ready to use.

Corn, Ham and Potato Scallop

Prep: 10 min Cook: 9 hr

6 cups 1-inch cubes peeled baking potatoes
1½ cups cubed fully cooked ham
1 can (15 ounces) whole kernel corn, drained
¼ cup chopped green bell pepper
2 teaspoons instant minced onion
1 can (10¾ ounces) condensed Cheddar cheese soup
½ cup milk
2 tablespoons Gold Medal all-purpose flour

1. Mix potatoes, ham, corn, bell pepper and onion in 3½- to 4-quart slow cooker.

2. Mix soup, milk and flour in small bowl. Beat with wire whisk until smooth. Pour soup mixture over potato mixture; stir gently to mix.

3. Cover and cook on low heat setting 7 to 9 hours or until potatoes are tender.

6 servings.

1 Serving: Calories 270 (Calories from Fat 70); Fat 8g (Saturated 3g); Cholesterol 30mg; Sodium 1030mg; Carbohydrate 39g (Dietary Fiber 3g); Protein 14g
% Daily Value: Vitamin A 22%; Vitamin C 20%; Calcium 8%; Iron 8%
Exchanges: 2½ Starch, 1 Medium-Fat Meat

BETTY'S TIPS

⚙ **Substitution**
Leftover cooked roast beef or turkey can be used in place of the ham.

⚙ **Success Hint**
Potatoes cook more quickly when cut into small pieces, so cubed potatoes will cook faster than quartered potatoes. The 1-inch chunks of potato in our recipe work well because they won't get too soft during the long cooking time.

⚙ **Serve-With**
This slow cooker recipe makes an ideal casual dinner. Serve it with warm biscuits and a spinach salad with cherry tomatoes and vinaigrette dressing.

Grilled Porkchop with Basil and Lemon Pepper Rub

Corn, Ham and Potato Scallop

Do-Ahead Ravioli Sausage Lasagna

Prep: 10 min   Cook: 10 min   Chill: 8 hr   Bake: 1 hr   Stand: 10 min

1¼ pounds bulk Italian sausage

1 jar (26 to 28 ounces) tomato pasta sauce (any variety)

1 package (25 to 27½ ounces) frozen cheese-filled ravioli

2½ cups shredded mozzarella cheese (10 ounces)

2 tablespoons grated Parmesan cheese

1. Cook sausage in 10-inch skillet over medium heat, stirring occasionally, until no longer pink; drain.

2. Spread ½ cup of the pasta sauce in ungreased rectangular pan, 13 × 9 × 2 inches. Arrange single layer of frozen ravioli over sauce; evenly pour 1 cup pasta sauce over ravioli. Sprinkle evenly with 1½ cups sausage and 1 cup of the mozzarella cheese. Repeat layers with remaining ravioli, pasta sauce and sausage.

3. Cover tightly with aluminum foil and refrigerate at least 8 hours but no longer than 24 hours.

4. Heat oven to 350°. Bake covered 45 minutes. Remove foil; sprinkle with remaining 1½ cups mozzarella and the Parmesan cheese. Bake about 15 minutes or until cheese is melted and lasagna is hot in center. Let stand 10 minutes before cutting.

8 servings.

1 Serving: Calories 540 (Calories from Fat 280); Fat 31g (Saturated 13g); Cholesterol 150mg; Sodium 1920mg; Carbohydrate 35g (Dietary Fiber 2g); Protein 32g
% Daily Value: Vitamin A 22%; Vitamin C 12%; Calcium 48%; Iron 14%
Exchanges: 2 Starch, 3½ High-Fat Meat, 1 Vegetable, 2 Fat

BETTY'S TIPS

⊙ **Success Hint**
Letting pasta casseroles stand a short time after baking lets the mixture cool slightly and allows for easier cutting and serving.

⊙ **Serve-With**
This easy, cheesy casserole is a crowd pleaser. Serve with thick slices of garlic bread and a tossed green salad.

Do-Ahead Ravioli Sausage Lasagna

Baked Ham with Balsamic Brown Sugar Glaze

Prep: 15 min Bake: 2 hr 15 min Stand: 10 min

1 fully cooked smoked bone-in ham (6 to 8 pounds)
1 cup packed brown sugar
2 tablespoons balsamic or cider vinegar
½ teaspoon ground mustard
 Orange slices, if desired
 Maraschino cherries, if desired

1. Heat oven to 325°. Place ham, fat side up, on rack in shallow roasting pan. Insert meat thermometer so tip is in thickest part of ham and does not touch bone or rest in fat. Cover loosely and bake 1 hour 15 minutes to 2 hours 15 minutes or until thermometer reads 135° (13 to 17 minutes per pound).

2. About 20 minutes before ham is done, remove from oven. Pour drippings from pan. Remove any skin from ham. Mix brown sugar, vinegar and mustard; pat or brush on ham. Bake uncovered 20 minutes longer.

3. Cover ham loosely and let stand about 10 minutes or until thermometer reads 140°. Garnish with orange slices and cherries.

12 servings.

1 Serving: Calories 225 (Calories from Fat 55); Fat 6g (Saturated 2g); Cholesterol 60mg; Sodium 1320mg; Carbohydrate 20g (Dietary Fiber 0g); Protein 23g
% Daily Value: Vitamin A 0%; Vitamin C 0%; Calcium 2%; Iron 10%
Exchanges: 3 Lean Meat, 1 Fruit

BETTY'S TIPS

✿ **Success Hint**
 While the ham stands for 10 minutes, the temperature will continue to rise about 5°. You'll notice that the ham will be easier to carve as the juices set up.

✿ **Special Touch**
 Although this ham is delicious on its own, you may want to serve it with honey mustard, horseradish sauce, applesauce or a fruit chutney.

Baked Ham with Balsamic Brown Sugar Glaze

Baby Back Ribs with Spicy Barbecue Sauce

Prep: 10 min Cook: 20 min Grill: 20 Min

Spicy Barbecue Sauce (below)
4½ pounds pork loin back ribs
3 cups water

1. If using charcoal grill, place drip pan directly under grilling area and arrange coals around edge of firebox. Heat coals or gas grill for indirect heat.

2. Make Spicy Barbecue Sauce.

3. Cut ribs into serving pieces. Place ribs in 4-quart Dutch oven; add water. Heat to boiling; reduce heat. Cover and simmer 5 minutes; drain.

4. Cover and grill pork over drip pan or over unheated side of gas grill and 5 to 6 inches from medium heat 15 to 20 minutes, brushing with sauce every 3 minutes, until pork is no longer pink and meat begins to pull away from bones.

8 servings.

Spicy Barbecue Sauce
½ cup ketchup
¼ cup water
3 tablespoons packed brown sugar
2 tablespoons white vinegar
2 teaspoons celery seed
¼ teaspoon red pepper sauce
¼ teaspoon liquid smoke, if desired

Heat all ingredients in 1-quart saucepan over medium heat, stirring frequently; reduce heat to low. Simmer uncovered 15 minutes, stirring occasionally.

1 Serving: Calories 555 (Calories from Fat 405); Fat 45g (Saturated 18g); Cholesterol 170mg; Sodium 160mg; Carbohydrate 1g (Dietary Fiber 0g); Protein 36g
% Daily Value: Vitamin A 6%; Vitamin C 0%; Calcium 6%; Iron 12%
Exchanges: 5 High-Fat Meat, 1 Fat

BETTY'S TIPS

© **Success Hint**
At the supermarket, these ribs may be labeled as back ribs or pork ribs.

Baby Back Ribs with Spicy Barbecue Sauce

Backyard Brats with Two-Tomato Relish

Prep: 15 min Grill: 25 min

Two-Tomato Relish (below)

6 fresh bratwurst (1 pound)

⅓ cup Dijon mustard

2 teaspoons chopped fresh or ½ teaspoon dried oregano leaves

6 bratwurst buns, split

1. Make Two-Tomato Relish.

2. Heat coals or gas grill for direct heat. Cover and grill bratwurst 4 to 5 inches from medium heat about 25 minutes, turning occasionally, until no longer pink in center.

3. Mix mustard and oregano; spread on cut sides of buns. Serve bratwurst on buns with relish.

6 servings.

Two-Tomato Relish

2 medium tomatoes, finely chopped (1½ cups)

2 medium yellow pear tomatoes, finely chopped (½ cup)

1 tablespoon red wine vinegar

1 teaspoon chopped fresh or ¼ teaspoon dried oregano leaves

Mix all ingredients. Cover and refrigerate until serving.

1 Serving: Calories 410 (Calories from Fat 225); Fat 25g (Saturated 8g); Cholesterol 45mg; Sodium 1340mg; Carbohydrate 34g (Dietary Fiber 3g); Protein 15g
% Daily Value: Vitamin A 12%; Vitamin C 26%; Calcium 10%; Iron 16%
Exchanges: 2 Starch, 1 High-Fat Meat, 1 Vegetable, 3 Fat

BETTY'S TIPS

✪ **Serve-With**
Serve these robust sandwiches with Betty's Classic Creamy Coleslaw (page 51), corn on the cob and brownies à la mode.

✪ **Variation**
You can use Italian or Polish sausage instead of the bratwurst. Or for a lower-fat option, use turkey Polish sausage.

Backyard Brats with Two-Tomato Relish

Kielbasa and Vegetable Packets

Prep: 20 min Grill: 40 min

2 rings (1 pound each) fully cooked kielbasa sausage, each cut into 8 pieces

24 new potatoes (about 2½ pounds), cut in half

Top with One or More of These Vegetables:

4 medium bell peppers, each cut lengthwise into eighths

2 medium red onions, each cut into 8 wedges

8 small zucchini, cut into ½-inch slices

8 ears corn, husked and cut into fourths

Add One or More of These Seasonings:

Cajun seasoning

Garlic salt

Pepper

1. Heat coals or gas grill for direct heat. Place 2 pieces kielbasa and 6 potato halves on one side of eight 18 × 12-inch sheets of heavy-duty aluminum foil. Top each with either 4 bell pepper pieces, 2 onion wedges, 3 or 4 zucchini slices or 4 corn pieces. Sprinkle with one or more of the seasonings.

2. Fold foil over kielbasa and vegetables so edges meet. Seal edges, making tight ½-inch fold; fold again. Allow space on sides for heat circulation and expansion.

3. Cover and grill packets 4 to 5 inches from medium heat 30 to 40 minutes or until potatoes are tender.* Place packets on plates. Cut large X across top of each packet; fold back foil.

8 servings.

*Cooking time may vary depending on ingredients selected.

1 Serving: Calories 525 (Calories from Fat 290); Fat 32g (Saturated 12g); Cholesterol 65mg; Sodium 1290mg; Carbohydrate 47g (Dietary Fiber 5g); Protein 18g
% Daily Value: Vitamin A 8%; Vitamin C 28%; Calcium 2%; Iron 18%
Exchanges: 3 Starch, 1 High-Fat Meat, 1 Vegetable, 4 Fat

BETTY'S TIPS

✪ **Health Twist**
Low-fat kielbasa or smoked sausage can be used with equally delicious results.

✪ **The Finishing Touch**
Provide permanent markers so guests can write their names on their packets to guarantee they'll get the favorites they selected. Encourage guests to add a creative design as well!

Kielbasa and Vegetable Packets

Sweet Potato, Peach and Pork Packets

Prep: 10 min Grill: 22 min

1 large sweet potato, peeled and thinly sliced
  Dash of salt
2 tablespoons butter or margarine
4 pork boneless smoked chops
2 medium peaches or nectarines, peeled and sliced
  Dash of ground cinnamon
4 medium green onions, sliced (¼ cup)

1. Heat coals or gas grill for direct heat. Cut four 18 × 12-inch pieces of heavy-duty aluminum foil. Spray with cooking spray. Place one-fourth of the sweet potato slices on one side of each foil piece. Sprinkle with salt. Cut butter into small pieces; sprinkle over sweet potato. Top with pork chops and peaches. Sprinkle with cinnamon.

2. Fold foil over pork mixture so edges meet. Seal edges, making tight ½-inch fold; fold again. Allow space on sides for heat circulation and expansion.

3. Cover and grill packets 4 to 5 inches from medium heat 20 to 22 minutes or until sweet potatoes and peaches are tender. Place packets on plates. Cut large X across top of each packet; fold back foil. Sprinkle with onions.

4 servings.

1 Serving: Calories 245 (Calories from Fat 110); Fat 12g (Saturated 6g); Cholesterol 55mg; Sodium 1050mg; Carbohydrate 17g (Dietary Fiber 3g); Protein 17g
% Daily Value: Vitamin A 100%; Vitamin C 14%; Calcium 2%; Iron 8%
Exchanges: ½ Starch, ½ Fruit, 2 Lean Meat, 1½ Fat

BETTY'S TIPS

☺ Substitution
Sliced apples can be used instead of the peaches or nectarines. It is not necessary to peel them.

☺ Did You Know?
Smoked pork chops can be found at the fresh meat counter at the grocery store. They do not require a lot of cooking because the smoking process has done that for you. Just cook them until they are thoroughly heated.

Sweet Potato, Peach and Pork Packets

Honey BBQ Pork Packets

Prep: 20 min Grill: 20 min

½ cup Lloyd's® barbeque sauce

¼ cup honey

2 teaspoons ground cumin

4 pork boneless rib or loin chops, ¾ to 1 inch thick (about 1¼ pounds)

2 large ears corn, each cut into 6 pieces

1 cup baby-cut carrots, cut lengthwise in half

2 cups refrigerated cooked new potato wedges (from 1-pound 4-ounce bag)

2 medium green onions, sliced (2 tablespoons)

1 teaspoon salt

1. Heat coals or gas grill for direct heat. Spray half of one side of four 18 × 12-inch sheets of heavy-duty aluminum foil with cooking spray.

2. Mix barbeque sauce, honey and cumin in small bowl. Place 1 pork chop, 3 pieces corn, ¼ cup carrots, ½ cup potato wedges and 1½ teaspoons green onions on center of each sprayed foil sheet; sprinkle with ¼ teaspoon salt. Spoon 3 tablespoons sauce mixture over pork and vegetables on each sheet.

3. Fold foil over pork and vegetables so edges meet. Seal edges, making tight ½-inch fold; fold again. Allow space on sides for heat circulation and expansion.

4. Grill packets 4 to 6 inches from medium heat 15 to 20 minutes, turning once, until pork is slightly pink in center. Place packets on plates. Cut large X across top of each packet; fold back foil.

4 servings.

1 Serving: Calories 385 (Calories from Fat 70); Fat 8g (Saturated 3g); Cholesterol 55mg; Sodium 960mg; Carbohydrate 59g (Dietary Fiber 4g); Protein 23g
% Daily Value: Vitamin A 100%; Vitamin C 14%; Calcium 2%; Iron 10%
Exchanges: 3 Starch, 1½ Very Lean Meat, 2 Vegetable

BETTY'S TIPS

✪ **Substitution**

Look for the cooked potato wedges in the refrigerated section of the supermarket. If they are not available, cut 2 medium potatoes into wedges and place in microwavable bowl. Cover and microwave on High for about 5 minutes or until crisp-tender. Place potatoes in packet and grill as directed.

Honey BBQ Pork Packets

Southwest Pork Packets

Prep: 15 min Stand: 5 min Bake: 25 min

2   cups uncooked instant rice
1   can (14½ ounces) chicken broth
1   tablespoon Mexican seasoning
1   can (15 ounces) whole kernel corn, drained
1   small bell pepper, chopped (½ cup)
4   medium green onions, sliced (¼ cup)
4   pork boneless rib or loin chops, ¾ to 1 inch thick (1¼ pounds)
2   teaspoons Mexican seasoning
    Salsa, if desired

1. Heat oven to 450°. Cut four 18 × 12-inch sheets of heavy-duty aluminum foil. Spray half of one side of each sheet with cooking spray.

2. Mix rice, broth and 1 tablespoon Mexican seasoning in large bowl; let stand about 5 minutes or until broth is absorbed. Stir in corn, bell pepper and onions.

3. Sprinkle each pork chop with ½ teaspoon Mexican seasoning; place in center of sprayed half of foil. Spoon rice mixture over pork. Fold foil over pork and rice so edges meet. Seal edges, making tight ½-inch fold; fold again. Allow space on sides for heat circulation and expansion. Place packets on large cookie sheet.

4. Bake 20 to 25 minutes or until pork is slightly pink in center. Place packets on plates. Cut large X across top of each packet; fold back foil. Serve with salsa.

4 servings.

1 Serving: Calories 475 (Calories from Fat 90); Fat 10g (Saturated 3g); Cholesterol 55mg; Sodium 730mg; Carbohydrate 70g (Dietary Fiber 4g); Protein 30g
% Daily Value: Vitamin A 6%; Vitamin C 24%; Calcium 6%; Iron 26%
Exchanges: 4 Starch, 2 Lean Meat, 2 Vegetable

BETTY'S TIPS

⊙ **Serve-With**
Quickly complete this meal with piping-hot corn muffins drizzled with honey along with a salad of orange slices and avocado wedges drizzled with vinaigrette dressing.

⊙ **Variation**
These pork packets are also great cooked on the grill. Heat coals or gas grill for direct heat. Grill packets 4 to 6 inches from medium heat 15 to 20 minutes or until pork is slightly pink in center. Or instead of using foil packets, try the heavy-duty foil bags made especially for grilling.

Southwest Pork Packets

Main Dish Beef

Main Dish Beef

Steaks, Pasta and Pleasure

Grilled Steak with Feta (page 208)

Wild Rice and Beef Casserole (page 211)

Steak and Onions with Blue Cheese Butter

Prep: 10 min Chill: 30 min Grill: 15 min

Blue Cheese Butter (below)
1 large red onion, peeled
1 tablespoon olive or vegetable oil
1 tablespoon Worcestershire sauce
4 beef tenderloin steaks, about 1 inch thick (about 1 pound)
$\frac{1}{4}$ teaspoon salt
$\frac{1}{8}$ teaspoon pepper

1. Make Blue Cheese Butter. Heat coals or gas grill for direct heat.

2. Pierce onion with eight 4-inch metal or wooden skewers, poking skewers through onion so they are parallel and at $\frac{1}{2}$-inch intervals. Cut onion between skewers into 8 slices (skewers will hold onion slices together). Brush oil and Worcestershire sauce on onion slices and beef. Sprinkle beef with salt and pepper.

3. Cover and grill onion slices on skewers 4 to 5 inches from medium heat 5 minutes. Turn onions; add beef to grill. Cover and grill 7 to 12 minutes, turning beef once, until beef is desired doneness. Top beef with Blue Cheese Butter. Serve with onion slices.

4 servings.

Blue Cheese Butter

2 tablespoons butter or margarine, softened
2 tablespoons crumbled blue cheese
2 teaspoons chopped fresh chives

Mix all ingredients in small serving bowl. Cover and refrigerate about 30 minutes or until firm.

1 Serving: Calories 280 (Calories from Fat 160); Fat 18g (Saturated 8g); Cholesterol 85mg; Sodium 290mg; Carbohydrate 4g (Dietary Fiber 1g); Protein 26g
% Daily Value: Vitamin A 8%; Vitamin C 2%; Calcium 4%; Iron 12%
Exchanges: 4 Lean Meat, $1\frac{1}{2}$ Fat

Steak and Onions with Blue Cheese Butter

Betty's Classic Peppercorn T-Bones

Prep: 10 min Grill: 14 min

6 beef T-bone steaks, 1 inch thick (about 1½ pounds)

3 cloves garlic, cut in half

1½ tablespoons black peppercorns, crushed

⅓ cup butter or margarine, softened

1½ tablespoons Dijon mustard

¾ teaspoon Worcestershire sauce

¼ teaspoon lime juice

Salt and pepper, if desired

1. Heat coals or gas grill for direct heat. Trim fat on beef steaks to ¼-inch thickness. Rub garlic on beef.

Press peppercorns into beef. Mix remaining ingredients except salt and pepper; set aside.

2. Cover and grill beef 4 to 5 inches from medium heat 10 to 14 minutes for medium doneness, turning once. Sprinkle with salt and pepper. Serve with butter mixture.

6 servings.

1 Serving: Calories 200 (Calories from Fat 135); Fat 15g (Saturated 8g); Cholesterol 65mg; Sodium 200mg; Carbohydrate 1g (Dietary Fiber 0g); Protein 15g
% Daily Value: Vitamin A 8%; Vitamin C 0%; Calcium 0%; Iron 8%
Exchanges: 2 High-Fat Meat

Betty's Classic Peppercorn T-Bones

Grilled Steak with Parsley Pesto

Orange-Thyme Marinade

Quick

Grilled Steak
with Parsley Pesto

Prep: 5 min Grill: 14 min

¼ cup chopped fresh parsley
¼ cup olive or vegetable oil
4 cloves garlic, cut into pieces
4 beef T-bone steaks, about 1 inch thick (about 8 ounces each)
1 teaspoon salt
½ teaspoon pepper

1. Heat coals or gas grill for direct heat. Place parsley, oil and garlic in food processor or blender. Cover and process until smooth.

2. Cut outer edge of fat on beef steaks diagonally at 1-inch intervals to prevent curling (do not cut into beef).

3. Cover and grill beef 3 to 4 inches from medium heat 5 minutes for medium-rare or 7 minutes for medium, brushing frequently with parsley mixture. Turn; brush generously with parsley mixture. Grill 5 to 7 minutes longer until desired doneness. Sprinkle with salt and pepper. Discard any remaining parsley mixture.

4 servings.

1 Serving: Calories 300 (Calories from Fat 180); Fat 20g (Saturated 5g); Cholesterol 80mg; Sodium 660mg; Carbohydrate 1g (Dietary Fiber 0g); Protein 29g
% Daily Value: Vitamin A 6%; Vitamin C 4%; Calcium 2%; Iron 16%
Exchanges: 4 Medium-Fat Meat

BETTY'S TIPS

❂ **Success Hint**
When handling the steaks during grilling, use tongs or a spatula instead of a fork so you don't pierce the beef, allowing the juices to cook out.

Orange-Thyme Marinade

Prep: 15 min Marinate: 6 hr

1 teaspoon grated orange peel
½ cup orange juice
2 tablespoons balsamic or red wine vinegar
1 tablespoon vegetable oil
2 medium green onions, finely chopped (2 tablespoons)
1 tablespoon chopped fresh thyme leaves
¼ teaspoon salt
⅛ teaspoon pepper

1. Mix all ingredients in shallow glass or plastic dish or resealable plastic food-storage bag. Add 2 pounds beef or pork; turn to coat with marinade. Cover dish or seal bag and refrigerate at least 6 hours but no longer than 24 hours.

2. Remove meat from marinade; reserve marinade. Grill meat as desired, brushing occasionally with marinade. Heat remaining marinade to boiling; boil and stir 1 minute. Serve marinade with grilled meat.

¾ cup marinade.

2 Tablespoons: Calories 30 (Calories from Fat 20); Fat 2g (Saturated 0g); Cholesterol 0mg; Sodium 100mg; Carbohydrate 3g (Dietary Fiber 0g); Protein 0g
% Daily Value: Vitamin A 0%; Vitamin C 14%; Calcium 0%; Iron 0%
Exchanges: ½ Fat

BETTY'S TIPS

❂ **Substitution**
If you like, use ½ teaspoon dried thyme leaves in place of the fresh.

❂ **Did You Know?**
Basic to French cuisine, thyme is a perennial herb that is native to southern Europe and the Mediterranean. It has a pungent, lemony flavor and aroma and is one of the basic ingredients in bouquet garni.

Grilled Steak with Feta

Prep: 10 min Marinate: 8 hr Grill: 20 min
(Photo on page 203)

Greek Marinade (right)
1 beef boneless sirloin steak, about 1 inch thick (2 pounds)
2 medium red onions, cut into ½-inch slices
1 package (4 ounces) crumbled feta cheese (1 cup)
Chopped fresh parsley, if desired

1. Make Greek Marinade in shallow glass or plastic dish or resealable plastic food-storage bag. Pierce beef with fork several times on both sides. Add beef and onions to marinade; turn to coat with marinade. Cover dish or seal bag and refrigerate, turning beef occasionally, at least 8 hours but no longer than 24 hours.

2. Heat coals or gas grill for direct heat. Remove beef from marinade; reserve marinade. Cover and grill beef and onions 4 to 5 inches from medium heat 15 to 20 minutes for medium doneness, brushing occasionally with marinade and turning once. Discard any remaining marinade.

3. Cut beef across grain into thin slices. Sprinkle beef with feta and parsley; serve with onion slices.

8 servings.

Greek Marinade
½ cup dry red wine or beef broth
1 tablespoon packed brown sugar
3 tablespoons olive or vegetable oil
1½ teaspoons dried oregano leaves
½ teaspoon salt
¼ teaspoon ground cinnamon
2 cloves garlic, finely chopped

Mix all ingredients.

1 Serving: Calories 225 (Calories from Fat 110); Fat 12g (Saturated 4g); Cholesterol 70mg; Sodium 380mg; Carbohydrate 5g (Dietary Fiber 1g); Protein 25g
% Daily Value: Vitamin A 2%; Vitamin C 0%; Calcium 8%; Iron 12%
Exchanges: 3 Lean Meat, 1 Vegetable, 1 Fat

BETTY'S TIPS

✪ **Substitution**
For a special occasion, individual beef tenderloins (about 4 ounces each) can be substituted for the beef boneless sirloin. Grill about 10 to 15 minutes for medium doneness.

✪ **Did You Know?**
Dry red wines, such as Cabernet, Merlot, Pinot Noir and Zinfandel, can be used in this marinade.

Mediterranean Pot Roast

Prep: 10 min Cook: 6 hr Stand: 15 min

1 beef boneless chuck roast (3 pounds)

1 teaspoon salt

1 tablespoon Italian seasoning

1 large clove garlic, finely chopped

⅓ cup oil-packed sun-dried tomatoes, drained and chopped

½ cup sliced pitted Kalamata or ripe olives

½ cup beef broth

½ cup frozen small whole onions (from 1-pound bag)

1. Spray 12-inch skillet with cooking spray; heat over medium-high heat. Cook beef in skillet about 5 minutes, turning once, until brown. Sprinkle with salt, Italian seasoning and garlic; remove from skillet.

2. Place beef, seasoned side up, in 4- to 5-quart slow cooker. Spread tomatoes and olives over beef. Add broth and onions.

3. Cover and cook on low heat setting 5 to 6 hours or until beef is tender.

4. Remove beef from slow cooker; cover and let stand 15 minutes. Slice beef; serve with onions and beef juices from slow cooker.

8 to 10 servings.

1 Serving: Calories 340 (Calories from Fat 190); Fat 21g (Saturated 8g); Cholesterol 105mg; Sodium 530mg; Carbohydrate 3g (Dietary Fiber 1g); Protein 35g
% Daily Value: Vitamin A 4%; Vitamin C 4%; Calcium 2%; Iron 24%
Exchanges: 5 Lean Meat, 1 Vegetable, 1 Fat

BETTY'S TIPS

☺ **Substitution**
Italian seasoning is a blend of herbs commonly used in Italian cuisine, such as oregano, basil and garlic. Pizza seasoning, which contains a similar blend plus bell peppers, can also be used in this mixture.

☺ **Serve-With**
Fluffy homemade mashed potatoes-skins on or off-is the perfect partner for beef roast.

Mediterranean Pot Roast

Cheddar Burgers and Veggies

Prep: 20 min Grill: 20 min

1½ pounds ground beef

1½ cups shredded Cheddar cheese (6 ounces)

1½ tablespoons Worcestershire sauce

3 medium green onions, chopped (3 tablespoons)

2 teaspoons peppered seasoned salt

3 medium yellow Yukon potatoes, thinly sliced

2 cups baby-cut carrots

18 cherry tomatoes, cut in half, if desired

6 medium green onions, sliced (⅓ cup)

1. Heat coals or gas grill for direct heat. Spray half of one side of six 18 × 12-inch sheets of heavy-duty aluminum foil with cooking spray.

2. Mix beef, cheese, Worcestershire sauce, chopped onions and 1½ teaspoons of the peppered seasoned salt. Shape mixture into 6 patties, about 1 inch thick.

3. Place potatoes on sprayed sides of foil sheets. Top with beef patty, carrots, tomatoes and sliced onions; sprinkle with remaining ½ teaspoon seasoned salt. Fold foil over patties and vegetables so edges meet.

Seal edges, making tight ½-inch fold; fold again. Allow space on sides for heat circulation and expansion.

4. Grill packets 4 to 6 inches from medium heat 17 to 20 minutes or until potatoes are tender. Place packets on plates. Cut a large × across top of packet; fold back foil.

6 servings.

1 Serving: Calories 440 (Calories from Fat 235); Fat 26g (Saturated 12g); Cholesterol 95mg; Sodium 770mg; Carbohydrate 24g (Dietary Fiber 4g); Protein 31g
% Daily Value: Vitamin A 100%; Vitamin C 22%; Calcium 18%; Iron 20%
Exchanges: 1 Starch, 3 Medium-Fat Meat, 2 Vegetable, 2 Fat

BETTY'S TIPS

✪ Substitution

If you don't have peppered seasoned salt, use 1 teaspoon seasoned salt or ½ teaspoon salt for each teaspoon of peppered seasoned salt.

Cheddar Burgers and Veggies

Wild Rice and Beef Casserole

Prep: 5 min Cook: 10 min Bake: 40 min
(Photo on page 203)

1 pound ground beef
1 package (6.2 ounces) fast-cooking long-grain and wild rice mix
1 can (10¾ ounces) condensed tomato soup
¼ cup milk
¼ teaspoon pepper
1 cup shredded Cheddar cheese (4 ounces)

1. Heat oven to 350°. Spray 2-quart casserole with cooking spray.

2. Cook ground beef in 10-inch skillet over medium heat 8 to 10 minutes, stirring occasionally, until brown; drain. Meanwhile, make rice mix as directed on package—except omit butter. Stir rice mixture, soup, milk and pepper into ground beef. Spoon into casserole.

3. Cover and bake 30 minutes. Sprinkle with cheese. Bake uncovered 5 to 10 minutes or until cheese is melted and mixture is hot.

4 servings.

1 Serving: Calories 460 (Calories from Fat 240); Fat 27g (Saturated 13g); Cholesterol 95mg; Sodium 690mg; Carbohydrate 24g (Dietary Fiber 1g); Protein 31g
% Daily Value: Vitamin A 14%; Vitamin C 8%; Calcium 18%; Iron 16%
Exchanges: 1½ Starch, 4 Medium-Fat Meat, 1 Fat

BETTY'S TIPS

⚙ **Time-Saver**
Did you know you can purchase precooked ground beef crumbles? Just stir them into the remaining ingredients and slash 10 minutes prep time. Look for plain and flavored varieties in the meat or freezer section of your store.

⚙ **Health Twist**
Save 17 grams of fat, 10 milligrams of cholesterol and 150 calories per serving by substituting ground turkey breast for the ground beef and using reduced-fat Cheddar cheese.

Mashed Potato Toppers

Prep: 10 min Cook: 30 min

12 medium round red or white potatoes
(4 pounds)
Italian Vegetable Sauté (opposite) and/or
Saucy Italian Beef (opposite)
²⁄₃ to 1 cup milk
½ cup butter or margarine, softened
1 teaspoon salt
¼ teaspoon pepper

Serve with One or More of These Toppings:

1 cup shredded Cheddar, Parmesan or Swiss
cheese
½ cup sliced ripe olives
Freshly ground pepper

1. Place potatoes in 4-quart saucepan; add enough water to just cover potatoes. Heat to boiling; reduce heat. Cover and simmer 20 to 30 minutes or until potatoes are tender; drain. Shake pan with potatoes over low heat to dry (this will help mashed potatoes be fluffier).

2. While potatoes are cooking, make Italian Vegetable Sauté and/or Saucy Italian Beef.

3. Mash potatoes in pan until no lumps remain. Add milk in small amounts, mashing after each addition (amount of milk needed to make potatoes smooth and fluffy depends on kind of potatoes used). Add butter, salt and pepper. Mash vigorously until potatoes are light and fluffy.

4. Allow 1 cup potatoes per serving. Top each serving with about ½ cup Italian Vegetable Sauté or Saucy Italian Beef. Serve with desired Toppings.

8 servings.

Nutrition information is not provided for this recipe because of the variety of food options.

BETTY'S TIPS

⊘ **Do-Ahead**
To make ahead and keep hot, spray inside of slow cooker with cooking spray and spoon mashed potatoes into slow cooker; cover and keep warm on low heat up to 2 hours.

⊘ **Serve-With**
Roasted-Vegetable Alfredo Sauce, on page 190, would also be delicious as a mashed potato topper.

⊘ **The Finishing Touch**
Serve these flavorful potatoes in a martini glass for an elegant touch. You can use colorful, plastic disposable glasses to save on cleanup after a party

Italian Vegetable Sauté

Prep: 12 min Cook: 10 min

½ cup Italian Parmesan or Italian dressing
2 medium zucchini, cut into ¼-inch slices (3 cups)
2 medium red bell peppers, thinly sliced
1½ cups sliced mushrooms
1 medium red onion, sliced
2 tablespoons dry white wine or chicken broth
¼ cup shredded Parmesan cheese

1. Cook dressing, zucchini, bell peppers, mushrooms and onion in 12-inch skillet over medium-high heat about 5 minutes, stirring frequently, until dressing has almost evaporated.

2. Stir in wine. Cook 2 to 5 minutes, stirring frequently, until vegetables are crisp-tender. Sprinkle with cheese.

About 5 cups vegetables.

Saucy Italian Beef

Prep: 12 min Cook: 6 min

¾ pound beef boneless sirloin or flank steak, cut into thin strips
1 tablespoon olive or vegetable oil
1 small green bell pepper, sliced
1 or 2 cloves garlic, finely chopped
1 can (14½ ounces) diced tomatoes with Italian herbs, undrained
1 can (8 ounces) pizza sauce
1 jar (4½ ounces) sliced mushrooms, drained

1. Cut beef into thin strips (beef is easier to cut if partially frozen, 30 to 60 minutes). Heat oil in 10-inch nonstick skillet over medium-high heat. Cook beef, bell pepper and garlic in oil, stirring occasionally, until beef is brown; drain.

2. Stir in tomatoes, pizza sauce and mushrooms. Cook 2 to 4 minutes or until hot.

About 5 cups beef mixture.

Mashed Potato Toppers with Italian Vegetable Sauté and Saucy Italian Beef

Betty... MAKES IT EASY

Burger and Veggie Packets

Prep: 15 min Bake: 20 min

1 pound extra-lean ground beef
1 tablespoon Worcestershire sauce
1½ teaspoons garlic pepper
½ teaspoon onion powder
2 cups frozen sugar snap peas, carrots, onions and mushrooms (from 1-pound bag)
32 frozen steak fries (from 28-ounce bag)
4 frozen half-ears corn-on-the-cob

1. Heat oven to 450°. Cut four 18 × 12-inch sheets of aluminum foil.

2. Mix beef, Worcestershire sauce, 1 teaspoon of the garlic pepper and the onion powder. Shape mixture into 4 patties, about ¼ inch thick.

3. Place 1 patty on center of each foil sheet. Top each with ½ cup vegetables and 8 steak fries. Place 1 piece of corn next to each patty. Sprinkle the remaining ½ teaspoon garlic pepper over vegetables. Fold foil over patties and vegetables. Seal edges at top, making tight ½-inch fold; fold again. Repeat folding at sides. Allow space on sides for heat circulation and expansion. Place packets on large cookie sheet.

4. Bake 15 to 20 minutes or until patties are no longer pink in center and juice of beef is clear. Place packets on plates. Open end of each packet to release steam, then open top of packet.

4 servings.

1 Serving: Calories 620 (Calories from Fat 200); Fat 22g (Saturated 7g); Cholesterol 70mg; Sodium 280mg; Carbohydrate 60g (Dietary Fiber 7g); Protein 30g
% Daily Value: Vitamin A 80%; Vitamin C 22%; Calcium 4%; Iron 26%
Exchanges: 3 Starch, 2 Medium-Fat Meat, 3 Vegetable, 3 Fat

Fold foil over patties and vegetables. Seal edges at top, making tight ½-inch fold; fold again. Repeat folding at sides. Allow space on sides for heat circulation and expansion.

Open end of each packet to release steam, then open top of packet.

Burger and Veggie Packets

Sizzling Fajitas

Sizzling Fajitas

Prep: 30 min Marinate: 8 hr Grill: 20 min

Fajita Marinade (right)

2 beef boneless top sirloin steaks, 1½ inches thick (1½ pounds each)

4 large onions, sliced

4 medium green or red bell peppers, cut into ¼-inch strips

¼ cup vegetable oil

24 flour tortillas (8 to 10 inches in diameter)

Serve with One or More of These Toppings:

1 jar (16 ounces) picante sauce (2 cups)

2 cups shredded Cheddar or Monterey Jack cheese (8 ounces)

3 cups purchased guacamole

1½ cups sour cream

Fajita Marinade

¼ cup vegetable oil

¼ cup red wine vinegar

1 teaspoon sugar

1 teaspoon dried oregano leaves

1 teaspoon chili powder

½ teaspoon garlic powder

½ teaspoon salt

¼ teaspoon pepper

Mix all ingredients.

1 Serving: Calories 610 (Calories from Fat 250); Fat 28g (Saturated 8g); Cholesterol 75mg; Sodium 830mg; Carbohydrate 60g (Dietary Fiber 6g); Protein 36g
% Daily Value: Vitamin A 12%; Vitamin C 40%; Calcium 18%; Iron 32%
Exchanges: 3 Starch, 3 Medium-Fat Meat, 3 Vegetable, 1½ Fat

BETTY'S TIPS

☺ Did You Know?

You can find ready-to-eat guacamole in the refrigerated section near tortillas and salsa, with the refrigerated dips or in the freezer section of most large supermarkets. You also may be able to purchase freshly made guacamole from a Mexican restaurant in your area.

☺ The Finishing Touch

Make cones out of various sizes and colors of tortillas to use as fun containers for the toppings. Secure the cones with toothpicks and place in sturdy glasses or containers.

1. Make Fajita Marinade in shallow glass or plastic dish or resealable plastic food-storage bag. Remove excess fat from beef. Pierce beef with fork several times on both sides. Add beef to marinade; turn to coat with marinade. Cover dish or seal bag and refrigerate, turning beef occasionally, at least 8 hours but no longer than 24 hours.

2. Heat coals or gas grill for direct heat. Remove beef from marinade; reserve marinade. Cover and grill beef 4 to 5 inches from medium heat 15 to 20 minutes for medium doneness, brushing occasionally with marinade and turning once. Toss onions and bell peppers with oil; place in grill basket. Add vegetables to grill with beef for last 6 to 8 minutes of grilling, turning vegetables once or twice, until crisp-tender.

3. While beef is grilling, heat oven to 325°. Wrap tortillas in aluminum foil. Heat in oven about 15 minutes or until warm. Remove tortillas from oven; keep wrapped.

4. Cut beef across grain into very thin slices. For each fajita, layer beef, onion mixture and desired Toppings on tortilla. Roll or fold tortilla around filling. Serve with desired Toppings.

12 servings.

Kid-Pleasin' Chili

Prep: 5 min   Cook: 40 min

Family-Pleasin' Chili

2	pounds ground beef
2	cans (15 to 16 ounces each) kidney beans, rinsed and drained
2	cans (10¾ ounces each) condensed tomato soup
2	soup cans water
2	tablespoons instant minced onion
4 to 6	teaspoons chili powder

1. Cook beef in 4-quart Dutch oven over medium heat 8 to 10 minutes, stirring occasionally, until brown; drain.

2. Stir in remaining ingredients. Heat to boiling, reduce heat. Cover and simmer 30 minutes, stirring occasionally.

8 servings (or enough chili for 2 recipes, 4⅓ cups each).

1 Serving: Calories 400 (Calories from Fat 160); Fat 18g (Saturated 7g); Cholesterol 65mg; Sodium 770mg; Carbohydrate 37g (Dietary Fiber 8g); Protein 31g
% Daily Value: Vitamin A 16%; Vitamin C 10%; Calcium 4%; Iron 30%
Exchanges: 2 Starch, 3 Medium-Fat Meat, 1 Vegetable

BETTY'S TIPS

⊕ **Variation**
This recipe is very mild to please younger members of your family. For a zestier chili, add ½ teaspoon garlic salt, ½ teaspoon ground cumin, ¼ teaspoon pepper and a few drops of red pepper sauce.

⊕ **Do-Ahead**
To keep half of this chili to use for Fiesta Taco Casserole (opposite), tightly cover and refrigerate 4⅓ cups chili up to 48 hours. Or cool mixture 1 hour, place in labeled airtight freezer container and freeze up to 2 months. Thaw in refrigerator or microwave when you need a quick-to-fix meal.

Fiesta Taco Casserole

Prep: 15 min Bake: 30 min

2 cups coarsely broken tortilla chips

½ recipe (4⅓ cups) Kid-Pleasin' Chili (opposite), thawed if frozen

½ cup sour cream

4 medium green onions, sliced (¼ cup)

1 medium tomato, chopped (¾ cup)

1 cup shredded Cheddar or Monterey Jack cheese (4 ounces)

Additional tortilla chips, if desired

1. Heat oven to 350°. Place broken tortilla chips in ungreased 2-quart casserole. Top with chili. Dollop with sour cream; spread evenly. Sprinkle with onions, tomato and cheese.

2. Bake uncovered 20 to 30 minutes or until hot and bubbly. Arrange additional tortilla chips around edge of casserole.

4 servings.

1 Serving: Calories 770 (Calories from Fat 385); Fat 43g (Saturated 16g); Cholesterol 115mg; Sodium 1200mg; Carbohydrate 65g (Dietary Fiber 11g); Protein 42g
% Daily Value: Vitamin A 32%; Vitamin C 18%; Calcium 24%; Iron 42%
Exchanges: 4 Starch, 4 High-Fat Meat, 1 Vegetable, 1 Fruit, ½ Fat

BETTY'S TIPS

⊙ **Substitution**
Looking for a different cheese to try? Shredded Mexican cheese blend can be used instead of Cheddar or Monterey Jack cheese.

⊙ **Serve-With**
To accompany this tasty casserole, set out bowls of guacamole, sliced green onions, chopped lettuce and your family's favorite salsa. Wedges of corn bread would be a great addition to this easy Mexican meal.

Fiesta Taco Casserole

Meatball Sandwich Casserole

Prep: 15 min Bake: 45 min

18 slices French bread, about ¼ inch thick

3 tablespoons olive or vegetable oil

1 package (18 ounces) frozen Italian-flavor or regular meatballs, 1 inch in diameter (36 meatballs), thawed

3 cups frozen stir-fry bell peppers and onions (from 1-pound bag), thawed and drained

1½ cups tomato pasta sauce (any variety)

1 cup shredded mozzarella cheese (4 ounces)

1. Heat oven to 350°. Spray pie plate, 10 × 1½ inches, with cooking spray. Brush one side of bread slices with olive oil. Line bottom and side of pie plate with bread, oil side up and slightly overlapping. Bake about 5 minutes or until edges are light golden brown.

2. Toss together meatballs, bell pepper mixture and pasta sauce in large bowl. Spoon meatball mixture into baked crust.

3. Bake uncovered 30 to 35 minutes or until hot in center. Sprinkle with cheese. Bake about 5 minutes or until cheese is melted.

6 servings.

1 Serving: Calories 610 (Calories from Fat 250); Fat 28g (Saturated 9g); Cholesterol 95mg; Sodium 1330mg; Carbohydrate 63g (Dietary Fiber 4g); Protein 31g
% Daily Value: Vitamin A 16%; Vitamin C 26%; Calcium 26%; Iron 28%
Exchanges: 4 Starch, 2½ Medium-Fat Meat, 1 Vegetable

BETTY'S TIPS

⚙ **Substitution**

You can make your own meatballs, if you prefer, or use frozen turkey meatballs.

Shredded Italian cheese blend instead of mozzarella cheese is a good choice, too.

⚙ **Time-Saver**

If you have a mister for olive oil or olive oil-flavored cooking spray, lightly spray one side of bread slices for a quick coating of oil.

Meatball Sandwich Casserole

Barbecue Beef and Corn Shepherd's Pie

Prep: 10 min Cook: 15 min Stand: 5 min

1   pound ground beef
8   medium green onions, sliced (½ cup)
1   cup barbecue sauce
1   can (11 ounces) whole kernel corn with red and green peppers, drained
1   can (4 ounces) chopped green chilies, undrained
½   package (7-ounce size) Betty Crocker Cheddar and bacon mashed potatoes (1 pouch)
1½ cups hot water
⅓   cup milk
2   tablespoons butter or margarine
½   cup shredded Cheddar cheese (2 ounces)
1   cup corn chips

1. Cook ground beef and ¼ cup of the onions in 10-inch nonstick skillet over medium-high heat, stirring occasionally, until beef is brown; drain well. Stir in barbecue sauce, ¾ cup of the corn and the chilies. Heat to boiling; reduce heat to low to keep warm.

2. Meanwhile, cook potatoes as directed on package for 4 servings, using 1 pouch Potatoes and Seasoning, hot water, milk and butter. Stir in remaining onions and corn; let stand 5 minutes.

3. Spoon potatoes onto center of beef mixture, leaving 2½- to 3-inch rim around edge of skillet; sprinkle cheese over potatoes and beef mixture. Cover and let stand about 5 minutes or until cheese is melted. Sprinkle corn chips around edge of skillet.

6 servings.

1 Serving: Calories 440 (Calories from Fat 190); Fat 21g (Saturated 9g); Cholesterol 65mg; Sodium 1000mg; Carbohydrate 45g (Dietary Fiber 3g); Protein 21g
% Daily Value: Vitamin A 14%; Vitamin C 16%; Calcium 12%; Iron 16%
Exchanges: 3 Starch, 2 Medium-Fat Meat, 1 Fat

BETTY'S TIPS

☺ Substitution
Ground pork or ground turkey can be substituted for the ground beef.

☺ Did You Know?
Barbecue sauces vary widely in flavor, from a manufacturer's original flavor to hickory, mesquite, honey, spicy, honey-mustard, sweet, sassy and low-sodium varieties. Although this recipe was developed with an original-flavored sauce, which is typically thick, red and slightly sweet, try it with your family's favorite.

Barbecue Beef and Corn Shepherd's Pie

One-Pan Pasta and Meatballs

Prep: 5 min Cook: 22 min

1 cup water
1 jar (26 to 28 ounces) tomato pasta sauce (any variety)
1½ cups uncooked elbow springs pasta (4½ ounces)
20 frozen fully cooked Italian-flavor or regular meatballs, 1 inch in diameter (from 18-ounce bag)
1 can (2¼ ounces) sliced ripe olives, drained
Grated Parmesan cheese, if desired

1. Heat water and pasta sauce to boiling in 10-inch skillet. Stir in pasta, meatballs and olives. Heat to boiling; reduce heat to medium.

2. Cover and cook 15 to 20 minutes, stirring occasionally, until pasta is tender. Sprinkle with cheese.

4 servings.

1 Serving: Calories 595 (Calories from Fat 200); Fat 22g (Saturated 7g); Cholesterol 75mg; Sodium 1530mg; Carbohydrate 80g (Dietary Fiber 5g); Protein 24g
% Daily Value: Vitamin A 28%; Vitamin C 22%; Calcium 18%; Iron 30%
Exchanges: 5 Starch, 1 High-Fat Meat, 1 Vegetable, 1½ Fat

BETTY'S TIPS

☼ Substitution

Don't care for olives? Substitute 1 small green bell pepper, cut into ½-inch pieces, or a 6-ounce jar of sliced mushrooms, drained, instead.

Rotini pasta can be used instead of elbow springs pasta. Both spiral pastas work well in this recipe.

Cheesy Pasta, Veggies and Beef

Prep: 5 min Cook: 22 min

1 pound ground beef
1 bag (1 pound) frozen pasta, broccoli, corn and carrots in garlic-seasoned sauce
1 can (10¾ ounces) condensed Cheddar cheese soup
1 cup water
Macaroni & cheese-flavored cheese topping or cheese-flavored tiny fish-shaped crackers, if desired

1. Cook beef in 10-inch skillet over medium heat 8 to 10 minutes, stirring occasionally, until brown; drain.

2. Stir pasta mixture, soup and water into beef. Heat to boiling; reduce heat. Cover and simmer 5 to 7 minutes, stirring occasionally, until vegetables are tender. Sprinkle with cheese topping.

4 servings.

1 Serving: Calories 320 (Calories from Fat 200); Fat 22g (Saturated 9g); Cholesterol 75mg; Sodium 740mg; Carbohydrate 6g (Dietary Fiber 0g); Protein 24g
% Daily Value: Vitamin A 32%; Vitamin C 0%; Calcium 6%; Iron 10%
Exchanges: 3 High-Fat Meat, 1 Vegetable

BETTY'S TIPS

☼ Success Hint

Do you prefer your cooked ground beef in small crumbles or large crumbles? For small crumbles, keep breaking up beef with a spoon and stir frequently while cooking. For large crumbles, break up beef into the size of pieces you want when you first start cooking it. Don't break it up while stirring and stir less often. Larger crumbles will take longer to cook completely through.

☼ Serve-With

Serve this super-easy skillet meal with a crisp salad and fresh fruit and sherbet or sorbet for dessert.

Cheesy Pasta, Veggies and Beef

One-Pan Pasta and Meatballs

Slow Cooker Sloppy Joes

Prep: 15 min Cook: 9 hr

3 pounds ground turkey or beef
1 large onion, coarsely chopped (1 cup)
1½ medium stalks celery, chopped (1½ cups)
1 cup barbecue sauce
1 can (26½ ounces) sloppy joe sauce
24 hamburger buns

1. Cook turkey and onion in 4-quart Dutch oven over medium heat about 10 minutes, stirring occasionally, until turkey is no longer pink; drain.

2. Mix turkey mixture and remaining ingredients except buns in 3½- to 4-quart slow cooker.

3. Cover and cook on low heat setting 7 to 9 hours (or high heat setting 3 to 4 hours) or until vegetables are tender.

4. Uncover and cook on high heat setting until desired consistency. Stir well before serving. Fill buns with turkey mixture.

24 sandwiches (or enough Sloppy Joes for 3 recipes, about 2½ cups each).

1 Sandwich: Calories 230 (Calories from Fat 65); Fat 7g (Saturated 2g); Cholesterol 25mg; Sodium 540mg; Carbohydrate 32g (Dietary Fiber 2g); Protein 12g
% Daily Value: Vitamin A 4%; Vitamin C 4%; Calcium 8%; Iron 12%
Exchanges: 2 Starch, 1 Lean Meat, 1 Vegetable

BETTY'S TIPS

✪ **Do-Ahead**

This recipe gives you a head start on three meals, Sloppy Joes, Hot Potato Stuffers (opposite) and one other. In addition to these two recipes, try this tasty turkey mixture over hot cooked rice or pasta. Or spoon over tortilla chips and top with shredded lettuce and cheese.

Slow Cooker Sloppy Joes

Quick

Sloppy Joes Hot Potato Stuffers

Prep: 7 min Microwave: 16 min Stand: 5 min

4 medium baking potatoes

2½ cups Slow Cooker Sloppy Joes (opposite), thawed if frozen

1 cup shredded Cheddar cheese (4 ounces)

Sour cream, if desired

Betty Crocker Bac-Os bacon flavor bits, if desired

Chopped onion, if desired

Chopped green bell pepper, if desired

Sliced ripe olives, if desired

1. Pierce potatoes with sharp knife. Arrange potatoes in spoke pattern with narrow ends in center on microwavable paper towel. Microwave on High 12 to 14 minutes, turning once, until tender. Cover and let stand 5 minutes.

2. Cut slit in each potato two-thirds of the way to bottom; gently press ends together to create a "well." Place potatoes on microwavable plate. Top potatoes with Sloppy Joes and cheese. Microwave 1 to 2 minutes or until cheese is melted. Serve with remaining ingredients as toppings.

4 servings.

1 Serving: Calories 560 (Calories from Fat 225); Fat 25g (Saturated 10g); Cholesterol 105mg; Sodium 1080mg; Carbohydrate 54g (Dietary Fiber 4g); Protein 34g
% Daily Value: Vitamin A 22%; Vitamin C 26%; Calcium 20%; Iron 14%
Exchanges: 3 Starch, 3 Medium-Fat Meat, 2 Vegetable, 1 Fat

BETTY'S TIPS

✿ **Variation**

Here's an easy meal for nights when the family is eating in shifts, because you can microwave a serving for one person at a time. After microwaving potatoes as directed in step 1, cut a slit in a potato, place on a microwavable plate and microwave on High 4 to 5 minutes to reheat. Top with Sloppy Joes and cheese; microwave 45 to 60 seconds longer or until cheese is melted.

Sloppy Joes Hot Potato Stuffers

Fajita Lasagna

Prep: 15 min Bake: 30 min Stand: 15 min

1 bag (1 pound) frozen stir-fry bell peppers and onions, thawed

1 pound ground beef

1 can (29 ounces) tomato sauce

1 envelope (1.4 ounces) fajita seasoning mix

12 no-boil lasagna noodles, each about 6 to 8 inches long and 3 inches wide

3 cups shredded Colby-Monterey Jack cheese (12 ounces)

1 can (2¼ ounces) sliced ripe olives, drained

1. Heat oven to 350°. Spray bottom and sides of rectangular baking dish, 13 × 9 × 2 inches, with cooking spray. Drain thawed bell pepper mixture; set aside.

2. Cook ground beef in 10-inch skillet over medium-high heat, stirring occasionally, until brown; drain. Stir in tomato sauce and seasoning mix; heat to boiling. Spread ½ cup sauce mixture in baking dish. Arrange 4 noodles crosswise, slightly overlapping, on sauce. Spread 1½ cups sauce over noodles, completely covering noodles. Spread pepper mixture evenly over sauce; sprinkle with 1 cup of the cheese.

3. Arrange 4 noodles crosswise, slightly overlapping, on cheese. Spread about 1½ cups sauce over noodles, completely covering noodles. Sprinkle 1 cup of the cheese and the olives over sauce. Arrange 4 noodles crosswise, slightly overlapping, on olives. Spread remaining sauce over noodles, completely covering noodles. Sprinkle with remaining 1 cup cheese.

4. Spray piece of aluminum foil large enough to cover baking dish with cooking spray. Tightly cover baking dish with foil, sprayed side down. Bake about 30 minutes or until hot and bubbly. Let stand 15 minutes before cutting.

8 servings.

1 Serving: Calories 460 (Calories from Fat 205); Fat 23g (Saturated 12g); Cholesterol 75mg; Sodium 1220mg; Carbohydrate 40g (Dietary Fiber 4g); Protein 27g
% Daily Value: Vitamin A 36%; Vitamin C 36%; Calcium 32%; Iron 20%
Exchanges: 2½ Starch, 2½ Medium-Fat Meat, 1 Vegetable, 1 Fat

BETTY'S TIPS

☺ **Success Hint**
For easier cutting, we're using ground beef in this recipe instead of the usual steak found in fajitas. When we tested this recipe using slices of steak, we found that cutting the lasagna into serving pieces was difficult.

☺ **Did You Know?**
No-boil lasagna noodles are so convenient to have on hand. Most large grocery stores carry boxes of them right next to the regular lasagna noodles and other pastas.

☺ **Serve-With**
Add guacamole, salsa and sour cream for a festive touch.

Fajita Lasagna

The Perfect Complement

Side Dishes for Every Occasion

Spicy Grilled Corn (page 228)

Foolproof Gravy (page 235)

Spicy Grilled Corn

Prep: 15 min Grill: 30 min
(Photo on page 227)

⅓ cup butter or margarine, softened
3 tablespoons Old El Paso taco seasoning mix
(from 1.25-ounce envelope)
12 ears corn with husks

1. Heat coals or gas grill for direct heat. Mix butter and taco seasoning mix. Carefully pull back husk of each ear of corn; remove silk. Spread butter mixture over corn. Pull husks back over ears; tie husks securely with thin piece of husk or string.

2. Grill corn uncovered 4 to 6 inches from medium heat 20 to 30 minutes, turning frequently, until tender.

12 servings.

1 Serving: Calories 165 (Calories from Fat 55); Fat 6g (Saturated 1g); Cholesterol 0mg; Sodium 200mg; Carbohydrate 27g (Dietary Fiber 3g); Protein 4g
% Daily Value: Vitamin A 12%; Vitamin C 6%; Calcium 0%; Iron 4%
Exchanges: 1½ Starch, 1 Fat

BETTY'S TIPS

⊛ **Success Hint**
For the best flavor, buy corn the day you plan to serve it. Keep it cold until you're ready to cook it.

⊛ **Variation**
You can also microwave corn on the cob. Husk the corn and place each ear on microwave-safe plastic wrap or waxed paper. Brush the corn with the butter mixture, then wrap. Microwave 4 ears of corn 6 to 8 minutes, turning once. Let stand 2 minutes. Repeat with remaining corn.

Smoked Sausage Baked Beans

Prep: 10 min Bake: 1 hr

2 cans (55 ounces each) baked beans
1 ring (1 pound) fully cooked smoked sausage, cubed
2 jalapeño chilies, seeded and finely chopped
1 tablespoon ground cumin
1 tablespoon chili powder

1. Heat oven to 350°. Mix all ingredients in large bowl; spoon into ungreased 4-quart casserole.

2. Bake uncovered 45 to 60 minutes or until thoroughly heated and bubbly.

24 servings.

1 Serving: Calories 180 (Calories from Fat 65); Fat 7g (Saturated 3g); Cholesterol 20mg; Sodium 770mg; Carbohydrate 26g (Dietary Fiber 6g); Protein 9g
% Daily Value: Vitamin A 26%; Vitamin C 4%; Calcium 8%; Iron 26%
Exchanges: 2 Starch, ½ Medium-Fat Meat

BETTY'S TIPS

⊛ **Pack 'n Go**
You can make these beans in a slow cooker, then bring it along to keep the beans warm. Mix all ingredients in 3½- to 4-quart slow cooker. Cover and cook on low heat setting 4 to 5 hours (or high heat setting 2 to 2½ hours) or until thoroughly heated and desired consistency.

Smoked Sausage Baked Beans

Balsamic Grilled Butternut Squash

Prep: 15 min Grill: 20 min

1   medium butternut squash, peeled and cut into 1-inch cubes
⅓ cup balsamic vinaigrette dressing
¼ teaspoon Italian seasoning
⅛ teaspoon coarse pepper
1   medium bell pepper, cut into 1-inch pieces (1 cup)

1. Heat coals or gas grill for direct heat. Place all ingredients except bell pepper in large bowl; toss to coat. Place squash in grill basket, reserving dressing in bowl.

2. Cover and grill squash 4 to 6 inches from medium heat 10 minutes. Add bell pepper to dressing in bowl; toss to coat. Add to grill basket. Cover and grill 5 to 10 minutes, shaking grill basket to turn vegetables occasionally, until squash and bell pepper are crisp-tender.

3. Pour vegetables from grill basket into remaining dressing in bowl; toss to coat. Serve immediately.

4 servings.

1 Serving: Calories 175 (Calories from Fat 70); Fat 8g (Saturated 1g); Cholesterol 5mg; Sodium 190mg; Carbohydrate 24g (Dietary Fiber 3g); Protein 2g
% Daily Value: Vitamin A 100%; Vitamin C 45%; Calcium 10%; Iron 6%
Exchanges: 1 Starch, ½ Fruit, 1½ Fat

BETTY'S TIPS

❂ **Variation**
Use sweet potatoes instead of the squash. The cooking time will be about the same.

❂ **Health Twist**
Winter squash, such as butternut, is a good source of iron and vitamins A and C, and it is high in fiber and low in fat and calories.

❂ **Did You Know?**
Butternut squash is the one that is shaped sort of like a peanut. This orange-fleshed winter squash has a delicate sweet flavor and is great for grilling.

Balsamic Grilled Butternut Squash

Grilled Sweet Potatoes with Chipotle-Honey Sauce

Prep: 10 min Grill: 10 min

Chipotle-Honey Sauce (right)
6 medium sweet potatoes
⅓ cup olive or vegetable oil
2 teaspoons coarse salt

1. Spray grill rack with cooking spray. Heat coals or gas grill for direct heat. Make Chipotle-Honey Sauce; set aside.

2. Cut each sweet potato lengthwise into 4 or 5 slices; brush both sides with oil. Place potatoes on grill rack; sprinkle with 1 teaspoon of the salt.

3. Cover and grill 4 to 6 inches from medium heat 8 to 10 minutes, turning once and sprinkling with remaining salt, until potatoes are tender. Serve with sauce.

6 servings.

Chipotle-Honey Sauce
1 cup honey
4 chipotle chilies in adobo sauce, finely chopped
2 tablespoons adobo sauce (from can of chilies)

Mix all ingredients.

1 Serving: Calories 380 (Calories from Fat 80); Fat 9g (Saturated 1g); Cholesterol 0mg; Sodium 740mg; Carbohydrate 77g (Dietary Fiber 4g); Protein 2g
% Daily Value: Vitamin A 100%; Vitamin C 24%; Calcium 4%; Iron 4%
Exchanges: 1 Starch, 4 Fruit, 1½ Fat

BETTY'S TIPS

✿ **Substitution**
Instead of making the Chipotle Honey Sauce, mix ½ cup honey, ½ cup hickory-flavored or regular barbecue sauce and ¼ teaspoon ground red pepper (cayenne) for a **Honey-Barbecue Sauce.**

Grilled Sweet Potatoes with Chipotle-Honey Sauce

Green Beans with Shiitake Mushrooms

Prep: 15 min Cook: 16 min

1½ pounds fresh green beans
¼ cup slivered almonds
6 ounces fresh shiitake mushrooms
1 tablespoon olive or vegetable oil
1 tablespoon sesame oil
3 cloves garlic, finely chopped
2 tablespoons soy sauce

1. Remove ends of beans. Leave beans whole or cut into 1-inch pieces. Place steamer basket in ½ inch water in saucepan or skillet (water should not touch bottom of basket). Place green beans in steamer basket. Cover tightly and heat to boiling; reduce heat. Steam 10 minutes.

2. Cook almonds in ungreased heavy skillet over medium-low heat 5 to 7 minutes, stirring frequently until browning begins, then stirring constantly until golden brown and fragrant.

3. Remove tough stems of mushrooms; cut mushrooms into ¼-inch slices. Heat olive and sesame oils in 12-inch skillet over medium heat. Cook mushrooms and garlic in oil 3 minutes, stirring occasionally. Stir in soy sauce and green beans. Cook 2 to 3 minutes or until green beans are crisp-tender. Sprinkle with almonds.

6 servings.

1 Serving: Calories 95 (Calories from Fat 65); Fat 7g (Saturated 1g); Cholesterol 0mg; Sodium 310mg; Carbohydrate 9g (Dietary Fiber 4g); Protein 3g
% Daily Value: Vitamin A 12%; Vitamin C 4%; Calcium 6%; Iron 8%
Exchanges: 2 Vegetable, 1 Fat

BETTY'S TIPS

☺ Substitution
If you're pressed for time, you can purchase two 12-ounce bags of precut, washed fresh green beans. You'll find them in the produce section of your supermarket.

☺ Did You Know?
Once cultivated only in Japan and Korea, shiitake mushrooms are now cultivated in the United States. The meaty flesh has a full-bodied, some even say steaklike, flavor. The stems are tough but add a wonderful flavor to stocks and sauces. (Discard the stems after they've been used for flavoring.)

Green Beans with Shiitake Mushrooms

Broccoli and Carrots with Creamy Parmesan Sauce

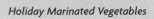

Holiday Marinated Vegetables

Broccoli and Carrots with Creamy Parmesan Sauce

Prep: 10 min Cook: 12 min

½ pound broccoli, cut into flowerets and stems (2 cups)
2 cups baby-cut carrots
Creamy Parmesan Sauce (below)
1 tablespoon chopped fresh chives

1. Heat 1 inch water to boiling in 2-quart saucepan. Add broccoli and carrots. Heat to boiling. Boil 5 to 7 minutes or until crisp-tender; drain and keep warm.

2. While vegetables are cooking, make Creamy Parmesan Sauce. Sprinkle chives over sauce. Serve with vegetables.

4 servings.

Creamy Parmesan Sauce

1 package (3 ounces) cream cheese
¼ cup grated Parmesan cheese
¼ cup milk
1 tablespoon butter or margarine

Cook all ingredients in 1-quart saucepan over medium heat, stirring constantly, until smooth and heated through.

1 Serving: Calories 175 (Calories from Fat 115); Fat 13g (Saturated 8g); Cholesterol 35mg; Sodium 250mg; Carbohydrate 12g (Dietary Fiber 4g); Protein 7g
% Daily Value: Vitamin A 100%; Vitamin C 50%; Calcium 16%; Iron 6%
Exchanges: 2½ Vegetable, 2½ Fat

BETTY'S TIPS

✿ **Substitution**
Olive oil can be substituted for the butter or margarine in the sauce recipe.

✿ **Success Hint**
Select broccoli flowerets of the same size and baby carrots of the same size to ensure even cooking. Very large pieces will take longer to cook, and very small pieces will take less time to cook.

Holiday Marinated Vegetables

Prep: 10 min Chill: 3 hr

⅔ cup Balsamic Vinaigrette (page 56) or Italian vinaigrette dressing
4 cups cooked broccoli or Brussels sprouts
2 cups cherry tomatoes, cut in half
3 cups mushroom halves or fourths (8 ounces)
Lettuce leaves, if desired

1. Pour Balsamic Vinaigrette over broccoli and tomatoes in large glass or plastic bowl. Cover and refrigerate at least 3 hours but no longer than 24 hours.

2. Add mushrooms to vegetables; toss until well coated. Drain before serving. Serve vegetables on lettuce.

8 servings.

1 Serving: Calories 170 (Calories from Fat 125); Fat 14g (Saturated 2g); Cholesterol 0mg; Sodium 40mg; Carbohydrate 11g (Dietary Fiber 2g); Protein 2g
% Daily Value: Vitamin A 18%; Vitamin C 42%; Calcium 2%; Iron 6%
Exchanges: 2 Vegetable, 2½ Fat

BETTY'S TIPS

✿ **Time-Saver**
For a shortcut, use a bottled vinaigrette that you buy at the grocery store. The flavors are endless, and if calories and fat are an issue, you choose low-fat or no-fat dressings.

✿ **Special Touch**
Serve these festive marinated vegetables on individual serving plates that you've lined with kale leaves or red leaf lettuce. Sprinkle with toasted pine nuts for extra pizzazz.

Spinach Milan-Style

Spinach Milan-Style

Prep: 10 min Cook: 10 min

2 pounds fresh spinach
2 tablespoons butter or margarine
2 cloves garlic, finely chopped
$\frac{1}{4}$ cup pine nuts
$\frac{1}{2}$ teaspoon ground nutmeg
$\frac{1}{2}$ teaspoon salt
$\frac{1}{4}$ teaspoon pepper
2 tablespoons water

1. Wash spinach thoroughly; drain. Remove stems and any yellow leaves.

2. Melt butter in 4-quart Dutch oven over medium heat. Cook garlic in butter about 5 minutes, stirring frequently, until just golden. Stir in pine nuts, nutmeg, salt and pepper.

3. Reduce heat to low. Gradually add spinach; sprinkle with water. Cover and cook about 5 minutes or until spinach is wilted.

4 servings.

1 Serving: Calories 145 (Calories from Fat 110); Fat 12g (Saturated 4g); Cholesterol 15mg; Sodium 470mg; Carbohydrate 8g (Dietary Fiber 5g); Protein 6g
% Daily Value: Vitamin A 100%; Vitamin C 38%; Calcium 16%; Iron 26%
Exchanges: 2 Vegetable, 2 Fat

BETTY'S TIPS

⊙ **Substitution**
Slivered almonds or pecan halves can be substituted for the pine nuts.

⊙ **Time-Saver**
Look for bags of prewashed regular or baby spinach leaves in the produce aisle; you'll save 5 to 10 minutes of preparation time.

Foolproof Gravy

Prep: 5 min Cook: 5 min
(Photo on page 227)

$\frac{1}{4}$ cup turkey drippings (fat and juices from roasted turkey)
$\frac{1}{4}$ cup Gold Medal all-purpose flour
2 cups liquid (juices from roasted turkey, broth, water)
   Browning sauce, if desired
$\frac{1}{2}$ teaspoon salt
$\frac{1}{2}$ teaspoon pepper

1. Pour drippings from turkey roasting pan into bowl, leaving brown particles in pan. Return $\frac{1}{4}$ cup drippings to roasting pan. (Measure accurately because too little fat makes gravy lumpy.) Beat in flour with wire whisk. (Measure accurately so gravy is not greasy.)

2. Cook over medium heat, stirring constantly, until mixture is smooth and bubbly; remove from heat. Stir in liquid. Heat to boiling, stirring constantly. Boil and stir 1 minute. Stir in a few drops of browning sauce. Stir in salt and pepper.

2 cups gravy.

$\frac{1}{4}$ Cup: Calories 65 (Calories from Fat 45); Fat 5g (Saturated 1g); Cholesterol 5mg; Sodium 400mg; Carbohydrate 4g (Dietary Fiber 0g); Protein 2g
% Daily Value: Vitamin A 0%; Vitamin C 0%; Calcium 0%; Iron 2%
Exchanges: $1\frac{1}{2}$ Fat

BETTY'S TIPS

⊙ **Success Hint**
The trick to smooth, creamy gravy is to use a wire whisk when adding the flour to the drippings. Beat the drippings rapidly with the whisk while adding the flour, and you won't get lumps.

⊙ **Special Touch**
For added flavor, use vegetable cooking water, tomato juice, vegetable juice or wine as part of the liquid.

Betty...

Dig It!

A new variety or color of potato seems to appear at the supermarket with every shopping trip. We're cooking this mealtime staple in new and interesting ways, too. Read this potato primer to see how this once-humble vegetable has become a top tuber!

REDS

With a blushing red skin and creamy white interior, red potatoes have a smooth, moist texture that makes them perfect in salads and good for steaming, boiling and roasting, too.

RUSSETS

The most widely used potato in the U.S., these brown-skinned, white-fleshed potatoes are a staple on tables everywhere. They are all-purpose potatoes, great for baking, mashing, frying and roasting.

PURPLE/BLUE

These colorful potatoes are native to South America. They have a slightly nutty flavor and can vary in color from indigo to pale purple. Both the skin and flesh have color in some varieties; in others, the interior is white and just the skin has color. These potatoes are good in salads and side dishes as well as for soups and French fries. They're also good mashed. The most color is preserved, however, when they're microwaved, steamed or baked.

WHITE

Less starchy than russet potatoes, these round or long white potatoes have a beige skin and white flesh. Regarded as an all-purpose potato, white potatoes can be used in most every kind of preparation.

YELLOW

Most popular in European countries, yellow potatoes, such as Yukon Gold and Yellow Finn varieties, are now showing up in American cuisine. These dense, creamy-textured potatoes differ from our white-fleshed common russet with their light, fluffy texture. Terrific in salads, potato dishes (au gratin, scalloped), soups and chowders, yellows can also be mashed.

FINGERLING

These potatoes are small, short potatoes that range from 1 to 2 inches in diameter and 2 to 3 inches in length. Because of their petite size and thin skin, there's no need to peel them. Great in salads or roasted, they come in a variety of colors.

POTATO PREP

- Leaving the skins on potatoes makes prep easier. Simply scrub skins with a vegetable brush, clean cloth or sponge. Potatoes with skins also keep many nutrients that are lost if skins are removed.

- Potatoes that have wrinkles, wilted skins, a green tint or soft dark areas should not be used.

- When cooking them whole, choose potatoes of uniform size.

- Cut potatoes can be stored in cold water up to 2 hours before cooking to prevent darkening. After 2 hours, however, potatoes start to lose some of their water-soluble nutrients.

SMASHING MASHED POTATO TIPS

- Russet potatoes will make fluffier mashed potatoes.

- Yellow, white and red potatoes will need a little extra TLC to turn them into mashed because they become more gluelike faster.

- Leaving the skin on adds flavor and nutrients.

- Be sure to heat drained potatoes over low heat about 1 minute, shaking often to remove excess moisture.

- Beat potatoes until light and fluffy. Overbeating them will cause them to become sticky and gluelike.

- You can use almost any type of milk, depending on your tastes: fat-free (skim) milk, half-and-half, cream or even sour cream. If using sour cream, don't heat before adding.

- Warm the milk before adding to the potatoes.

Betty's Best Mashed Potatoes

Classic mashed potatoes at their best. We've added new flavor twists as well as success tips so your mashed potatoes will be perfect every time.

	2	pounds potatoes
1/3 to 1/2	cup milk
	1/4	cup butter or margarine, softened
	1/2	teaspoon salt
	Dash of pepper

1. Place potatoes in 2-quart saucepan; add enough water just to cover potatoes. Heat to boiling; reduce heat. Cover and simmer 20 to 30 minutes or until potatoes are tender; drain. Shake pan with potatoes over low heat to dry (this will help mashed potatoes be fluffier.)

2. Mash potatoes in pan until no lumps remain. Add milk in small amounts, mashing after each addition (amount of milk needed to make potatoes smooth and fluffy depends on kind of potatoes used).

3. Add butter, salt and pepper. Mash vigorously until potatoes are light and fluffy. If desired, sprinkle with small pieces of butter or sprinkle with paprika, chopped fresh parsley or chives.

4 to 6 servings.

Blue Cheese Mashed Potatoes: Stir in 1/4 cup crumbled blue cheese in step 3.

Garlic Mashed Potatoes: Cook 6 cloves garlic, peeled, with the potatoes.

Horseradish Mashed Potatoes: Add 2 tablespoons prepared mild or hot horseradish with the butter, salt and pepper in step 3.

Nutrition information is not provided for this recipe because of the variety of food options.

Betty's Best Mashed Potatoes

Slow Cooker Apple-Pecan Bread Stuffing

Prep: 20 min   Cook: 5 hr

  4 cups soft bread crumbs (about 6 slices bread)
  1 cup crushed saltine crackers (about eighteen 2-inch squares)
1½ cups chopped apples
  1 cup chopped pecans
  1 large onion, chopped (1 cup)
  2 medium stalks celery, chopped (1 cup)
⅔ cup vegetable or chicken broth
¼ cup butter or margarine, melted
½ teaspoon pepper
½ teaspoon rubbed sage
  2 eggs
     Chopped fresh parsley, if desired

1. Spray inside of 2- to 3½-quart slow cooker with cooking spray. Mix bread crumbs, cracker crumbs, apples, pecans, onion and celery in cooker. Mix remaining ingredients except parsley until well blended; pour into cooker. Toss to coat ingredients.

2. Cover and cook on low heat setting 4 to 5 hours or until stuffing is slightly puffed and brown around the edges. Sprinkle with parsley.

8 servings.

1 Serving: Calories 260 (Calories from Fat 160); Fat 18g (Saturated 2g); Cholesterol 0mg; Sodium 380mg; Carbohydrate 24g (Dietary Fiber 3g); Protein 5g
% Daily Value: Vitamin A 8%; Vitamin C 2%; Calcium 4%; Iron 8%
Exchanges: 1 Starch, ½ Fruit, 3½ Fat

BETTY'S TIPS

✪ Success Hint
Making soft bread crumbs is easy because you just tear the bread into small pieces. It's best to use a firm bread that is a couple of days old. Fresh, soft bread will give you a stuffing that is too moist and soggy.

✪ Variation
A delicious meatless second meal can be made from any leftover stuffing. Simply shape the stuffing into patties and heat in butter until brown on both sides. Serve with your favorite green veggie and juicy tomato slices.

Slow Cooker Sweet Potatoes

Prep: 15 min   Cook: 8 hr

  6 medium sweet potatoes or yams (2 pounds), peeled and cut into 1-inch cubes
1½ cups applesauce
⅔ cup packed brown sugar
  3 tablespoons butter or margarine, melted
  1 teaspoon ground cinnamon
½ cup chopped nuts, toasted

1. Place sweet potatoes in 2- to 3½-quart slow cooker. Mix remaining ingredients except nuts; spoon over potatoes.

2. Cover and cook on low heat setting 6 to 8 hours or until potatoes are very tender.

3. Meanwhile, cook nuts in ungreased heavy skillet over medium-low heat 5 to 7 minutes, stirring frequently until browning begins, then stirring constantly until golden brown and fragrant; set aside. Sprinkle nuts over sweet potatoes.

6 servings.

1 Serving: Calories 370 (Calories from Fat 110); Fat 12g (Saturated 4g); Cholesterol 15mg; Sodium 60mg; Carbohydrate 66g (Dietary Fiber 5g); Protein 4g
% Daily Value: Vitamin A 100%; Vitamin C 24%; Calcium 6%; Iron 8%
Exchanges: 1 Starch, 3½ Fruit, 2 Fat

BETTY'S TIPS

✪ Success Hint
Many varieties of sweet potatoes are available. Although the variety of sweet potatoes with dark orange skin is often labeled as "yams," true yams are not generally available in our supermarkets. The very light-colored sweet potatoes are not as sweet and are drier than the darker-skinned ones. We like the darker sweet potatoes (or "yams") for this dish.

✪ Serve-With
While the turkey roasts in the oven, cook this Thanksgiving favorite in the slow cooker. If your home is this year's holiday gathering spot for family and friends, you can double or triple this recipe and cook it in a 5- to 6-quart cooker.

Slow Cooker Sweet Potatoes

Slow Cooker Apple-Pecan Bread Stuffing

The Perfect Complement   239

Slow Cooker Wild Rice with Cranberries

Prep: 15 min Cook: 5 hr + 15 min

1½ cups uncooked wild rice
1 tablespoon butter or margarine, melted
½ teaspoon salt
¼ teaspoon pepper
4 medium green onions, sliced (¼ cup)
2 cans (14 ounces each) vegetable broth
1 can (4 ounces) sliced mushrooms, undrained
½ cup slivered almonds
⅓ cup dried cranberries

1. Mix all ingredients except almonds and cranberries in 2- to 3½-quart slow cooker.

2. Cover and cook on low heat setting 4 to 5 hours or until wild rice is tender.

3. Meanwhile, cook almonds in ungreased heavy skillet over medium-low heat 5 to 7 minutes, stirring frequently until browning begins, then stirring constantly until golden brown and fragrant; set aside. Stir almonds and cranberries into rice mixture. Cover and cook on low heat setting 15 minutes.

6 servings.

1 Serving: Calories 260 (Calories from Fat 65); Fat 7g (Saturated 2g); Cholesterol 5mg; Sodium 900mg; Carbohydrate 45g (Dietary Fiber 5g); Protein 9g
% Daily Value: Vitamin A 10%; Vitamin C 2%; Calcium 4%; Iron 8%
Exchanges: 3 Starch, ½ Fat

BETTY'S TIPS

✪ **Substitution**
Many supermarkets now carry a wide variety of dried fruits. Dried blueberries or cherries are delicious substitutes for the cranberries.

✪ **Success Hint**
Toasting the almonds not only enhances the flavor and color of the almonds but also helps prevent them from becoming soggy after they are stirred into the wild rice mixture.

Slow Cooker Wild Rice with Cranberries

The Best Baked Goods

Cookies, Muffins and Breads

Glazed Raisin-Cinnamon Biscuits (page 252)

Grilled Garlic Bread with Rosemary (page 262)

Fresh Mint Chocolate Chip Cookies

Prep: 15 min Bake: 13 min per sheet

1⅓   cups sugar
¾   cup butter or margarine, softened
1   tablespoon finely chopped fresh mint leaves
1   egg
2   cups Gold Medal all-purpose flour
1   teaspoon baking soda
½   teaspoon salt
1   package (10 ounces) mint-chocolate chips (1½ cups)

1. Heat oven to 350°. Beat sugar, butter, mint and egg in large bowl with electric mixer on medium speed, or mix with spoon. Stir in flour, baking soda and salt. Stir in chocolate chips.

2. Drop dough by rounded tablespoonfuls about 2 inches apart onto ungreased cookie sheet. Bake 11 to 13 minutes or until golden brown. Cool 1 to 2 minutes; remove from cookie sheet to wire rack.

About 3½ dozen cookies.

1 Cookie: Calories 120 (Calories from Fat 55); Fat 6g (Saturated 3g); Cholesterol 15mg; Sodium 90mg; Carbohydrate 15g (Dietary Fiber 0g); Protein 1g
% Daily Value: Vitamin A 2%; Vitamin C 0%; Calcium 2%; Iron 2%
Exchanges: ½ Starch, ½ Fruit, 1 Fat

BETTY'S TIPS

⊘ **Substitution**
You can substitute ¼ teaspoon mint extract for the chopped mint leaves.

⊘ **Serve-With**
Fresh mint makes these cookies so very cool and refreshing. They would be great on a hot summer afternoon served with iced tea.

⊘ **Variation**
For **Mint Raspberry Chocolate Chip Cookies**, use raspberry chocolate chips instead of the mint variety.

Chewy Oatmeal Snack Bars

Prep: 10 min Cook: 5 min Chill: 2 hr

½   cup butter or margarine
⅔   cup packed brown sugar
⅔   cup maple-flavored syrup
⅔   cup crunchy peanut butter
1   teaspoon vanilla
3   cups quick-cooking oats
1   cup wheat germ
1   cup graham cracker crumbs
1   cup cherry- or orange-flavored sweetened dried cranberries

1. Grease bottom and sides of rectangular pan, 13 × 9 × 2 inches, with shortening. Melt butter in 2-quart saucepan over medium heat. Stir in brown sugar and maple syrup; heat to boiling. Boil 1 minute, stirring frequently; remove from heat. Stir in peanut butter and vanilla until mixture is smooth.

2. Stir remaining ingredients into peanut butter mixture, mixing well. Press evenly in pan. Cover and refrigerate about 2 hours or until firm. For bars, cut into 6 rows by 4 rows. Store covered in refrigerator.

24 bars.

1 Bar: Calories 160 (Calories from Fat 80); Fat 9g (Saturated 3g); Cholesterol 10mg; Sodium 90mg; Carbohydrate 31g (Dietary Fiber 16g); Protein 5g
% Daily Value: Vitamin A 2%; Vitamin C 0%; Calcium 2%; Iron 6%
Exchanges: 1 Starch, 1 Fruit, ½ Fat

BETTY'S TIPS

⊘ **Substitution**
Honey can be used instead of the maple syrup, and old-fashioned oats can be used instead of the quick-cooking oats.

⊘ **Success Hint**
These bars can be stored at room temperature, but the texture will be softer. For an easy grab-and-go treat, after cutting bars, wrap them separately in plastic wrap and store in a resealable plastic bag in the fridge. They'll keep up to a week, but there may not be any left by then!

Chewy Oatmeal Snack Bars

Fresh Mint Chocolate Chip Cookies

Key Lime Bars

Prep: 15 min Bake: 35 min Cool: 30 min Chill: 3 hr

1½ cups graham cracker crumbs (20 squares)
⅓ cup butter or margarine, melted
3 tablespoons sugar
1 package (8 ounces) cream cheese, softened
1 can (14 ounces) sweetened condensed milk
¼ cup Key lime juice or regular lime juice
1 tablespoon grated lime peel
    Additional lime peel, if desired

1. Heat oven to 350°. Grease bottom and sides of square pan, 9 × 9 × 2 inches, with shortening.

2. Mix cracker crumbs, butter and sugar thoroughly with fork. Press evenly in bottom of pan. Refrigerate while preparing cream cheese mixture.

3. Beat cream cheese in small bowl with electric mixer on medium speed until light and fluffy. Gradually beat in milk until smooth. Beat in lime juice and lime peel. Spread over layer in pan.

4. Bake about 35 minutes or until center is set. Cool 30 minutes. Cover loosely and refrigerate at least 3 hours until chilled. For bars, cut into 6 rows by 6 rows. Garnish with additional lime peel. Store covered in refrigerator.

36 bars.

1 Bar: Calories 110 (Calories from Fat 55); Fat 6g (Saturated 3g); Cholesterol 15mg; Sodium 70mg; Carbohydrate 12g (Dietary Fiber 0g); Protein 2g
% Daily Value: Vitamin A 4%; Vitamin C 0%; Calcium 4%; Iron 0%
Exchanges: ½ Starch, ½ Fruit, 1 Fat

BETTY'S TIPS

⊙ **Variation**
If you love lemon, you can substitute lemon juice and lemon peel for the Key lime juice and lime peel.

Key Lime Bars

Butterscotch-Macadamia Nut Bars

Prep: 15 min Bake: 30 min Cool: 1 hr

¾ cup butter or margarine
1½ cups packed brown sugar
1 tablespoon vanilla
2 eggs
2 cups Gold Medal all-purpose flour
1½ teaspoons baking powder
1 cup coarsely chopped macadamia nuts
1 cup butterscotch-flavored chips

1. Heat oven to 350°. Grease bottom and sides of rectangular pan, 13 × 9 × 2 inches, with shortening. Heat butter and brown sugar in 3-quart saucepan over low heat about 5 minutes, stirring occasionally, until butter is melted; remove from heat.

2. Pour sugar mixture into large bowl. Add vanilla and eggs; beat with electric mixer on medium speed until blended, or mix with spoon. Add flour and baking powder; beat until well blended. Stir in ½ cup each of the nuts and butterscotch chips. Pour mixture into pan. Sprinkle with remaining nuts and chips.

3. Bake 25 to 30 minutes or until top is golden brown and center is set. Cool completely, about 1 hour. For bars, cut into 8 rows by 6 rows.

48 bars.

1 Bar: Calories 110 (Calories from Fat 55); Fat 6g (Saturated 3g); Cholesterol 15mg; Sodium 50mg; Carbohydrate 13g (Dietary Fiber 0g); Protein 1g
% Daily Value: Vitamin A 2%; Vitamin C 0%; Calcium 2%; Iron 2%
Exchanges: 1 Starch, 1 Fat

BETTY'S TIPS

⊘ **Substitution**
Toasted sliced almonds can be substituted for the macadamia nuts.

⊘ **Success Hint**
Because of their high fat content, macadamia nuts should be stored in the refrigerator or freezer to prevent them from becoming rancid.

⊘ **The Finishing Touch**
For a fun twist, serve these bars on skewers, threading them alternately with berries or dried fruit.

Butterscotch-Macadamia Nut Bars

Christmas Tree Brownies

Prep: 15 min Bake: 55 min Cool: 1 hr

1   package Betty Crocker Supreme® chocolate
     chunk brownie mix
3   tablespoons water
½   cup vegetable oil
2   eggs
     Vanilla Butter Frosting (below)
     Candy-coated chocolate candies
8   pretzel nuggets

1. Heat oven to 325°. Grease bottom only of round pan,
9 × 1½ inches, with shortening. Make brownie mix as
directed on package, using water, oil and eggs. Pour
into pan. Bake 50 to 55 minutes or until toothpick inserted 2 inches from side of pan comes out almost
clean. Cool completely, about 1 hour.

2. Make Vanilla Butter Frosting; spread frosting evenly
over brownies.

3. To serve, cut into 8 wedges. Decorate wedges with
candies to look like Christmas tree lights. Center
pretzel nugget on bottom edge of each brownie
wedge for tree trunk.

8 servings.

Vanilla Butter Frosting
 ½   cup butter or margarine, softened
 2   cups powdered sugar
 1   teaspoon vanilla
1 to 2 tablespoons milk
3 or 4 drops green food color

Mix butter, powdered sugar and vanilla with spoon
until smooth. Stir in milk until spreadable. Stir in
food color.

1 Serving: Calories 700 (Calories from Fat 280); Fat 31g (Saturated 11g);
Cholesterol 85mg; Sodium 300mg; Carbohydrate 102g (Dietary Fiber 0g);
Protein 4g
% Daily Value: Vitamin A 10%; Vitamin C 0%; Calcium 6%; Iron 12%
Exchanges: Not Recommended

BETTY'S TIPS

⊙ **Variation**
Bake brownies in a square or rectangular pan, as directed
on the package. Prepare frosting, adding 1 teaspoon mint extract. Cut brownies into squares and decorate with foil-
wrapped rectangular chocolate mints, unwrapped and
chopped.

Christmas Tree Brownies

Chocolate Chip Cookie Dough Brownies

Prep: 15 min Bake: 40 min Cool: 1 hr

1 package Betty Crocker Original Supreme® brownie mix (with chocolate syrup pouch)

⅓ cup vegetable oil

¼ cup water

2 eggs

1 pouch Betty Crocker® chocolate chip cookie mix

½ cup butter or margarine, softened

1 egg

Dark Chocolate Frosting (right)

1. Heat oven to 350°. Grease bottom only of rectangular baking pan, 13 × 9 × 2 inches, with shortening. Make brownie mix as directed on package, using oil, water and 2 eggs. Spread in pan.

2. Make cookie mix as directed on pouch, using butter and 1 egg. Drop dough by rounded tablespoonfuls evenly onto brownie batter; press down lightly.

3. Bake 35 to 40 minutes or until toothpick inserted 2 inches from side of pan comes out almost clean. Cool completely, about 1 hour. Frost with Dark Chocolate Frosting. For brownies, cut into 8 rows by 6 rows.

48 brownies.

Dark Chocolate Frosting

3 tablespoons butter or margarine

2 tablespoons corn syrup

2 tablespoons water

2 ounces unsweetened baking chocolate, chopped

2 teaspoons vanilla

¾ to 1 cup powdered sugar

Heat butter, corn syrup and water to boiling in 1-quart saucepan; remove from heat. Stir in chocolate until melted. Beat in vanilla and enough powdered sugar, using wire whisk, until spreadable.

1 Brownie: Calories 180 (Calories from Fat 80); Fat 9g (Saturated 3g); Cholesterol 20mg; Sodium 100mg; Carbohydrate 23g (Dietary Fiber 0g); Protein 2g
% Daily Value: Vitamin A 6%; Vitamin C 0%; Calcium 2%; Iron 4%
Exchanges: ½ Starch, 1 Fruit, 2 Fat

BETTY'S TIPS

❂ **Time-Saver**
The Dark Chocolate Frosting is certainly delicious, but if time is short, simply serve these chewy bars plain or lightly sprinkled with powdered sugar.

❂ **Did You Know?**
This is one of those little secrets we know you'll love! Cutting brownies or any bar with a chewy and dense texture is much easier when using a plastic knife.

Chocolate Chip Cookie Dough Brownies

Betty's Classic Oatmeal Brownies

Betty's Classic Oatmeal Brownies

Prep: 15 min Bake: 50 min Cool: 2 hr

2½ cups quick-cooking or old-fashioned oats
¾ cup Gold Medal all-purpose flour
¾ cup packed brown sugar
½ teaspoon baking soda
¾ cup butter or margarine, melted
1 package Betty Crocker Original Supreme brownie mix (with chocolate syrup pouch)
⅓ cup water
⅓ cup vegetable oil
2 or 3 eggs
½ cup chopped nuts

1. Heat oven to 350°. Grease bottom only of rectangular pan, 13 × 9 × 2 inches, with shortening, or spray with cooking spray.

2. Mix oats, flour, brown sugar and baking soda in medium bowl; stir in butter. Reserve 1 cup of the oat mixture. Press remaining oat mixture in pan. Bake 10 minutes; cool 5 minutes.

3. Stir brownie mix, chocolate syrup, water, oil and 2 eggs for fudgelike brownies (or 3 eggs for cakelike brownies) in medium bowl, using spoon, until well blended. Stir in nuts. Spread over baked layer; sprinkle with reserved oat mixture.

4. Bake 35 to 40 minutes or until toothpick inserted 2 inches from side of pan comes out clean or almost clean. Cool completely, about 2 hours. For brownies, cut into 8 rows by 6 rows. Store tightly covered.

48 brownies.

1 Brownie: Calories 135 (Calories from Fat 55); Fat 6g (Saturated 3g); Cholesterol 15mg; Sodium 80mg; Carbohydrate 19g (Dietary Fiber 1g); Protein 2g
% Daily Value: Vitamin A 2%; Vitamin C 0%; Calcium 0%; Iron 2%
Exchanges: 1 Starch, 1 Fat

BETTY'S TIPS

✪ Pack 'n Go
These totally transportable brownies are sure to be a big hit at your next get-together. Pack a plastic knife (rather than a sharp knife) to easily cut the brownies.

✪ Did You Know?
Quick-cooking and old-fashioned rolled oats are interchangeable unless a recipe calls for a specific type. Instant oatmeal products, on the other hand, are not the same and should not be used for baking.

Coconut, Pineapple and Macadamia Scones

Prep: 10 min Bake: 14 min

2½ cups Original Bisquick mix
¼ cup sugar
¼ cup firm butter or margarine
½ cup flaked coconut
½ cup chopped macadamia nuts
¼ cup whipping (heavy) cream
1 egg
1 can (8 ounces) pineapple tidbits, well drained

1. Heat oven to 425°. Spray cookie sheet with cooking spray. Mix Bisquick mix and sugar in large bowl. Cut in butter, using pastry blender or crisscrossing 2 knives, until crumbly. Stir in remaining ingredients.

2. Pat dough into 10 × 7-inch rectangle on cookie sheet (if dough is sticky, dip fingers in Bisquick mix). Cut into 12 rectangles, but do not separate. Sprinkle with additional sugar and coconut if desired.

3. Bake 12 to 14 minutes or until golden brown; carefully separate scones. Serve warm.

12 scones.

1 Scone: Calories 240 (Calories from Fat 125); Fat 14g (Saturated 6g); Cholesterol 35mg; Sodium 410mg; Carbohydrate 25g (Dietary Fiber 1g); Protein 3g
% Daily Value: Vitamin A 4%; Vitamin C 0%; Calcium 6%; Iron 6%
Exchanges: 1 Starch, ½ Fruit, 3 Fat

BETTY'S TIPS

✪ **Substitution**
Crazy for nuts? Try substituting pecans or almonds for the macadamia nuts in this sweet scone. Or use a combination of nuts.

✪ **Serve-With**
Toss together a bowl of assorted fresh fruit pieces or pour glasses of your favorite juice blend to serve with these tropical scones. Don't forget the butter and honey or jam!

Cherry-Chocolate Chip Scones

Prep: 20 min Bake: 15 min

2 cups Original Bisquick mix
⅓ cup finely chopped dried cherries
⅓ cup miniature semisweet chocolate chips
3 tablespoons sugar
⅓ cup whipping (heavy) cream
1 egg
About 1 tablespoon milk
About 1 tablespoon coarse sugar

1. Heat oven to 425°. Grease cookie sheet with shortening. Stir Bisquick mix, cherries, chocolate chips, 3 tablespoons sugar, the whipping cream and egg until soft dough forms.

2. Place dough on surface sprinkled with Bisquick mix; gently roll in Bisquick mix to coat. Shape into a ball; knead 10 times. Pat dough into 8-inch circle on cookie sheet. Brush dough with milk; sprinkle with 1 tablespoon sugar. Cut into 8 wedges, but do not separate.

3. Bake 12 to 15 minutes or until golden brown; carefully separate wedges. Serve warm.

8 scones.

1 Scone: Calories 230 (Calories from Fat 90); Fat 10g (Saturated 4g); Cholesterol 40mg; Sodium 440mg; Carbohydrate 33g (Dietary Fiber 1g); Protein 3g
% Daily Value: Vitamin A 2%; Vitamin C 0%; Calcium 6%; Iron 6%
Exchanges: 1 Starch, 1 Fruit, 2 Fat

BETTY'S TIPS

✪ **Substitution**
Pick your favorite fruit! Dried apricots, cranberries and blueberries are great stand-ins for the dried cherries.

✪ **Did You Know?**
Scones are a Scottish quick bread that come in a variety of shapes-triangles, circles, squares, diamonds and rectangles. They can be sweet or savory and are traditionally served for tea and now more often at breakfast and brunches.

Coconut, Pineapple and Macadamia Scones

Cherry-Chocolate Chip Scones

Glazed Raisin-Cinnamon Biscuits

Prep: 15 min Bake: 10 min
(Photo on page 241)

2½ cups Original Bisquick mix
½ cup raisins
⅔ cup milk
2 tablespoons granulated sugar
1 teaspoon ground cinnamon
  Vanilla Glaze (right)

1. Heat oven to 450°. Stir all ingredients except Vanilla Glaze just until soft dough forms.

2. Place dough on surface generously dusted with Bisquick mix; gently roll in Bisquick mix to coat. Shape into ball; knead 10 times. Roll ½ inch thick. Cut with 2½-inch cutter dipped in Bisquick mix. Place 2 inches apart on ungreased cookie sheet.

3. Bake 8 to 10 minutes or until golden brown. While biscuits are baking, make Vanilla Glaze. Spread glaze over warm biscuits.

12 to 15 biscuits.

Vanilla Glaze
⅔ cup powdered sugar
1 tablespoon warm water
¼ teaspoon vanilla

Beat all ingredients with spoon until smooth.

1 Biscuit: Calories 165 (Calories from Fat 35); Fat 4g (Saturated 1g); Cholesterol 0mg; Sodium 360mg; Carbohydrate 30g (Dietary Fiber 1g); Protein 2g
% Daily Value: Vitamin A 0%; Vitamin C 0%; Calcium 6%; Iron 4%
Exchanges: 1 Starch, 1 Fruit, 1 Fat

BETTY'S TIPS

✸ Substitution
Dried sweetened cranberries can be used in place of the raisins. Their slight tartness gives these biscuits a different flavor.

✸ Success Hint
If you don't have a round biscuit cutter, a glass that's 2½ inches in diameter is a good substitute.

✸ Variation
To make **Glazed Raisin-Cinnamon Drop Biscuits**, instead of kneading and rolling, drop dough by 12 to 15 rounded spoonfuls onto ungreased cookie sheet. Bake 10 to 12 minutes or until golden brown.

Orange-Almond Streusel Muffins

Prep: 20 min Bake: 15 min

Streusel Topping (right)
1   teaspoon grated orange peel
½   cup orange juice
⅓   cup packed brown sugar
¼   cup vegetable oil
½   teaspoon almond extract
1   egg
2   cups Original Bisquick mix
¼   cup sliced almonds

1. Heat oven to 400°. Grease bottoms only of 12 medium muffin cups, 2½ × 1¼ inches with shortening; or line muffin cups with paper baking cups. Make Streusel Topping; set aside.

2. Mix orange peel, orange juice, brown sugar, oil, almond extract and egg in large bowl. Stir in Bisquick mix just until moistened. Stir in almonds. Divide batter evenly among muffin cups. Sprinkle with topping.

3. Bake 13 to 15 minutes or until golden brown. Immediately remove from pan to wire rack. Serve warm.

12 muffins.

Streusel Topping
1   tablespoon Original Bisquick mix
2   tablespoons packed brown sugar
2   tablespoons sliced almonds
1   tablespoon butter or margarine

Mix Bisquick mix, brown sugar and almonds in medium bowl. Cut in butter, using fork, until crumbly.

1 Muffin: Calories 190 (Calories from Fat 90); Fat 10g (Saturated 2g); Cholesterol 20mg; Sodium 310mg; Carbohydrate 22g (Dietary Fiber 1g); Protein 3g
% Daily Value: Vitamin A 0%; Vitamin C 2%; Calcium 4%; Iron 6%
Exchanges: 1 Starch, ½ Fruit, 2 Fat

BETTY'S TIPS

☺ **Serve-With**
Serve these muffins warm with honey butter or cream cheese. Add fresh fruit and hot tea for a light breakfast or snack.

Orange-Almond Streusel Muffins

Raspberry-White Chocolate Muffins

Chocolate-Pistachio Bread

Raspberry-White Chocolate Muffins

Prep: 6 min Bake: 18 min Cool: 5 min

2 cups Original Bisquick mix
½ cup white baking chips
⅓ cup sugar
⅔ cup milk
2 tablespoons vegetable oil
1 egg
1 cup raspberries

1. Heat oven to 400°. Grease bottoms only of 12 medium muffin cups, 2½ X 1¼ inches, with shortening; or line muffin cups with paper baking cups.

2. Stir all ingredients except raspberries in large bowl just until moistened. Fold in raspberries. Divide batter evenly among muffin cups.

3. Bake 15 to 18 minutes or until golden brown. Cool 5 minutes; remove from pan to wire rack. Serve warm.

12 muffins.

1 Muffin: Calories 305 (Calories from Fat 215); Fat 24g (Saturated 13g); Cholesterol 175mg; Sodium 440mg; Carbohydrate 8g (Dietary Fiber 0g); Protein 14g
% Daily Value: Vitamin A 18%; Vitamin C 2%; Calcium 22%; Iron 4%
Exchanges: ½ Starch, 2 High-Fat Meat, 1 Fat

BETTY'S TIPS

✿ **Substitution**
For those who have blackberries or blueberries on hand, those berries can be used instead of the raspberries.

✿ **Special Touch**
For a sweet finish, dip muffin tops into melted butter and then into coarse sugar crystals or granulated sugar. Another dazzler—drizzle tops with melted white baking chips.

Chocolate-Pistachio Bread

Prep: 15 min Bake: 55 min Cool: 2 hr 10 min

⅔ cup granulated sugar
½ cup butter or margarine, melted
¾ cup milk
1 egg
1½ cups Gold Medal all-purpose flour
1 cup chopped pistachio nuts
½ cup semisweet chocolate chips
⅓ cup baking cocoa
2 teaspoons baking powder
¼ teaspoon salt
Coarse sugar crystals (decorating sugar), if desired

1. Heat oven to 350°. Grease bottom and sides of loaf pan, 9 X 5 X 3 inches, with shortening. Mix granulated sugar, butter, milk and egg in large bowl until well blended. Stir in remaining ingredients except sugar crystals. Pour into pan. Sprinkle with sugar crystals.

2. Bake 50 to 55 minutes or until toothpick inserted in center comes out clean. Cool 10 minutes. Loosen sides of loaf from pan; remove from pan to wire rack. Cool completely, about 2 hours, before slicing.

1 loaf (24 slices).

1 Slice: Calories 145 (Calories from Fat 70); Fat 8g (Saturated 4g); Cholesterol 20mg; Sodium 100mg; Carbohydrate 16g (Dietary Fiber 1g); Protein 3g
% Daily Value: Vitamin A 4%; Vitamin C 0%; Calcium 4%; Iron 6%
Exchanges: 1 Starch, 1½ Fat

BETTY'S TIPS

✿ **Substitution**
Chopped walnuts can be substituted for the pistachio nuts for delicious **Chocolate-Walnut Bread.**

✿ **Do-Ahead**
You may tightly wrap and store this bread in the refrigerator for up to 1 week.

Betty... MAKES IT EASY

Apple-Cream Cheese Coffee Cake

Prep: 25 min Bake: 15 min Cool: 2 hr 10 min

Cream Cheese Filling (right)
1 package (3 ounces) cream cheese
¼ cup firm butter or margarine
2 cups Original Bisquick mix
⅓ cup milk
2 tablespoons sugar
½ teaspoon ground cinnamon
1 can (21 ounces) apple pie filling
¼ cup chopped walnuts

Fold strips over filling, overlapping strips.

1. Heat oven to 425°. Lightly grease cookie sheet with short-ening. Make Cream Cheese Filling.

2. Cut cream cheese and butter into Bisquick mix in medium bowl, using pastry blender or crisscrossing 2 knives, until crumbly. Stir in milk until soft dough forms. Place dough on surface well dusted with Bisquick mix; roll in Bisquick mix to coat. Knead 8 to 10 times.

3. Roll dough into 12 × 8-inch rectangle. Place on cookie sheet. Spread Cream Cheese Filling down center of rec-tangle. Make 2½-inch cuts at 1-inch intervals on 12-inch sides of rectangle. Fold strips over filling, overlapping strips. Mix sugar and cinnamon; sprinkle over top.

4. Bake 12 to 15 minutes or until golden; cool 10 minutes. Carefully place on wire rack; cool completely, about 2 hours. Spoon pie filling down center of coffee cake. Sprinkle with walnuts. Store covered in refrigerator.

Cream Cheese Filling
1 package (8 ounces) cream cheese, softened
⅓ cup sugar
1 teaspoon grated lemon peel
2 teaspoons lemon juice

Beat all ingredients with electric mixer on medium speed until smooth.

10 servings.

1 Serving: Calories 365 (Calories from Fat 190); Fat 21g (Saturated 11g); Cholesterol 45mg; Sodium 470mg; Carbohydrate 40g (Dietary Fiber 1g); Protein 5g
% Daily Value: Vitamin A 12%; Vitamin C 0%; Calcium 8%; Iron 8%
Exchanges: 2 Starch, 1 Fruit, 3 Fat

Apple-Cream Cheese Coffee Cake

Blueberry-Banana Oat Bread

Prep: 10 min Bake: 55 min Cool: 2 hr 10 min

2¼ cups Original Bisquick mix

⅔ cup sugar

⅓ cup quick-cooking oats

1 cup mashed very ripe bananas (2 medium)

¼ cup milk

2 eggs

1 cup fresh or frozen (thawed and drained) blueberries

1. Heat oven to 350°. Grease bottom only of loaf pan, 9 × 5 × 3 inches, with shortening.

2. Stir Bisquick mix, sugar, oats, bananas, milk and eggs in large bowl until moistened; beat vigorously 30 seconds. Gently stir in blueberries. Pour into pan.

3. Bake 50 to 55 minutes or until toothpick inserted in center comes out clean. Cool 10 minutes. Loosen loaf from sides of pan; remove from pan and place top side up on wire rack. Cool completely, about 2 hours, before slicing.

1 loaf (24 slices).

1 Slice: Calories 90 (Calories from Fat 20); Fat 2g (Saturated 1g); Cholesterol 20mg; Sodium 170mg; Carbohydrate 16g (Dietary Fiber 1g); Protein 2g
% Daily Value: Vitamin A 0%; Vitamin C 0%; Calcium 2%; Iron 2%
Exchanges: 1 Starch

BETTY'S TIPS

⊙ **Substitution**
Try using fresh raspberries instead of the blueberries in this flavorful moist bread.

⊙ **Success Hint**
Most quick breads are removed from their pans to a wire rack. This produces a drier, crisper surface. If left in the pan, the bread would become steamed and soft.

To store, wrap tightly and keep at room temperature up to 4 days or refrigerate up to 10 days.

Blueberry-Banana Oat Bread

Cinnamon Bubble Loaf

Prep: 10 min   Bake: 30 min   Stand: 10 min

2   tablespoons granulated sugar
1½ teaspoons ground cinnamon
3½ cups Original Bisquick mix
½   cup milk
⅓   cup granulated sugar
3   tablespoons butter or margarine, softened
1   teaspoon vanilla
1   egg
2   tablespoons butter or margarine, melted
    Powdered Sugar Glaze (below), if desired

1. Heat oven to 375°. Grease bottom and sides of loaf pan, 9 × 5 × 3 inches, with shortening. Mix 2 tablespoons sugar and the cinnamon; set aside.

2. Stir Bisquick mix, milk, ⅓ cup sugar, 3 tablespoons butter, the vanilla and egg in medium bowl until soft dough forms. Shape dough into 1-inch balls; roll in cinnamon-sugar. Place dough randomly in pan. Sprinkle with any remaining cinnamon-sugar; drizzle melted butter over dough balls.

3. Bake 25 to 30 minutes or until golden brown. Let stand in pan 10 minutes. Remove from pan to wire rack. Make Powdered Sugar Glaze; drizzle over loaf. Cut into slices. Serve warm.

1 loaf (12 slices).

Powdered Sugar Glaze
½   cup powdered sugar
2 to 3   teaspoons water

Mix ingredients until thin enough to drizzle.

1 Slice: Calories 240 (Calories from Fat 90); Fat 10g (Saturated 4g); Cholesterol 30mg; Sodium 540mg; Carbohydrate 35g (Dietary Fiber 1g); Protein 3g
% Daily Value: Vitamin A 4%; Vitamin C 0%; Calcium 8%; Iron 6%
Exchanges: 1 Starch, 1 Fruit, 2 Fat

BETTY'S TIPS

✿ **Time-Saver**
Save time by letting the kids help! Mix the sugar and cinnamon in a plastic food-storage bag and have the little ones shake the pieces of dough in the mixture.

✿ **Serve-With**
Treat your friends to this yummy bread for breakfast after a sleepover. Add orange juice, bananas and grapes to complete the meal.

Cinnamon Bubble Loaf

Betty's Classic Cheddar Cheese Biscuits

Easy Puff Twists

Quick

Betty's Classic Cheddar Cheese Biscuits

Prep: 10 min Bake: 10 min

  2   cups Original Bisquick
  ⅔   cup milk
  ½   cup shredded Cheddar cheese (2 ounces)
  ¼   cup butter or margarine, melted
  ¼   teaspoon garlic powder, if desired

1. Heat oven to 450°. Mix Bisquick, milk and cheese until soft dough forms; beat vigorously 30 seconds. Drop dough by 10 to 12 spoonfuls about 2 inches apart onto ungreased cookie sheet.

2. Bake 8 to 10 minutes or until golden brown. Mix butter and garlic powder; brush on warm biscuits before removing from cookie sheet. Serve warm.

10 to 12 biscuits.

1 Biscuit: Calories 220 (Calories from Fat 110); Fat 12g (Saturated 5g); Cholesterol 20mg; Sodium 580mg; Carbohydrate 23g (Dietary Fiber 0g); Protein 4g
% Daily Value: Vitamin A 4%; Vitamin C 0%; Calcium 10%; Iron 6%
Exchanges: 1½ Starch, 2 Fat

BETTY'S TIPS

✿ **Health Twist**
For 2 grams of fat and 100 calories per serving, use Reduced Fat Bisquick, fat-free (skim) milk and reduced-fat Cheddar cheese. Omit butter. Increase garlic powder to ½ teaspoon and stir in with the Bisquick. Spray warm biscuits with butter-flavored cooking spray if desired.

✿ **Variation**
To make **Herbed Cheese Biscuits**, stir in ¾ teaspoon dried dill weed, crumbled dried rosemary leaves or Italian seasoning with the Bisquick.

Easy Puff Twists

Prep: 25 min Bake: 8 min per sheet

  ⅔   cup grated Parmesan cheese
  1   tablespoon paprika
  1   package (17.3 ounces) frozen puff pastry, thawed
  1   egg, slightly beaten

1. Heat oven to 425°. Cover 2 cookie sheets with cooking parchment paper or heavy brown paper. Mix cheese and paprika. Roll 1 sheet of pastry into 12 × 10-inch rectangle on lightly floured surface with floured cloth-covered rolling pin.

2. Brush egg over pastry. Sprinkle with 3 tablespoons of the cheese mixture; press gently into pastry. Turn pastry over. Brush egg over other side of pastry. Sprinkle with 3 tablespoons of the cheese mixture; press gently into pastry. Fold pastry lengthwise in half.

3. Cut pastry crosswise into ½-inch strips. Unfold strips; roll each end in opposite direction to twist. Place twists on cookie sheet. Bake 7 to 8 minutes or until puffed and golden brown. Remove from cookie sheet to wire rack. Repeat with remaining sheet of pastry, egg and cheese mixture. Serve twists warm or cool.

48 twists.

1 Twist: Calories 60 (Calories from Fat 35); Fat 4g (Saturated 2g); Cholesterol 15mg; Sodium 55mg; Carbohydrate 5g (Dietary Fiber 0g); Protein 1g
% Daily Value: Vitamin A 2%; Vitamin C 0%; Calcium 2%; Iron 2%
Exchanges: ½ Starch, ½ Fat

BETTY'S TIPS

✿ **Variation**
For a garlicky twist, mix 2 teaspoons garlic powder with the Parmesan cheese mixture.

✿ **Special Touch**
For an appetizer-size bread that will melt in your mouth, cut twists in half before baking. Serve with cheese and fruit.

Grilled Garlic Bread with Rosemary

Prep: 10 min Grill: 15 min
(Photo on page 241)

1 loaf (1 pound) unsliced French bread
½ cup butter or margarine, softened
2 tablespoons chopped fresh or 2 teaspoons dried rosemary leaves
1 tablespoon chopped fresh parsley or 1 teaspoon parsley flakes
¼ to ½ teaspoon garlic powder

1. Heat coals or gas grill for direct heat. Cut bread loaf into 1-inch slices without cutting through bottom of loaf. Mix remaining ingredients; spread on both sides of bread slices. Wrap bread loaf in heavy-duty aluminum foil.

2. Cover and grill bread 5 to 6 inches from medium heat 10 to 15 minutes, turning once, until hot.

12 slices.

1 Slice: Calories 165 (Calories from Fat 80); Fat 9g (Saturated 5g); Cholesterol 20mg; Sodium 270mg; Carbohydrate 19g (Dietary Fiber 1g); Protein 3g
% Daily Value: Vitamin A 6%; Vitamin C 0%; Calcium 2%; Iron 6%
Exchanges: 1 Starch, 1 Fat

BETTY'S TIPS

✪ **Substitution**
Basil would make a nice substitution for the rosemary if you prefer its mild flavor.

✪ **Variation**
If you prefer to bake this bread, heat the oven to 400° and prepare bread as directed. Wrap the bread in aluminum foil and bake about 15 minutes or until hot.

Pesto Biscuits

Prep: 15 min Bake: 12 min
(Photo on page xi)

2 cups Gold Medal all-purpose flour
3 teaspoons baking powder
½ teaspoon salt
⅓ cup shortening
¼ cup basil pesto
   About ½ cup milk
   Finely shredded Parmesan cheese, if desired

1. Heat oven to 450°. Mix flour, baking powder and salt in large bowl. Cut in shortening and pesto, using pastry blender or crisscrossing 2 knives, until mixture looks like fine crumbs. Stir in just enough milk so dough leaves side of bowl and forms a ball.

2. Place dough on lightly floured surface. Knead lightly 10 times. Roll or pat ½ inch thick. Cut with floured 2½-inch cookie or biscuit cutter. Place about 1 inch apart on ungreased cookie sheet. Sprinkle with cheese.

3. Bake 10 to 12 minutes or until golden brown. Immediately remove from cookie sheet. Serve warm.

10 biscuits.

1 Biscuit: Calories 190 (Calories from Fat 100); Fat 11g (Saturated 3g); Cholesterol 0mg; Sodium 330mg; Carbohydrate 20g (Dietary Fiber 1g); Protein 4g
% Daily Value: Vitamin A 0%; Vitamin C 0%; Calcium 12%; Iron 8%
Exchanges: 1 Starch, 1 Vegetable, 2 Fat

BETTY'S TIPS

✪ **Variation**
Use 1½-inch cookie cutters to make bite-size biscuits and serve as an appetizer with red or green hot pepper (jalapeño) jelly.

✪ **Special Touch**
It's easy to get even your butter into the act of being festive. Slice chilled butter ¼ inch thick and cut slices with mini-cookie cutters. Use cutters with open tops so you can push the butter through. Simple shapes, such as stars and hearts, work best. Place butter on waxed paper; refrigerate until ready to serve. Butter scraps can be softened and reshaped or used in baking.

Indulgent Desserts

Cakes, Pies and More

Gingerbread-Orange Pudding Cake (page 265)

S'mores Dip (page 279)

Rum-Coconut Pound Cake

Prep: 15 min Bake: 1 hr Cool: 2 hr 30 min

1 package Betty Crocker SuperMoist® butter recipe yellow cake mix

1 package (4-serving size) vanilla instant pudding and pie filling mix

1 cup water

½ cup butter or margarine, softened

4 eggs

2 teaspoons rum extract

½ cup Betty Crocker Rich & Creamy® vanilla ready-to-spread frosting

½ teaspoon rum extract

¼ cup chopped pecans

¼ cup flaked coconut, toasted

1. Heat oven to 350°. Grease 12-cup bundt cake pan or 10 × 4-inch angel food cake pan (tube pan), with shortening; lightly flour. Beat cake mix, pudding mix, water, butter, eggs and 2 teaspoons rum extract in large bowl with electric mixer on low speed 30 seconds. Beat on medium speed 2 minutes. Pour into pan.

2. Bake 50 to 60 minutes or until toothpick inserted in center comes out clean. Cool 30 minutes; re-move from pan to wire rack. Cool completely, about 2 hours.

3. Place frosting in small microwavable bowl. Microwave uncovered on Medium (50%) 15 seconds. Stir in ½ teaspoon rum extract. Spread over top of cake, allowing some to drizzle down side. Sprinkle pecans and coconut over top of cake. Store loosely covered.

16 servings.

1 Serving: Calories 290 (Calories from Fat 115); Fat 13g (Saturated 6g); Cholesterol 70mg; Sodium 380mg; Carbohydrate 40g (Dietary Fiber 0g); Protein 3g
% Daily Value: Vitamin A 6%; Vitamin C 0%; Calcium 4%; Iron 4%
Exchanges: 1 Starch; 1½ Fruit; 3 Fat

BETTY'S TIPS

☺ **Success Hint**
 To toast coconut, bake uncovered in ungreased shallow pan in 350° oven 5 to 7 minutes, stirring occasionally, until golden brown.

Rum-Coconut Pound Cake

Gingerbread-Orange Pudding Cake

Prep: 15 min Bake: 40 min Cool: 30 min
(Photo on page 263)

1 package Betty Crocker® gingerbread cake and cookie mix
1 cup water
1 egg
⅔ cup packed brown sugar
½ cup water
½ cup orange juice
¼ cup butter or margarine
1½ teaspoons grated orange peel
Whipped cream or vanilla ice cream, if desired

BETTY'S TIPS

✪ Success Hint
When grating citrus fruits, make sure to grate just the brightly colored outer portion of the peel and not the white portion underneath. The white portion, or "pith," is bitter tasting.

✪ Special Touch
Instead of cutting this dessert into the usual 8 rectangles, try triangles. First cut the dessert into 4 squares, then cut each square diagonally in half to make triangles.

1. Heat oven to 350°. Mix gingerbread mix, 1 cup water and egg in ungreased square baking dish, 8 × 8 × 2 inches, using fork, until blended. Stir vigorously about 2 minutes, scraping corners frequently, until well mixed. Sprinkle brown sugar evenly over batter.

2. Heat ½ cup water, the orange juice and butter in 2-quart saucepan over high heat, stirring frequently, until mixture is hot and butter is melted. Stir in orange peel. Slowly pour over batter and brown sugar (some batter will rise to top).

3. Bake 35 to 40 minutes or until toothpick inserted in center comes out clean. Carefully remove from oven because cake floats on top of pudding layer (top of baked cake will have cracks). Cool 30 minutes. Serve warm with whipped cream.

8 servings.

1 Serving: Calories 410 (Calories from Fat 160); Fat 18g (Saturated 8g); Cholesterol 55mg; Sodium 430mg; Carbohydrate 59g (Dietary Fiber 0g); Protein 3g
% Daily Value: Vitamin A 10%; Vitamin C 6%; Calcium 2%; Iron 6%
Exchanges: Not Recommended

Nutty Chocolate Chip Picnic Cake

Double-Chocolate Cake with Broiled Topping

Nutty Chocolate Chip Picnic Cake

Prep: 15 min Bake: 35 min Cool: 1 hr

½ cup miniature semisweet chocolate chips
⅓ cup packed brown sugar
⅓ cup chopped pecans
1 package Betty Crocker SuperMoist devil's food cake mix
1⅓ cups water
½ cup vegetable oil
3 eggs

1. Heat oven to 350°. Grease bottom only of rectangular pan, 13 × 9 × 2 inches, with shortening, or spray with cooking spray.

2. Mix chocolate chips, brown sugar and pecans; set aside. Make cake mix as directed on package, using water, oil and eggs. Pour into pan. Sprinkle with chocolate chip mixture.

3. Bake 30 to 35 minutes or until toothpick inserted in center comes out clean. Cool completely, about 1 hour. Store tightly covered.

15 servings.

1 Serving: Calories 380 (Calories from Fat 200); Fat 22g (Saturated 6g); Cholesterol 50mg; Sodium 290mg; Carbohydrate 43g (Dietary Fiber 1g); Protein 4g
% Daily Value: Vitamin A 2%; Vitamin C 0%; Calcium 4%; Iron 10%
Exchanges: Not Recommended

BETTY'S TIPS

☺ **Serve-With**
Planning a party at home? Serve this take-along cake with your favorite ice cream. Chocolate, vanilla and caramel are just a few delicious possibilities.

☺ **Special Touch**
For an extra dose of decadence, drizzle the cake with caramel or hot fudge topping. Or frost with your favorite frosting.

Double-Chocolate Cake with Broiled Topping

Prep: 10 min Bake: 28 min Broil: 2 min

1 pouch Betty Crocker Snackin' Cake® chocolate chunk cake mix
¾ cup water
¼ cup quick-cooking oats
¼ cup packed brown sugar
2 tablespoons butter or margarine
2 tablespoons flaked coconut
2 tablespoons chopped pecans

1. Heat oven to 350°. Bake cake mix as directed on package, using ¾ cup water.

2. While cake is baking, mix oats and brown sugar in medium bowl. Cut in butter, using pastry blender or crisscrossing 2 knives, until mixture is well blended. Stir in coconut and pecans. Sprinkle over hot cake.

3. Set oven control to broil. Broil cake with top 4 to 6 inches from heat 1 to 2 minutes or until topping is light golden brown. Serve warm or cool.

8 servings.

1 Serving: Calories 385 (Calories from Fat 200); Fat 22g (Saturated 6g); Cholesterol 60mg; Sodium 230mg; Carbohydrate 45g (Dietary Fiber 2g); Protein 4g
% Daily Value: Vitamin A 4%; Vitamin C 0%; Calcium 6%; Iron 10%
Exchanges: Not Recommended

BETTY'S TIPS

☺ **Substitution**
The golden chocolate chip flavor of Betty Crocker Snackin' Cake mix can be substituted.

☺ **Serve-With**
Serve with scoops of vanilla ice cream and a drizzle of caramel, butterscotch or hot fudge sauce.

Chewy Turtle Snack Cake

Prep: 15 min Bake: 40 min Cool: 1 hr 30 min

¾ cup sugar

¼ cup plus 2 tablespoons butter or margarine, softened

2 ounces sweet baking chocolate, melted and cooled

1 cup Gold Medal all-purpose flour

½ teaspoon baking soda

⅛ teaspoon salt

½ teaspoon vanilla

¼ cup plus 2 tablespoons buttermilk

3 tablespoons water

2 eggs

Caramel Topping (below)

1 bag (10 to 11½ ounces) large semisweet chocolate chips, chunks or miniature kisses

½ cup chopped pecans

1. Heat oven to 350°. Grease bottom and sides of rectangular pan, 13 × 9 × 2 inches, with shortening; lightly flour.

2. Beat sugar and butter in large bowl with electric mixer on high speed about 3 minutes, scraping bowl occasionally, until fluffy. Beat in melted chocolate, flour, baking soda, salt, vanilla, buttermilk, water and eggs on medium speed until mixed. Pour into pan.

3. Bake about 20 minutes or until toothpick inserted in center comes out clean. Make Caramel Topping; spread over hot cake. Sprinkle with chocolate chips and pecans. Bake about 20 minutes longer or until chocolate chips are melted. Cool completely, about 1 hour 30 minutes.

16 servings.

Caramel Topping

½ cup butter or margarine

1 bag (14 ounces) caramels

1 can (5 ounces) evaporated milk

Heat all ingredients over medium heat, stirring constantly, until smooth.

1 Serving: Calories 415 (Calories from Fat 205); Fat 23g (Saturated 13g); Cholesterol 60mg; Sodium 210mg; Carbohydrate 48g (Dietary Fiber 2g); Protein 6g
% Daily Value: Vitamin A 10%; Vitamin C 0%; Calcium 6%; Iron 6%
Exchanges: Not Recommended

BETTY'S TIPS

✿ **Substitution**

No buttermilk on hand? Place 1¼ teaspoons lemon juice or white vinegar in a measuring cup, then add ¼ cup plus 2 tablespoons milk and stir. Let stand a few minutes before adding to the other ingredients.

✿ **Variation**

For **Chewy Chocolate-Peanut Turtle Snack Cake**, use ½ cup chopped dry-roasted peanuts instead of pecans and chocolate caramels instead of regular caramels.

Chewy Turtle Snack Cake

Mini Almond Cheesecakes

Prep: 15 min   Bake: 25 min   Cool: 15 min   Chill: 2 hr

12   vanilla wafers
 1   package (8 ounces) cream cheese, softened
 1   package (3 ounces) cream cheese, softened
¼   cup sugar
 2   tablespoons amaretto or ½ teaspoon almond extract
 2   eggs
¼   cup chopped almonds, toasted

1. Heat oven to 350°. Line 12 medium muffin cups, 2½ × 1¼ inches, with paper baking cups. Place 1 wafer, flat side down, in each cup.

2. Beat cream cheese and sugar in medium bowl with electric mixer on medium speed until fluffy. Beat in amaretto. Beat in eggs, one at a time. Fill cups ¾ full with cream cheese mixture. Sprinkle with almonds.

3. Bake 20 to 25 minutes or until centers are firm. Immediately remove from pan to wire rack. Cool 15 minutes. Cover and refrigerate at least 2 hours but no longer than 48 hours.

12 servings.

1 Serving: Calories 160 (Calories from Fat 110); Fat 12g (Saturated 6g); Cholesterol 65mg; Sodium 110mg; Carbohydrate 9g (Dietary Fiber 0g); Protein 4g
% Daily Value: Vitamin A 8%; Vitamin C 0%; Calcium 2%; Iron 4%
Exchanges: ½ Starch, 2½ Fat

BETTY'S TIPS

❂ **Substitution**
Two tablespoons rum or ½ teaspoon rum extract can be substituted for the amaretto.

❂ **Success Hint**
To toast nuts, heat oven to 350°. Spread nuts in ungreased shallow pan. Bake about 10 minutes, stirring occasionally, until golden brown and fragrant. Watch carefully because nuts brown quickly. Or cook nuts in ungreased heavy skillet over medium-low heat 5 to 7 minutes, stirring frequently until browning begins, then stirring constantly until golden brown and fragrant.

❂ **Do-Ahead**
These wonderful make-ahead cheesecakes can be refrigerated up to 48 hours or tucked away in the freezer. To freeze, refrigerate cheesecakes 1 hour or until completely cooled, then place in a labeled airtight freezer container and freeze up to 2 months. About 2 hours before serving, remove container lid and place frozen cheesecakes in refrigerator to thaw.

Mini Almond Cheesecakes

Almond Shortcake with Triple-Berry Sauce

Prep: 20 min Bake: 12 min Cool: 1 hr

2 cups Gold Medal all-purpose flour
½ cup sugar
3 teaspoons baking powder
½ teaspoon salt
½ cup butter or margarine
¾ cup milk
1 teaspoon almond extract
2 eggs, slightly beaten
1 tablespoon sugar
½ cup sliced almonds
   Triple-Berry Sauce (right)

1. Heat oven to 450°. Grease bottom and sides of rectangular pan, 13 × 9 × 2 inches, with shortening. Mix flour, ½ cup sugar, the baking powder and salt in medium bowl. Cut in butter, using pastry blender or crisscrossing 2 knives, until mixture looks like fine crumbs. Stir in milk, almond extract and eggs just until blended. Spread in pan. Sprinkle with 1 tablespoon sugar and the almonds.

2. Bake 10 to 12 minutes or until light golden brown. Cool completely, about 1 hour. Serve shortcake with Triple-Berry Sauce.

12 servings.

Triple-Berry Sauce
¾ cup sugar
4 teaspoons cornstarch
1½ cups water
4 to 6 drops red food color, if desired
4 cups sliced strawberries
1⅓ cups raspberries
1⅓ cups blueberries

Mix sugar and cornstarch in 2-quart saucepan. Stir in water. Cook over medium heat, stirring constantly, until mixture thickens and boils. Boil and stir 1 minute. Remove from heat; cool 10 minutes. Stir in food color and berries. Cover and refrigerate until serving.

1 Serving: Calories 320 (Calories from Fat 110); Fat 12g (Saturated 5g); Cholesterol 55mg; Sodium 290mg; Carbohydrate 49g (Dietary Fiber 2g); Protein 5g
% Daily Value: Vitamin A 8%; Vitamin C 26%; Calcium 10%; Iron 8%
Exchanges: 2 Starch, 1 Fruit, 2 Fat

BETTY'S TIPS

⚙ **Pack 'n Go**
This family-pleasing dessert is totally totable. Cover the pan of cooled shortcake and pack the Triple-Berry Sauce in a separate container.

⚙ **Variation**
If brunch is in the plans, the almond shortcake makes a great coffee cake. Serve it slightly warm from the oven with butter and strawberry jam.

⚙ **Special Touch**
Add a spoonful of whipped topping to each serving for an extra-special treat.

Almond Shortcake with Triple-Berry Sauce

Fruity Cake Bowls

Prep: 20 min Bake: 30 min Cool: 30 min

- 6 waffle ice-cream bowls, 3½ inches in diameter
- ¾ cup Gold Medal all-purpose flour
- ½ cup sugar
- ¼ cup butter or margarine, softened
- ¼ cup milk
- ½ teaspoon baking powder
- ½ teaspoon vanilla
- 1 egg
- 1½ cups cherry pie filling
  Refrigerated whipped cream topping (from 7-ounce can)
- 6 maraschino cherries with stems, if desired

1. Heat oven to 325°. Place each waffle bowl in 6-ounce custard cup or jumbo muffin cup (for support while baking). Place custard cups on cookie sheet.

2. Beat flour, sugar, butter, milk, baking powder, vanilla and egg in medium bowl with electric mixer on low speed 30 seconds, scraping bowl constantly. Beat on high speed 2 minutes, scraping bowl occasionally. Spoon about ¼ cup batter into each waffle bowl.

3. Bake 25 to 30 minutes or until toothpick inserted in center comes out clean. Remove bowls from custard cups to wire rack. Cool completely, about 30 minutes.

4. Spoon ¼ cup pie filling into each bowl. Add about 2 tablespoons whipped topping to each. Top each serving with a cherry.

6 servings.

1 Serving: Calories 470 (Calories from Fat 130); Fat 14g (Saturated 6g); Cholesterol 35mg; Sodium 170mg; Carbohydrate 82g (Dietary Fiber 3g); Protein 7g
% Daily Value: Vitamin A 8%; Vitamin C 0%; Calcium 6%; Iron 14%
Exchanges: Not recommended

BETTY'S TIPS

❂ **Pack 'n Go**
Make the cake bowls ahead and transport them in a large container. Bring along the pie filling and a can of whipped topping. Top the bowls when you arrive at your destination.

❂ **Success Hint**
This recipe can easily be doubled if you're feeding a large bunch. If you don't have enough custard cups, one batch of bowls can cool while the other batch bakes.

❂ **Variation**
Feel free to use any flavor of pie filling you like in this recipe.

If you're going to serve this at home, try topping with ice cream or frozen yogurt instead of the whipped topping.

Fruity Cake Bowls

Nutty Banana Cream Pie-in-a-Bowl

Prep: 10 min Bake: 15 min Cool: 30 min Chill: 4 hr

Peanut Crunch (below)

1   package (4-serving size) banana instant pudding and pie filling mix

2   cups cold milk

3   ripe medium bananas, sliced

1   container (8 ounces) frozen whipped topping, thawed (3 cups)

1. Make Peanut Crunch. Make pudding mix in large bowl as directed on package, using 2 cups milk.

2. Layer half of the Peanut Crunch, pudding, bananas and whipped topping in 2-quart serving bowl; repeat layers. Cover and refrigerate at least 4 hours. Store covered in refrigerator.

8 servings.

Peanut Crunch

1   cup Gold Medal all-purpose flour

¼   cup packed brown sugar

½   cup butter or margarine

½   cup peanuts

Heat oven to 400°. Mix flour and brown sugar in large bowl. Cut in butter, using pastry blender or criss-crossing 2 knives, until mixture is crumbly. Stir in peanuts. Press evenly on bottom of ungreased square pan, 9 × 9 × 2 inches. Bake about 15 minutes or until light brown. Stir to break up. Cool completely, about 30 minutes.

1 Serving: Calories 375 (Calories from Fat 170); Fat 19g (Saturated 10g); Cholesterol 35mg; Sodium 290mg; Carbohydrate 46g (Dietary Fiber 2g); Protein 7g
% Daily Value: Vitamin A 12%; Vitamin C 8%; Calcium 10%; Iron 6%
Exchanges: Not Recommended

BETTY'S TIPS

✪ **Pack 'n Go**
Assemble this pudding pie in a portable bowl with a lid and tote in an insulated pack with ice packs. Return any left-over pudding to the cooler.

✪ **Success Hint**
To quickly cool the Peanut Crunch, spread it in a larger pan and place the pan in the freezer.

✪ **Special Touch**
Garnish with a whole strawberry or maraschino cherry.

Nutty Banana Cream Pie-in-a-Bowl

Dutch Apple Wedges

Prep: 15 min Bake: 55 min Cool: 30 min

    1   cup Gold Medal all-purpose flour
    1/3 cup sugar
    1/2 cup butter or margarine
         Crumb Topping (below)
    1/3 cup sugar
    2   tablespoons Gold Medal all-purpose flour
    3/4 teaspoon ground cinnamon
    1 1/2 cups thinly sliced peeled tart cooking apples

1. Heat oven to 350°. Mix 1 cup flour and 1/3 cup sugar in medium bowl. Cut in butter, using pastry blender or crisscrossing 2 knives, until crumbly. Press in ungreased round pan, 9 × 1 1/2 inches. Bake 25 minutes.

2. Make Crumb Topping; set aside. Mix 1/3 cup sugar, 2 tablespoons flour and the cinnamon in medium bowl. Stir in apples until coated. Spoon over baked layer. Sprinkle with topping.

3. Bake about 30 minutes or until topping is light brown and apples are tender. Cool 30 minutes before serving. Serve warm or cool. Cut into 12 wedges.

12 servings.

Crumb Topping
    2/3 cup Gold Medal all-purpose flour
    1/2 cup packed brown sugar
    1/4 cup butter or margarine

Mix all ingredients until crumbly.

1 Serving: Calories 255 (Calories from Fat 110); Fat 12g (Saturated 7g); Cholesterol 30mg; Sodium 80mg; Carbohydrate 36g (Dietary Fiber 1g); Protein 2g
% Daily Value: Vitamin A 4%; Vitamin C 0%; Calcium 0%; Iron 6%
Exchanges: 1 Starch, 1 1/2 Fruit, 2 Fat

BETTY'S TIPS

✪ **Serve-With**
A small scoop of cinnamon or vanilla ice cream and a drizzle of warm caramel sauce turn comfort food into rich and decadent!

✪ **Did You Know?**
With so many apple varieties available, selecting the right one can be a challenge. Tart cooking apples include Granny Smith, Greening and Haralson. For sweet cooking apples, try Golden Delicious, Braeburn, Crispin/Mutsu or Honeycrisp.

Tempting Pumpkin Pie

Prep: 20 min Bake: 1 hr Cool: 30 min Chill: 4 hr

         Best Flaky Pastry (page 276)
    2   eggs
    1/2 cup sugar
    1   teaspoon ground cinnamon
    1/2 teaspoon salt
    1/2 teaspoon ground ginger
    1/8 teaspoon ground cloves
    1   can (15 ounces) pumpkin (not pumpkin pie mix)
    1   can (12 ounces) evaporated milk

1. Heat oven to 425°. Make Best Flaky Pastry—except trim overhanging edge of pastry 1/2 inch from rim of pie plate. Fold and roll pastry in toward middle of pie rather than under. Do not flute.

2. Beat eggs slightly in medium bowl with wire whisk or hand beater. Beat in remaining ingredients.

3. Cover edge of pie crust with 2- to 3-inch strip of aluminum foil to prevent excessive browning; remove foil during last 15 minutes of baking. To prevent spilling, place pastry-lined pie plate on oven rack. Pour filling into pie plate. Bake 15 minutes.

4. Reduce oven temperature to 350°. Bake about 45 minutes longer or until knife inserted in center comes out clean. Cool 30 minutes. Refrigerate about 4 hours or until chilled. Store covered in refrigerator.

8 servings.

1 Serving: Calories 280 (Calories from Fat 125); Fat 14g (Saturated 4g); Cholesterol 60mg; Sodium 290mg; Carbohydrate 34g (Dietary Fiber 2g); Protein 7g
% Daily Value: Vitamin A 100%; Vitamin C 2%; Calcium 16%; Iron 10%
Exchanges: 1 Starch, 1 Vegetable, 1 Fruit, 2 1/2 Fat

BETTY'S TIPS

✪ **Serve-With**
For ultimate decadence, serve slices of this pumpkin pie on a pool of caramel sauce.

✪ **Special Touch**
To make your own pie as pretty as this picture, cut scraps of rolled pastry with leaf-shaped cookie cutters. Sprinkle cutouts with sugar; drape over rolled-up foil (1/2 inch diameter) on a cookie sheet. Bake at 425° 3 to 5 minutes or until golden brown. Let cool. Once pie has baked and cooled, top with leaves.

Dutch Apple Wedges

Tempting Pumpkin Pie

Chocolate Pecan Pie

Prep: 20 min Bake: 50 min Cool: 30 min Chill: 2 hr
(Photo on page iii)

Best Flaky Pastry (right)
- $\frac{2}{3}$ cup sugar
- $\frac{1}{3}$ cup butter or margarine, melted
- 1 cup corn syrup
- 2 tablespoons bourbon, if desired
- $\frac{1}{2}$ teaspoon salt
- 3 eggs
- 1 cup pecan halves or broken pecans
- 1 bag (6 ounces) semisweet chocolate chips (1 cup)

1. Heat oven to 375°. Make Best Flaky Pastry.

2. Beat sugar, butter, corn syrup, bourbon, salt and eggs in large bowl with hand beater. Stir in pecans and chocolate chips. Pour into pastry-lined pie plate. Cover edge with 2- to 3-inch strip of aluminum foil to prevent excessive browning; remove foil during last 15 minutes of baking.

3. Bake 40 to 50 minutes or until set. Cool 30 minutes. Refrigerate about 2 hours until chilled.

8 servings.

Best Flaky Pastry
- 1 cup Gold Medal all-purpose flour
- $\frac{1}{4}$ teaspoon salt
- $\frac{1}{3}$ cup plus 1 tablespoon shortening or $\frac{1}{3}$ cup lard
- 2 to 3 tablespoons cold water

1. Mix flour and salt in medium bowl. Cut in shortening, using pastry blender or crisscrossing 2 knives, until particles are size of small peas. Sprinkle with cold water, 1 tablespoon at a time, tossing with fork until all flour is moistened and pastry almost leaves side of bowl (1 to 2 teaspoons more water can be added if necessary).

2. Gather pastry into a ball. Shape into flattened round on lightly floured surface. Roll pastry, using floured rolling pin, into circle 2 inches larger than upside-down pie plate, 9 × $1\frac{1}{4}$ inches. Fold pastry into fourths; place in pie plate. Unfold and ease into plate, pressing firmly against bottom and side. Trim overhanging edge of pastry 1 inch from rim of pie plate. Fold and roll pastry under, even with plate; flute as desired.

1 Serving: Calories 630 (Calories from Fat 315); Fat 35g (Saturated 14g); Cholesterol 105mg; Sodium 350mg; Carbohydrate 76g (Dietary Fiber 3g); Protein 6g
% Daily Value: Vitamin A 8%; Vitamin C 0%; Calcium 2%; Iron 10%
Exchanges: Not Recommended

BETTY'S TIPS

✿ **Substitution**
Rise to the occasion! If using self-rising flour, there is no need to add salt.

✿ **Health Twist**
Decrease the butter to $\frac{1}{4}$ cup and use only $\frac{1}{2}$ cup pecans.

✿ **Special Touch**
Garnish with whipped cream and Betty Crocker Dessert Decorations® chocolate leaves.

Chocolate Dream Tart

Prep: 10 min Bake: 40 min Cool: 1 hr

⅓ cup butter or margarine, softened
1 cup Gold Medal all-purpose flour
1 egg
1 tablespoon butter or margarine
1 can (14 ounces) sweetened condensed milk
1 bag (12 ounces) semisweet chocolate chips (2 cups)
½ cup chopped walnuts
1 teaspoon vanilla
Unsweetened whipped cream, if desired

1. Heat oven to 400°. Cut ⅓ cup butter into flour in medium bowl, using pastry blender or crisscrossing 2 knives, until mixture is crumbly. Mix in egg until dough forms. Press firmly and evenly against bottom and side of ungreased tart pan, 9 × 1 inch. Bake 12 to 15 minutes or until golden brown; cool on wire rack.

2. Reduce oven temperature to 350°. Melt 1 tablespoon butter in 2-quart saucepan over low heat. Stir in milk and chocolate chips. Cook over low heat, stirring occasionally, until chocolate is melted. Stir in walnuts and vanilla. Spread in baked crust.

3. Bake about 25 minutes or until edge is set but chocolate appears moist in center. Cool completely in pan on wire rack, about 1 hour. To serve, top each slice with whipped cream.

12 to 16 servings.

1 Serving: Calories 430 (Calories from Fat 200); Fat 22g (Saturated 12g); Cholesterol 50mg; Sodium 105mg; Carbohydrate 51g (Dietary Fiber 2g); Protein 7g
% Daily Value: Vitamin A 8%; Vitamin C 0%; Calcium 14%; Iron 8%
Exchanges: 2 Starch, ½ Other Carbohydrates, 5 Fat

BETTY'S TIPS

○ **Do-Ahead**
To make ahead, tightly cover the completely cooled tart and refrigerate up to 3 days. To freeze, tightly wrap the completely cooled tart and freeze up to 2 months. About 1 hour before serving, unwrap frozen tart and let stand at room temperature to thaw.

Chocolate Dream Tart

Dark Chocolate-Raspberry Fondue

Dark Chocolate-Raspberry Fondue

Prep: 15 min Cook: 5 min

⅔ cup whipping (heavy) cream
⅓ cup seedless raspberry preserves
1 tablespoon honey
1 bag (12 ounces) semisweet chocolate chunks
Assorted dippers (fresh fruit pieces, pretzels, shortbread cookies, pound cake cubes or angel food cake cubes), if desired

1. Mix whipping cream, raspberry preserves and honey in fondue pot or 2-quart saucepan. Heat over warm/simmer setting or medium-low heat, stirring occasionally, just until bubbles rise to surface (do not boil).

2. Add chocolate; stir with wire whisk until melted. Keep warm over warm/simmer setting. (If using saucepan, pour into fondue pot and keep warm over warm/simmer setting.) Serve with dippers.

16 servings (2 tablespoons each).

2 Tablespoons: Calories 155 (Calories from Fat 80); Fat 9g (Saturated 6g); Cholesterol 10mg; Sodium 10mg; Carbohydrate 19g (Dietary Fiber 1g); Protein 1g
% Daily Value: Vitamin A 2%; Vitamin C 0%; Calcium 2%; Iron 4%
Exchanges: 1 Fruit, 2 Fat

BETTY'S TIPS

✪ **Keep It Casual**
Serve the fondue in a shallow bowl instead of a fondue pot. Purchase already-cut bite-size pieces of fruit at the supermarket for dippers.

✪ **Make It Extra Special**
Use special fruits such as fresh figs or pears cut lengthwise or cut pound cake with mini star-shaped cookie cutters and purchase pirouette or other fancy cookies for dipping. Place fruits and cookies in pretty cocktail glasses and arrange with fondue pot on a tray lined with a doily, cheese leaves or parchment paper.

S'mores Dip

Prep: 5 min
(Photo on page 263)

2 jars (7 ounces each) marshmallow creme
3 containers (4 ounces each) snack-size chocolate fudge pudding
Graham crackers, if desired
Assorted fruits, if desired

1. Stir marshmallow creme until smooth. Layer marshmallow creme and pudding in clear glasses or bowls.

2. Serve dip with graham crackers and fruits.

About 3½ cups dip.

¼ Cup: Calories 135 (Calories from Fat 10); Fat 1g (Saturated 1g); Cholesterol 0mg; Sodium 40mg; Carbohydrate 31g (Dietary Fiber 0g); Protein 1g
% Daily Value: Vitamin A 0%; Vitamin C 0%; Calcium 2%; Iron 0%
Exchanges: 2 Fruit

BETTY'S TIPS

✪ **Serve-With**
Skewer banana chunks, strawberries, kiwifruit pieces, grapes and pineapple chunks on 4-inch drinking straws for funky fruit dippers.

✪ **Special Touch**
Kids and kids at heart will love this yummy dip! Serve it in a soda fountain-style sundae glass to show off the layers and swirls. For a fun finish, top with candy decorations, miniature candy-coated chocolate candies or chopped peanuts.

Cinnamon Truffles

Prep: 35 min Cook: 5 min Chill: 2 hr Stand: 30 min

1 bag (12 ounces) semisweet chocolate chips (2 cups)

1 tablespoon butter or margarine

¼ cup whipping (heavy) cream

1 teaspoon vanilla

½ teaspoon ground cinnamon

Powdered sugar, if desired

Baking cocoa, if desired

1 Truffle: Calories 90 (Calories from Fat 55); Fat 6g (Saturated 3g); Cholesterol 5mg; Sodium 5mg; Carbohydrate 9g (Dietary Fiber 1g); Protein 1g
% Daily Value: Vitamin A 0%; Vitamin C 0%; Calcium 0%; Iron 2%
Exchanges: ½ Starch, 1 Fat

1. Line cookie sheet with aluminum foil or parchment paper. Melt chocolate chips and butter in heavy 2-quart saucepan over low heat, stirring constantly; remove from heat.

2. Stir in whipping cream, vanilla and cinnamon. Refrigerate 30 to 60 minutes, stirring frequently, just until firm enough to roll into balls.

3. Drop mixture by tablespoonfuls onto cookie sheet. Shape into balls. (If mixture is too sticky, refrigerate until firm enough to shape.) Refrigerate about 1 hour until firm.

4. Sprinkle half of the truffles with powdered sugar and half with cocoa. Store in airtight container in refrigerator. Remove truffles from refrigerator about 30 minutes before servings; serve at room temperature.

About 2 dozen truffles.

BETTY'S TIPS

❂ **Keep It Casual**
Serve the truffles in paper candy cups placed in an ornament box.

❂ **Make It Extra Special**
Punch a small hole in the bottom of silver paper candy cups. Insert an 8- to 12-inch lollipop stick through the bottom of a cup and then into a truffle. Wrap thin ribbon around the stick. Place truffle "pops" in a simple silver cup or pitcher.

Cinnamon Truffles

Easy Peppermint Dessert

Prep: 40 min Cook: 15 min Cool: 2 hr Freeze: 11 hr

1 package (1 pound) creme-filled chocolate sandwich cookies, crushed (about 3 cups)

½ cup butter or margarine, melted

½ gallon peppermint stick, party mint or mint chip ice cream, softened

1 container (12 ounces) frozen whipped topping, thawed

½ cup butter or margarine

4 ounces unsweetened baking chocolate, chopped

2 cups sugar

1 can (12 ounces) evaporated milk

1 teaspoon vanilla

⅓ cup crushed peppermint candies or candy canes

1. Mix crushed cookies and melted butter. Press mixture firmly in bottom of ungreased rectangular pan, 13 × 9 × 2 inches.

2. Stir together ice cream and 2 cups of the whipped topping; spoon evenly onto chocolate cookie crust. Freeze about 3 hours or until firm.

3. Meanwhile, melt butter and chocolate in 2-quart saucepan over low heat, stirring constantly. Stir in sugar; gradually stir in milk. Heat to boiling over medium-high heat, stirring constantly. Cook and stir 5 minutes or until slightly thickened; stir in vanilla. Cool completely, about 2 hours.

4. Pour 2 cups of chocolate sauce evenly over ice cream. Freeze at least 8 hours but no longer than 2 weeks. Cover and refrigerate remaining sauce.

5. Reheat reserved sauce until just warm. To serve, cut into 5 rows by 3 rows. Top with sauce and remaining whipped topping; sprinkle with crushed candies.

15 servings.

1 Serving: Calories 630 (Calories from Fat 295); Fat 33g (Saturated 18g); Cholesterol 70mg; Sodium 380mg; Carbohydrate 79g (Dietary Fiber 3g); Protein 7g
% Daily Value: Vitamin A 16%; Vitamin C 0%; Calcium 18%; Iron 10%
Exchanges: Not Recommended

BETTY'S TIPS

✿ **Time-Saver**
Omit the homemade chocolate sauce and use 3 cups prepared hot fudge sauce.

✿ **Success Hint**
You will need about 12 round peppermint candies to equal ⅓ cup crushed candies.

✿ **Variation**
If you don't want to serve the dessert with chocolate sauce, pour all of the sauce over the ice cream mixture and freeze.

✿ **Special Touch**
Decorate individual servings with miniature candy canes.

Easy Peppermint Dessert

Frosty Orange Cappuccino Dessert

Prep: 30 min Bake: 10 min Cool: 30 min Freeze: 3 hr

2 cups crushed vanilla wafer cookies (50 cookies)

⅓ cup butter or margarine, melted

3 cups whipping (heavy) cream

4 teaspoons instant espresso or regular coffee (dry)

2 tablespoons hot water

2 packages (8 ounces each) cream cheese, softened

2 cans (14 ounces each) sweetened condensed milk

1 cup frozen (thawed) orange juice concentrate

⅔ cup chocolate-flavored syrup

1. Heat oven to 350°. Mix crushed cookies and butter. Press mixture firmly and evenly in bottom of ungreased rectangular pan, 13 × 9 × 2 inches. Bake about 10 minutes or until light golden brown. Cool completely, about 30 minutes.

2. Meanwhile, beat whipping cream in chilled large bowl with electric mixer on high speed until stiff peaks form; set aside. Stir coffee into hot water until dissolved; set aside.

3. Beat cream cheese in large bowl on medium speed until smooth. Beat in milk until blended. Spoon 1 cup cream cheese mixture into small bowl; stir in orange juice concentrate and 1 cup of the whipped cream.

4. Stir coffee mixture and chocolate syrup into remaining cream cheese mixture until smooth. Fold in remaining whipped cream. Pour chocolate mixture over crust. Drop orange mixture by spoonfuls over chocolate mixture; swirl mixtures with knife.

5. Freeze at least 3 hours until firm. For servings, cut into 5 rows by 3 rows.

15 servings.

1 Serving: Calories 630 (Calories from Fat 340); Fat 38g (Saturated 23g); Cholesterol 120mg; Sodium 280mg; Carbohydrate 64g (Dietary Fiber 1g); Protein 10g
% Daily Value: Vitamin A 28%; Vitamin C 46%; Calcium 26%; Iron 6%
Exchanges: Not Recommended

Frosty Orange Cappuccino Dessert

Praline Peach Cobbler

Prep: 10 min Bake: 50 min

1 cup graham cracker crumbs

1 cup finely chopped pecans

½ cup packed brown sugar

½ cup butter or margarine, melted

2 cans (29 ounces each) sliced peaches, drained

2 teaspoons prepared cinnamon-sugar

1 cup Original Bisquick

1 cup granulated sugar

1 cup milk

1. Heat oven to 350°. Spray rectangular pan, 13 × 9 × 2 inches, with cooking spray.

2. Mix cracker crumbs, pecans, brown sugar and butter. Press evenly in bottom of pan. Arrange peaches on crust; sprinkle with cinnamon-sugar. Mix Bisquick, granulated sugar and milk; pour over peaches.

3. Bake 45 to 50 minutes or until golden. Serve warm.

8 to 12 servings.

1 Serving: Calories 570 (Calories from Fat 235); Fat 26g (Saturated 9g); Cholesterol 35mg; Sodium 380mg; Carbohydrate 83g (Dietary Fiber 4g); Protein 5g
% Daily Value: Vitamin A 38%; Vitamin C 4%; Calcium 10%; Iron 10%
Exchanges: Not Recommended

BETTY'S TIPS

⚙ **Serve-With**
Whipped cream and half-and-half are natural partners to grace peach cobbler, but cinnamon, butter pecan and, yes, plain old vanilla ice cream would taste great, too.

⚙ **Did You Know?**
The graham cracker, pecan and brown sugar mixture gives a deliciously unexpected crunch to this delectable cobbler.

Praline Peach Cobbler

Light 'n' Creamy Tropical Dessert

Prep: 15 min Bake: 15 min Cool: 1 hr Chill: 4 hr

Almond Crust (below)
1 package (8 ounces) cream cheese, softened
⅔ cup sugar
1 teaspoon vanilla
1 can (20 ounces) pineapple tidbits in juice, drained and 1 cup juice reserved
1½ cups whipping (heavy) cream
2 cups miniature marshmallows
1 tablespoon cornstarch
1 papaya or mango, peeled, seeded and cut into pieces
1 kiwifruit, peeled and cut into pieces

1. Bake and cool Almond Crust.

2. Mix cream cheese, sugar and vanilla in large bowl with spoon. Reserve ½ cup of the pineapple. Stir remaining pineapple into cream cheese mixture.

3. Beat whipping cream in chilled medium bowl with electric mixer on high speed until stiff peaks form. Fold whipped cream and marshmallows into cream cheese mixture. Spread over crust. Cover and refrigerate at least 4 hours until set but no longer than 48 hours.

4. Gradually stir reserved 1 cup pineapple juice into cornstarch in 1-quart saucepan. Cook over medium heat, stirring constantly, until thickened and bubbly. Cook and stir 2 minutes longer. Cool completely, about 30 minutes. Fold in reserved ½ cup pineapple, the papaya and kiwifruit. For servings, cut into 5 rows by 3 rows. Serve with fruit mixture. Store covered in refrigerator.

15 servings.

Almond Crust
1½ cups Gold Medal all-purpose flour
1 cup butter or margarine, softened
½ cup powdered sugar
½ cup finely chopped slivered almonds

Heat oven to 400°. Beat flour, butter and powdered sugar in large bowl with electric mixer on low speed

1 minute, scraping bowl constantly. Beat on high speed about 2 minutes or until creamy. Stir in almonds. Press mixture evenly in bottom of ungreased rectangular pan, 13 × 9 × 2 inches. Bake 12 to 15 minutes or until edges are golden brown. Cool completely, about 30 minutes.

1 Serving: Calories 405 (Calories from Fat 245); Fat 27g (Saturated 16g); Cholesterol 75mg; Sodium 140mg; Carbohydrate 38g (Dietary Fiber 2g); Protein 4g
% Daily Value: Vitamin A 24%; Vitamin C 16%; Calcium 4%; Iron 6%
Exchanges: Not Recommended

BETTY'S TIPS

⊗ **Substitution**
One teaspoon almond extract can be substituted for the vanilla.

⊗ **Time-Saver**
Look in the produce section of the supermarket for slices or pieces of papaya and mango or a mixture of tropical fruits packed in jars. To use, cut up if necessary and drain before adding to the cornstarch mixture.

Light 'n' Creamy Tropical Dessert

helpful **nutrition** and **cooking** information

nutrition guidelines

We provide nutrition information for each recipe that includes calories, fat, cholesterol, sodium, carbohydrate, fiber and protein. Individual food choices can be based on this information.

Recommended intake for a daily diet of 2,000 calories as set by the Food and Drug Administration

Total Fat	Less than 65g
Saturated Fat	Less than 20g
Cholesterol	Less than 300mg
Sodium	Less than 2,400mg
Total Carbohydrate	300g
Dietary Fiber	25g

criteria used for calculating nutrition information

- The first ingredient was used wherever a choice is given (such as ⅓ cup sour cream or plain yogurt).
- The first ingredient amount was used wherever a range is given (such as 3- to 3½-pound cut-up broiler-fryer chicken).
- The first serving number was used wherever a range is given (such as 4 to 6 servings).
- "If desired" ingredients and recipe variations were not included (such as sprinkle with brown sugar, if desired).
- Only the amount of a marinade or frying oil that is estimated to be absorbed by the food during preparation or cooking was calculated.

ingredients used in recipe testing and nutrition calculations

- Ingredients used for testing represent those that the majority of consumers use in their homes: large eggs, 2% milk, 80%-lean ground beef, canned ready-to-use chicken broth and vegetable oil spread containing not less than 65 percent fat.

- Fat-free, low-fat or low-sodium products were not used, unless otherwise indicated.

- Solid vegetable shortening (not butter, margarine, nonstick cooking sprays or vegetable oil spread as they can cause sticking problems) was used to grease pans, unless otherwise indicated.

equipment used in recipe testing

We use equipment for testing that the majority of consumers use in their homes. If a specific piece of equipment (such as a wire whisk) is necessary for recipe success, it is listed in the recipe.

- Cookware and bakeware without nonstick coatings were used, unless otherwise indicated.

- No dark-colored, black or insulated bakeware was used.

- When a pan is specified in a recipe, a metal pan was used; a baking dish or pie plate means ovenproof glass was used.

- An electric hand mixer was used for mixing only when mixer speeds are specified in the recipe directions. When a mixer speed is not given, a spoon or fork was used.

cooking terms glossary

Beat: Mix ingredients vigorously with spoon, fork, wire whisk, hand beater or electric mixer until smooth and uniform.

Boil: Heat liquid until bubbles rise continuously and break on the surface and steam is given off. For rolling boil, the bubbles form rapidly.

Chop: Cut into coarse or fine irregular pieces with a knife, food chopper, blender or food processor.

Cube: Cut into squares ½ inch or larger.

Dice: Cut into squares smaller than ½ inch.

Grate: Cut into tiny particles using small rough holes of grater (citrus peel or chocolate).

Grease: Rub the inside surface of a pan with shortening, using pastry brush, piece of waxed paper or paper towel, to prevent food from sticking during baking (as for some casseroles).

Julienne: Cut into thin, matchlike strips, using knife or food processor (vegetables, fruits, meats).

Mix: Combine ingredients in any way that distributes them evenly.

Sauté: Cook foods in hot oil or margarine over medium-high heat with frequent tossing and turning motion.

Shred: Cut into long thin pieces by rubbing food across the holes of a shredder, as for cheese, or by using a knife to slice very thinly, as for cabbage.

Simmer: Cook in liquid just below the boiling point on top of the stove; usually after reducing heat from a boil. Bubbles will rise slowly and break just below the surface.

Stir: Mix ingredients until uniform consistency. Stir once in a while for stirring occasionally, often for stirring frequently and continuously for stirring constantly.

Toss: Tumble ingredients (such as green salad) lightly with a lifting motion, usually to coat evenly or mix with another food.

metric conversion chart

Volume

U.S. Units	Canadian Metric	Australian Metric
¼ teaspoon	1 mL	1 ml
½ teaspoon	2 mL	2 ml
1 teaspoon	5 mL	5 ml
1 tablespoon	15 mL	20 ml
¼ cup	50 mL	60 ml
⅓ cup	75 mL	80 ml
½ cup	125 mL	125 ml
⅔ cup	150 mL	170 ml
¾ cup	175 mL	190 ml
1 cup	250 mL	250 ml
1 quart	1 liter	1 liter
1½ quarts	1.5 liters	1.5 liters
2 quarts	2 liters	2 liters
2½ quarts	2.5 liters	2.5 liters
3 quarts	3 liters	3 liters
4 quarts	4 liters	4 liters

Weight

U.S. Units	Canadian Metric	Australian Metric
1 ounce	30 grams	30 grams
2 ounces	55 grams	60 grams
3 ounces	85 grams	90 grams
4 ounces (¼ pound)	115 grams	125 grams
8 ounces (½ pound)	225 grams	225 grams
16 ounces (1 pound)	455 grams	500 grams
1 pound	455 grams	½ kilogram

Measurements

Inches	Centimeters
1	2.5
2	5.0
3	7.5
4	10.0
5	12.5
6	15.0
7	17.5
8	20.5
9	23.0
10	25.5
11	28.0
12	30.5
13	33.0

Temperatures

Fahrenheit	Celsius
32°	0°
212°	100°
250°	120°
275°	140°
300°	150°
325°	160°
350°	180°
375°	190°
400°	200°
425°	220°
450°	230°
475°	240°
500°	260°

Note: The recipes in this cookbook have not been developed or tested using metric measures. When converting recipes to metric, some variations in quality may be noted.

Index

Underscored page references indicate Betty's Tips and tables. **Boldface** references indicate photographs.